# KEANO
## Portrait of a Hero

Stafford Hildred and Tim Ewbank

# KEANO

## Portrait of a Hero

JB

JOHN BLAKE

Published by John Blake Publishing Ltd, 3 Bramber Court,
2 Bramber Road, London W14 9PB, England

First published in paperback by Blake Publishing in 2004

ISBN 1 904034 72 1

British Library Cataloguing-in-Publication Data: A catalogue record
for this book is available from the British Library.

Design by www.envydesign.co.uk

Printed and bound in Great Britain by CPD (Wales)

1 3 5 7 9 10 8 6 4 2

Papers used by John Blake Publishing Ltd are natural, recyclable products
made from wood grown in sustainable forests. The manufacturing processes conform to
the environmental regulations of the country of origin.

Every attempt has been made to contact the relevant copyright holders, but some where
unobtainable. We would be grateful if the appropriate people could contact us.

# CONTENTS

# INTRODUCTION

ROY KEANE IS THE last person to turn a drama into a crisis. But if someone chooses to turn the greatest controversy of his remarkable life in football's frontline into a musical there is going to be nothing he can do to stop it.

And hilariously the bitter public row between Ireland soccer captain Roy Keane and the national team's manager Mick McCarthy just before the 2002 World Cup finals looks set to become immortalised in a musical 'McCarcatus', as the innovative new work is likely to be titled.

In a blaze of international headlines Keane stormed out of the tournament after a row with McCarthy, who is currently manager of Sunderland. Now *Father Ted* co-writer Arthur Matthews and author Mick Nugent have turned the passionate bust-up into an opera. Matthews came up with the idea to use this real-life incident as a basis for drama after seeing *Jerry Springer the Opera* in London.

He described the shouting match between Keane and McCarthy as 'My generation's civil war'. And added, 'The nation had not been split apart as much since Irishman fought Irishman in 1921 over the Anglo–Irish Treaty. We decided to give *McCartacus* a Roman feel, modified on the Spartacus epic. Keane and McCarthy are soldiers going to war with each other.' Jim Sheridan, director of *In the Name of the Father* and *My Left Foot* is pencilled in to direct the musical, which is expected to open in Dublin in the autumn of 2004.

Irish football fans are certain to be quick to queue for tickets – after all, the bitter split polarised opinion across the country. Was Keane a hero or a villain? People argued in pubs and clubs and football grounds across the land about whether the Irish captain, comfortably the country's most influential player, was a supreme professional or a disloyal disgrace to his country.

**ROY WAS FURIOUS THAT NO GOALKEEPERS WERE AVAILABLE FOR AN END-OF-TRAINING FIVE-A-SIDE GAME. HIS FURY WAS FURTHER AGGRAVATED BY THE EXPLANATION THAT THE KEEPERS WERE TIRED AFTER WORKING HARD. ROY'S REACTION WAS THAT THEY WERE THERE TO DO PRECISELY THAT – WORK HARD.**

Rarely has one footballer ever generated such fierce debate among his countrymen as Roy Keane did in the summer of 2002. The events were packed with drama from start to finish – and, of course, it is not over yet.

Manchester United's 2003–04 season saw the club fall away badly from its own high standards in the Premiership. The season was blighted for the club by the long controversy over key defender Rio Ferdinand and his missed drugs test. Manchester United felt the player was treated harshly by a ban that ruled him out of the second half of the season and after a promising start they finished disappointingly behind Arsenal and Chelsea in the Premiership. Their spirited success in the FA Cup, which included a tense semi-final victory over Arsenal, before beating Millwall in the final, provided some small consolation.

There was barely time for Roy to reflect on the considerable disappointments of Manchester United's season before he was collecting his thoughts to focus on Ireland's build-up and preparations for the World Cup. Naturally he was thrilled at the prospect. The tournament represented a pinnacle in any footballer's career and Roy Keane had been hugely instrumental in getting Ireland to the finals. He was proud to be going to Japan and Korea, and could stake a genuine claim to being perhaps Ireland's only world-class player. They were a young squad and Roy's vast experience would be essential.

The Republic of Ireland players, under manager Mick McCarthy, felt they could give anybody a good game and they harboured real hopes of progressing from their group. Drawn in Group E, they would face a German team – who, on recent form, were hardly world-beaters – Saudi Arabia, whom they could expect to beat, and an ever-improving Cameroon. In fact, the first match, on 1 June, was against Cameroon and a good initial result was vital. In other words, they needed to hit the ground running, fully acclimatised and properly prepared.

But from the moment the squad set off for the airport to fly to their training camp on the tiny Pacific island of Saipan, Roy Keane was starting to feel that all was not as it should be. For the players to have to push their way through a milling throng and a voracious media at Dublin airport prior to 17 hours of flying to Saipan via Amsterdam and Tokyo was, he felt, not the ideal way to start. And, once ensconced in the team's hotel in Saipan, further rumblings of Roy's discontent were not long in surfacing. They were eventually to reach the most explosive of crescendos and throw Ireland's preparations into utter disarray.

On 21 May, the first signs of a very public rift between Roy and the management became apparent when Roy hurled a plastic bottle of water in anger and frustration in a training ground spat with Packie Bonner, the goalkeeping coach. It transpired that Roy was furious that no goalkeepers were available for an end-of-training five-a-side game. His fury was further aggravated by the explanation that the keepers were tired after working hard. Roy's reaction was that they were there to do precisely that – work hard.

Other problems with the team's preparations were also eating away at Roy's sense of dedicated professionalism. The training pitch, he felt, was so hard it was like a concrete car park, which invited injury. Additionally, there were only two goals on the training ground, the skips containing the team's training gear were missing and there were no balls.

By now Roy had had enough. He decided that, if they weren't going to prepare properly, he was going home and told McCarthy so. During what turned out to be a long night, Roy telephoned his wife Theresa back in Manchester to talk things through with her. He also spoke to his agent Michael Kennedy and to Alex Ferguson, who was on holiday and had seen the news about the bust-up. Roy knew the Manchester United manager would understand his frustrations at what had gone on and what he was going through. Ferguson listened intently to what Roy had to say and advised him to stick it out, partly because of his family.

In all the see-sawing confusion, Celtic's young midfielder Colin Healy was lined up as a stand-by replacement for Roy. But just before the FIFA deadline for naming the squad was reached, Roy was back in the fold. The whole matter now seemed resolved. But on 23 May in an interview in the *Irish Times*, Roy sounded off about what he felt was the unprofessionalism surrounding the squad's preparations. Explaining in the article why he had said he was going home, Roy said, 'I've come over here to do well and I want people around me to do well. If I feel we're not wanting the same things, there's no point.'

> **'I'VE COME OVER HERE TO DO WELL AND I WANT PEOPLE AROUND ME TO DO WELL. IF I FEEL WE'RE NOT WANTING THE SAME THINGS, THERE'S NO POINT.'**
>
> **Roy Keane**

Roy's public criticism of the Irish training set-up infuriated McCarthy, but much worse was to follow. McCarthy decided to call a clear-the-air meeting with the players so that any grievances could be aired. But a still-enraged Roy exploded and hurled a torrent of abuse at McCarthy. 'Unfortunately it became a slanging match,' said a stunned McCarthy, who then took the decision to kick Roy out of the squad in disgrace.

With Roy Keane summarily dismissed, McCarthy turned to veteran defender Steve Staunton as his new captain. Staunton, like the other players, was clearly stunned by Roy's behaviour. 'It was unacceptable and I'm not going to say anything different to what's been said,' Staunton told BBC online. The banishing of Roy Keane sent shock waves that rippled from the Irish base on the sun-drenched island of Saipan all the way back to rain-lashed Ireland. At one Dublin shopping centre, Roy's expulsion from the Irish squad was announced over the PA system to astounded shoppers who struggled to come to terms with the news that the squad's star player had become an outcast.

Naturally Roy's vitriolic outburst and his sending home

prompted fierce debate in Irish society. Opinions were divided as to whether his expulsion was warranted, or whether he had valid reasons for his disenchantment with the preparations and was just being ultra-professional. The news had spread like wildfire and radio and TV programmes, quick to join in the debate, were flooded with calls from supporters expressing their anger and dismay and seeking reassurance that the loss of Keane did not mean it was all over for the team.

One of the callers to a radio phone-in was former international Ray Houghton who recalled that, in Italy in 1990 when Ireland reached the quarter-finals, both he and his roommate John Aldridge could not fit their suitcases through the door of their hotel bedroom in Rome because it was so small. But members of the FAI hierarchy were quartered in rooms that had 'two big double beds and an en suite'.

**'WE HAD GREAT HOPES FOR THIS WORLD CUP, BUT THEY'VE BEEN BLOWN APART BY IDIOTIC MANAGEMENT. ROY KEANE IS THE REASON THEY ARE OUT THERE.'**

Paul McGrath, ex-Manchester United star and Republic of Ireland international

Another ex-Manchester United Irish international, Paul McGrath, also rushed to Roy's defence. He said, 'I'm devastated for him, disgusted by it to be honest … it's wrecking my head. We had great hopes for this World Cup, but they've been blown apart by idiotic management. Roy Keane is the reason they are out there and I won't stray from that … as captain he should have the right to go to Mick and Packie and say how he feels. That's why he's captain.'

There was support also, not unpredictably, from Denis Irwin. Roy's former United and Republic of Ireland teammate and fellow Corkman said, 'Roy is serious about football, he wants his teammates to think the same way as him and he wants training to be perfect because they are playing in a World Cup. I'm sure Roy will be feeling a very lonely man.'

But the weight of calls to media outlets indicated that the sympathy largely lay with Mick McCarthy rather than with Roy. Unsurprisingly, the FAI soon stressed their endorsement of McCarthy's action. The FAI's John Delaney said, 'Mick got us qualification for the World Cup in one of the most difficult groups, with Holland and Portugal. Some may say Roy Keane got us there, others would say Shay Given or Steve Staunton – but Mick McCarthy is the manager and the FA fully stand by the decision.'

As the debate raged on, McCarthy's predecessor, Jack Charlton, who took Keane to the 1994 finals in the USA, commented, 'I think when Roy sits down and thinks about what he's done, he will have a few regrets. You don't walk out on a World Cup. He's one of the best players in the world and he should be at the finals. He had his complaints about their preparations, but that has nothing to do with the players. Roy's made a mistake and has got to live with the consequences. He's got to face the anger of the fans.'

Such was the furore that even sports-mad Irish prime minster Bertie Ahern weighed in, offering to intervene if either side thought it might be useful. But on the other side of the world Roy was making plans to fly home – pursued by the media.

Seemingly unfazed by the pre-tournament upheavals, Ireland went on to manage a thoroughly commendable 1-1 draw with Cameroon, illuminated by a magnificent strike by Matt Holland. 'The performance highlighted the togetherness that has come into the squad in the past two weeks,' said Mick McCarthy tellingly. Against Germany on 5 June, a deserved equaliser in injury time by Robbie Keane sent the Green Army into a delirium surpassed only by the euphoria of inflicting a 3-0 defeat on Saudi Arabia on 11 June, which took Ireland safely through the group stage. But the heartbreak of going out of the tournament to Spain five days later on penalties prompted a vigorous discussion of the Roy Keane debate all over again.

**'YOU DON'T WALK OUT ON A WORLD CUP. HE'S ONE OF THE BEST PLAYERS IN THE WORLD AND HE SHOULD BE AT THE FINALS.'**

**Jack Charlton, ex-Republic of Ireland manager**

So many questions were raised by Roy Keane's dismissal from the national team. How much better would Ireland have done if Roy had been there? Would they have progressed further? Would he have taken a penalty against Spain? If so, surely he would have done better than those who missed, wouldn't he? Would he have transformed Ireland's superiority into a victory over Spain, ensuring penalties would not have even come into the equation? Was Ireland's team spirit enhanced by Roy's absence? Or did his very exit bind the team together? Would Roy's presence have given Ireland a talisman for whom the team would have rallied round even more courageously? Would Roy's experience have made that vital difference to what was a young and raw Irish squad? All these questions and more were hotly debated by the fans.

One player in the German squad had absolutely no doubts about the effect of Roy Keane's dismissal. 'Of course the Irish would have been much stronger with Roy Keane,' he said. 'We felt great relief when we heard we would not be facing him. Every player in our squad knows about Roy Keane, his strength and his energy. He was the one player we were worried about. Then suddenly he was not going to be there. It made us very happy.'

Before the Irish squad headed home to a tumultuous reception, Mick McCarthy was inevitably asking himself the same questions, although he had no regrets about the action he had taken. 'The opportunity was there for him to play in this World Cup and he chose not to take it,' said McCarthy, pre-empting the Keane inquest from the media, after Ireland's exit.

The FAI's rapid announcement that McCarthy had been appointed to take the team on to the European Championship in 2004 seemed effectively to slam the door on Roy Keane's international career. But even then few would have dared to bet that Roy Keane had been seen in a Republic of Ireland shirt for the last time. Despite starring in the most turbulent episode in the history of Irish international football, Roy still believes his only 'sin' of World Cup 2002 was wanting the best for the team. The FAI will learn from the experience of losing their only world-class player from the tournament.

> **'THE OPPORTUNITY WAS THERE FOR HIM TO PLAY IN THIS WORLD CUP AND HE CHOSE NOT TO TAKE IT.'**
> Mick McCarthy, Republic of Ireland manager

Undoubtedly there will be changes to the way the squad is prepared as a result of Roy's outbursts. And there are many who, despite the events of May 2002, still believe that one day Roy Keane will be the manager of the Irish team.

One thing is certain. The events that resulted in Keane's dismissal from the squad will be remembered and talked about for years. Even in a footballing career that has been studded with controversy and incident, Keane's exit from the 2002 World Cup ranks as by far the most contentious event yet.

Typically Roy has expressed the opinion that he has no need to convince himself that he did anything wrong. And in footballing circles, not just in Ireland, he has not been short of support.

With McCarthy moving away from the Irish post, Keane's attitude certainly softened. After the likeable Brian Kerr confidently and competently took charge, Roy Keane decided to return to the Irish team. He would have preferred to do so with a minimum of fuss, but like everything concerned with the high-profile Manchester United skipper the decision was closely examined in the press. Newspapers were happy to rehash the whole controversial Saipan saga and many commentators insisted the decision was contrary to the views of his club manager Sir Alex Ferguson.

But the Man Utd boss sounded a clarion of support for his captain in an interview in May 2004. Sir Alex claimed he backed Keane's international return so that his highly valued player could one day live in peace in his native country. Keane's shock decision to play for Ireland again after a two-year absence was believed to have caused a rift with the Manchester United manager. But Ferguson insisted he was fully supportive of the 32-year-old, believing he had to pull on the green shirt again to ensure he was not hounded if and when he returned to his home country to live.

Ferguson said, 'I felt it was the right thing to happen and I backed it 100 per cent. The storm from the World Cup had passed over but Roy felt there was still some residue from that remaining. His family live there and his kids will be going back there some day soon. I was 100 per cent with him – irrespective of what anyone says, I was behind him and what he chose to do.'

Former Irish manager Jack Charlton insisted Roy Keane had plenty of bridges to build before he was welcomed back into

the fold. But Keane's former international teammate Kevin Sheedy pointed out that the Manchester United skipper will still be two months short of his 35th birthday when the first game of the 2006 World Cup finals kicks off. Sheedy believed there was nothing to prevent Roy Keane from having a huge impact on the Irish side. 'We are talking about a hypothetical situation because nobody can tell how the next two years will go for Roy in terms of injuries and everything else,' said Sheedy. 'But I doubt if he would have considered coming out of international retirement just for the sake of it. Roy would certainly have looked to that stage and he clearly believes he will still be capable of performing at the highest level in two years' time. Anyway, with modern training methods and recovery techniques, he will certainly have every chance of making it.'

CHAPTER 1

# CORK BORN AND BRED

THE MARRIAGE BETWEEN Maurice 'Mossie' and Marie Lynch was a happy one that linked two proud Irish families with a strong sporting heritage. Marie is a distant relation of the famous Jack Lynch, winner of no fewer than six All-Ireland medals for hurling and Gaelic football, and Taoiseach for two terms in the 1970s. The Lynches are an Irish family that dates back to the Normans and has left its mark all over the world. Patrick Lynch left Ireland to become Chile's foremost naval hero. Thomas Lynch became a plantation owner in America and was one of the signatories of the Declaration of Independence. Keanes are an equally historic Irish family. One of their darker ancestors was Blosky O'Kane who slew the heir to the throne in the twelfth century. The mercenary tradition was in the family long before Brian Clough made his famous signing. In the eighteenth century there were no fewer than fourteen military men called Kean or Keane serving in armies

The Keane house in the working-class Mayfield area of Cork City.

in Europe. And the famous nineteenth-century actor Edmund Kean was a distant relative. Mossie and Marie had five children and it was on 10 August 1971 that the fourth of the breed was born in the district of Mayfield on the northern fringe of the beautiful Irish city of Cork. Roy Maurice Keane was fortunate to be born into a large and loving family that has nurtured and protected him through the many twists and turns of fortune that follow life as captain of the most famous football club in the world.

Mrs Mary Kenneally never needed an alarm clock to wake her in the mornings two decades ago in her tidy council home at 102 Ballinderry Park. She could rely on the sound of a football hitting the side of her house at 7.30 every morning. The impact of leather on the wall was hard and very regular. Sometimes it would make the ornaments on her mantelpiece, which backs on to the wall, vibrate and threaten to crash down on the hearth. On those mornings she would open her front door, look round to her left and shout, 'Roy! Roy! Take it easy.'

The response from the young boy who was to become the Republic of Ireland's greatest footballer was generally a cheeky grin and a shrug of the shoulders. And Roy Keane would take his ball off across the road and up the six steps to the small grassy knoll of open space surrounded by a low grey wall between Mrs Kenneally's home and his own. Once there he would start to dribble round the five trees until one or more of his classmates would come out and join him.

'I never minded the early-morning calls,' smiled Mary Kenneally. 'My wall had no windows and there was enough concrete for the boys to play on. They were mostly good lads but Roy was always the first. He would arrive with the ball at his feet and that was how he always seemed to be.

'Before he'd had his breakfast he'd be out with the ball. He never went anywhere without that ball. We didn't mind because we had schoolkids ourselves. He was a popular boy. The whole family was popular. It's become a great incentive for the kids. They all say they're going to be the second Roy Keane.'

**'BEFORE HE'D HAD HIS BREAKFAST HE'D BE OUT WITH THE BALL. HE NEVER WENT ANYWHERE WITHOUT THAT BALL.'**
Mary Kenneally, childhood neighbour

The dedication was clearly there from an early age. Even as a young boy Roy Keane was well aware of his lack of height and to make the most of his heading ability he used to practise heading at a ball tied to his mother's washing line. Other times he'd be heading at the washing itself, which often earned him an earful of abuse when a muddy football hit its target.

Roy Keane's family had strong sporting links even before he started waking up Mrs Kenneally. His father Mossie was a fair footballer – particularly, as he put it once, when he had enjoyed a drink. 'I played some of my best games with five pints inside me,' he told one early interviewer. Mossie played with St Mary's and Temple United in Cork and Roy's three brothers Denis, Pat and Johnson, have all been enthusiastic soccer players at different levels. Marie's father was a fine footballer and he and two brothers all won FAI medals.

The council estate where Roy grew up is on the very edge of the ancient city of Cork just yards from sweeping open countryside where the brothers would roam as boys. The city has a proud tradition as the third largest in the island of Ireland after Dublin and Belfast, and even today Roy Keane always insists he comes from 'Cork first and Ireland second'. It has always been an important seaport and began life as a sprawling collection of houses on an island in the swampy estuary of the River Lee. Gradually the community grew up either side of the river bank. Today the river flows through the historic city in two great channels so that you find yourself continuously crossing bridges as you explore. As a boy young Roy Keane and his friends would take the number eight bus and venture into the bright lights of the city centre.

**ROY'S FATHER MOSSIE WAS A FAIR FOOTBALLER – PARTICULARLY, AS HE PUT IT ONCE, WHEN HE HAD ENJOYED A DRINK. 'I PLAYED SOME OF MY BEST GAMES WITH FIVE PINTS INSIDE ME,' HE TOLD ONE EARLY INTERVIEWER.**

Cork has a long tradition for independence and stubborn resistance. The people fought the Viking sea pirates who came to raid and burn and stayed to trade and marry. The Anglo-

Roy Keane with a young fan from Cork.

Norman invasion of 1172 resulted in both the Danish lords and the local chiefs having to submit to Henry II, but many of Ireland's frequent uprisings against foreign oppressors have taken root in Cork. The city was known as 'Rebel Cork' and it's a name that could equally well be applied to its favourite footballing son.

As a boy Roy Keane was always very much his own man. He might have been small for his age but he was never timid. And ingrained in him from his earliest years was a fierce feeling against any sort of injustice. Compromise was never a

**INGRAINED IN HIM FROM HIS EARLIEST YEARS WAS A FIERCE FEELING AGAINST ANY SORT OF INJUSTICE. IF ROY KEANE FELT SOMETHING WAS WRONG HE WOULD SAY SO.**

word in his vocabulary. If Roy Keane felt something was wrong he would say so.

Neighbour Mary Kenneally had cause to be grateful for Roy's refusal to accept anything he felt was wrong. She recalls, 'When my son Aaron was growing up he was small for his age and he ran into a bit of bullying. It was very upsetting and I didn't find out what was going on until afterwards. Aaron didn't like to say anything about it.

'But Roy stopped it. He was only a year or so older and he was small himself but he was a very tough young lad. He warned the bullies off and after that he used to protect Aaron. He looked after him and was very good to him. I will always be thankful for that. They weren't even close friends or anything. Roy just couldn't stand bullies. They used to gang up on weaker lads like Aaron and take their things from them. Roy really looked after him; he was like a guardian angel.'

Another neighbour backed up Mrs Kenneally's words: 'I saw what Roy Keane did that time, and another time when a younger lad was having his stuff messed around with. This fat kid who was a year younger than Aaron was constantly beaten up. His dad had a shop in Mayfield and this gang of kids used to wait for him at the gates of the school and hit him. They made him bring them sweets and other stuff from the shop in exchange for not getting beaten up. It went on for a while until Roy stopped it.

'He didn't say anything to anyone about it. Not even to his friends. He just made sure he walked to school with this fat kid and when the bullies lined up to take the sweets he stepped in between them and hit the leader in the mouth. He was bigger than Roy but Roy hit him really hard and his lip bled and he fell to his knees. He didn't hit Roy back and his friends just sort of drifted away. The fat kid had his mouth open as if he had just seen a ghost. I don't think anyone had ever stuck up for him before. Roy just could not bear to see any sort of bullying. If there were two boys hitting one he would just wade in to even up the odds. He was never very big at school but he was always very hard.'

Roy went to the local St John's Primary School, Scoil Eoin Aspal in Mayfield, and then on to Mayfield Community School. When Roy made a visit back to Mayfield Community School a few years ago he was mobbed by children who dream of emulating his success. And in the streets where he grew up he is still hero-worshipped by the youngsters. But today when the newspapers start writing about Roy Keane going from 'rags to riches' his proud parents get annoyed. Roy's mother Marie told one TV interviewer firmly that she did not appreciate such descriptions, insisting that her family were not poverty stricken just 'ordinary hard-working people'.

The whole family was well liked and is still well respected. They moved to nearby Lotamore Park when Roy was a teenager but still remained friendly with the neighbours and old friends they grew up with. Keiran Murphy, who lives around the corner from Roy Keane's old home, said, 'The Keanes are all right. They are an honest working family who anyone would be happy to know. Mossie used to work at the old textile factory Sunbeam Wolsey in Blackpool until it closed down and he became unemployed like a lot of us. They never had a lot but if you asked for anything they would always try to help you out. That's what it's like round here. I wouldn't live anywhere else.'

Other contemporaries from those days recall a shy, quiet lad with an impish smile and an enthusiasm for football that overrode all other ambitions. 'Roy always wanted to be a professional footballer,' said one old schoolfriend. 'Most of us changed our minds every week about what we would like to do when we grew up but he never altered.

'He would always want to play. We all liked football and we'd put down the coats and have a game loads of times. But at the end Roy was always wanting to go on a little longer. "Just till the next goal," he'd say when people were starting to drift off, "Just till the next goal." And when the next goal came he would want to play until the next one. It never ever went on long enough for Roy.

'Even when he was a young boy he knew he had to practise each part of his game. He had this thing about jumping high for headers because he knew if he could do that he could compensate for being small. And he would always tackle like a demon because he knew he was so light that he would be easy to brush off if he didn't go in hard and accurately.

'But I've seen him practising taking corners for ages on his own. He'd try to swing the ball in so an imaginary centre forward could leap up and head it in. Then he would go and fetch the ball and do it again. And again and again. I think that is why no one from his past, no one from Cork in fact, begrudges Roy Keane his success. If they know Roy Keane then they know he has earned it.'

Rockmount AFC, a schoolboys club on the north side of Cork, is rightly proud of the sporting contribution it has made to the city of Cork over the past 75 years. Countless numbers of youngsters down the years can credit an early love of football and sport in general to the encouragement they received with Rockmount.

Rockmount wasn't Roy Keane's local club but it was only natural that he should enjoy his first organised football with

Rockmount because he was following a strong family tradition. Keane's mother had two brothers, Mick and Pat Lynch, who had both played for Rockmount and managed their teams, and Keane's own brothers Denis and Johnson had also played for Rockmount.

Rockmount's football coaches had seen enough of Keane's brothers, especially Denis's energetic performances in left midfield, to welcome wholeheartedly yet another member of the family to the club. When young Roy finally came along one day, however, they couldn't help but notice he was very small and slender for his age. He was nine years old and many lads his age were already a lot bigger and sturdier. But his Rockmount mentors, coaches Timmy Murphy and the late Gene O'Sullivan, could not help but be impressed by the way the boy seemed to grow a few inches with pride when he first pulled on Rockmount's green-and-yellow strip for the first time.

**'NO ONE FROM HIS PAST, NO ONE FROM CORK IN FACT, BEGRUDGES ROY KEANE HIS SUCCESS. IF THEY KNOW ROY KEANE THEN THEY KNOW HE HAS EARNED IT.'**

A schoolfriend

It was obvious to them, too, that the lad was absolutely mad about football. He could think and talk of little else and stored away in his head as many soccer statistics as he could. As he was ferried around from football pitch to football pitch on the way to and from games, Keane would pester his coaches to test his knowledge with football quizzes and he loved to reel off the names and footballing stats of all the players of Tottenham Hotspur, the team he decided he would support. Keane's joy was unconfined when, three months before his tenth birthday, he watched on TV his favourites, Spurs, win an astonishing replay of the one hundredth FA Cup final in 1981. Ricardo Villa, a black-bearded Argentine imported to Spurs after the 1978 World Cup, scored one of Wembley's finest goals running 30 yards, beating three Manchester City defenders, and gliding the ball with calculated ease past City's goalkeeper Joe Corrigan.

It was a fairy-tale finish to a fantastic final that left a little boy in Mayfield, Cork, and millions of other TV viewers, open mouthed. If ever there was a moment that fostered dreams for Keane that one day he'd play in a Wembley cup final, then this was it. One of the Spurs players that day was Glenn Hoddle and it's not difficult to judge what the nine-year-old Keane's reaction would have been if he had been told that one day he would indeed grow up to play in a winning FA Cup final side at Wembley against a team that included Glenn Hoddle.

Keane's abundant enthusiasm to talk about anything to do with football, Murphy noted, was matched by a desire to get out on a pitch and play that was unquenchable. Once Keane had a ball at his feet it was also clear to Murphy that the little lad certainly had ability to go with his enthusiasm. When he didn't have the ball he was quite prepared to scrap for it with much bigger opponents. Although he was still only 9 Murphy had no qualms about sticking little Roy Keane into the Under-11 Rockmount team straight away. By the end of his first season Keane had done so well that he was voted player of the season.

Such was Roy Keane's appetite for playing soccer that there were weekends when he would turn out for an Under-10 game on a Saturday morning, take his place in the Under-11 team for a match in the afternoon, and play for the Under-12 side on the Sunday. Astonishingly, Murphy marvelled, Keane somehow seemed to have the stamina for it all in his lean and tiny frame. If there was a game available, young Keane was up for it and he would run and run and never seemed to flag.

Murphy was also impressed when he learned that such was Keane's desire to improve his game that he had hung a football from his mum's washing line in an effort to keep practising his heading. Murphy remembers the youngster was always bursting to train in all weathers. Torrential rain, bitter cold, even snow would never deter him and he was always the first with his boots on ready for training. Rockmount Park was, in fact, seven miles away so Keane and the other youngsters would sneak in and train under Murphy's watchful eye at Old Christian rugby club before the rugger players themselves turned up.

As he ran an experienced eye over the young footballers available to him, Murphy realised that a youthful team was developing under him of quite exceptional talent with Roy Keane emerging as a key member notable, just as he is today, for his non-stop running up and down the pitch. 'I used to call him the Boiler Man,' says Murphy. 'You know, the fellow who mans the furnace, who gets things heated up and keeps them that way. He was the motivator, the leader. When things were going bad for Rockmount, all you had to do was roar at Roy. He would do the rest.'

In all its long and illustrious history, Rockmount's stock as a footballing nursery has never been higher than when Roy Keane was a member of a team that became virtually invincible for half a dozen years. The record books show that the Rockmount boys won the League and Cup Double for six consecutive seasons. They were unbeaten from Under-11 to Under-15 and they can lay claim to forming the greatest schoolboy football team Cork has ever produced. It says much for their ability that no less than five of them went on to play international football at some level or other. Alan O'Sullivan, a more-than-useful left-winger, went on to Luton Town, striker Paul McCarthy went to

Brighton when the Sussex club were in the old First Division in England, and Damien Martin and Len Downey both went on to excel in the Munster League.

Keane struck up a special comradeship with Downey both on and off the field. Standing side by side, at that point in time they made for the most unlikely pair of pals. The physical contrast between them could hardly have been more marked: Downey tall, fair and strapping, and Keane small and wiry, the dark thatch of hair on top of his head still not taking him up to the height of Downey's shoulder. Both of them harboured ambitions to be full-time professional footballers and, as their friendship developed, an additional bond developed between them when they both appeared to get overlooked while other members of their team were scouted by soccer coaches and went on to take up football apprenticeships.

**BY THE END OF HIS FIRST SEASON AT ROCKMOUNT KEANE HAD DONE SO WELL THAT HE WAS VOTED PLAYER OF THE SEASON.**

In those days it was Paul McCarthy who was tipped to go on to become a top player and everyone at Rockmount was delighted for him when he was taken on by Brighton. Not long after he had registered, McCarthy – with the help of his father – set the wheels in motion for Roy Keane to come over to the Sussex coast and have a trial with Brighton. But Keane's chance evaporated after the club were swayed by a scout's appraisal that the boy was too small and had a suspect temperament. McCarthy recalls that Keane was indeed small but that he never backed away from trouble on the pitch and, if Brighton had cared to look beyond Keane's size, they would have seen a teenager whose passing was almost faultless and a midfield player who simply never gave the ball away.

Although conscious of his lack of size, Keane was not unduly troubled by it. He had seen his brothers physically develop late and grow and broaden into big lads, and he simply assumed it would be the same for him. It was others who seemed more concerned for him and Keane had to put up with unsolicited offers of advice ranging from eating special foods to hanging by his fingertips from doorways, banisters, or basketball rings to try to stretch himself.

One thing was for certain: Keane could look after himself. When he was 14 his attentions briefly turned to another sport for which his will to win, courage and determination was well suited. He was already enjoying his football and occasional forays into Gaelic football but now, just as Mike Tyson was starting to unleash his own explosive brand of savagery among the world's heavyweights, Keane was drawn to boxing.

**'I USED TO CALL HIM THE BOILER MAN. YOU KNOW, THE FELLOW WHO MANS THE FURNACE, WHO GETS THINGS HEATED UP AND KEEPS THEM THAT WAY. HE WAS THE MOTIVATOR, THE LEADER.'**
Rockmount coach Timmy Murphy

He joined Dillon's boxing club, one of the smaller boxing clubs in Cork situated at Dillon's Cross just outside the city, and very much a local club. 'He trained for one season at junior, beginner level,' recalls family friend Frank Nash. 'He had a couple of preliminary rounds more to accompany his brother than anything else. Every year there's an intake of new young boxers and they come and they train for a while and then they test out and the fall-out rate is huge. Normally what happens is that a young lad does training for several months and is then matched with a similar boxer from another club to test them out to see if they have the potential to enter real competition. You have to be dedicated and you have to have a bit of style even to move on to the amateur ranks. Roy decided his talents lay elsewhere.'

Keane had just four fights in the Irish Novice League and won them all but Frank Nash maintains, 'His appearance at the club was quite fleeting. There would be local contests and then contests under what is known as the Cork County Board of the Irish Amateur Boxing Association. He didn't move on to that level.'

**THE YOUNG KEANE HAD TO PUT UP WITH UNSOLICITED OFFERS OF ADVICE RANGING FROM EATING SPECIAL FOODS TO HANGING BY HIS FINGERTIPS FROM DOOR-WAYS, BANISTERS, OR BASKETBALL RINGS TO TRY TO STRETCH HIMSELF.**

In all Roy Keane spent nine happy, hugely successful years with Rockmount. He has only the fondest memories of his days as a Rockmount player and the club's chairman John Delea, who was Keane's manager in his last years with Rockmount, has become a much-valued and trusted friend.

By the time Keane left school after the Inter-Cert, so much of his life and time was devoted to soccer that he could see no life for himself other than that of becoming a footballer. The only other alternative was unemployment. Depressingly for a young man so utterly obsessed with soccer as Roy Keane, however, it appeared that as far as his football was concerned he would have to remain just an enthusiastic amateur.

At no time did Keane lose faith in his own ability, but his hopes of a full-time professional footballing career were beginning to look decidedly slim. On countless occasions he had heard that scouts from big clubs had been watching him with interest but still none had come in for him. He found it all so frustrating. In desperation, with Timmy Murphy's help, Keane began writing off to the big British clubs requesting a trial. But none, it seemed, were interested. Each rejection brought despondency but Keane never completely gave in to despair.

Having set his sights as high as playing for an English First Division team, it was naturally something of a comedown for Keane when he was offered terms as a part-time player for Cork City. True, it might not be Tottenham Hotspur, but at least it was a chance to play football as a part-time professional and to Keane that at least offered a far better alternative than kicking his heels as an unemployed teenager.

Cork City thought they had him signed and sealed when they spoke to Keane at his home and went through the registration paperwork with him. But around the same time as Cork City were making their approach to Keane, a local carpenter called

**With some of his adoring fans.**

Eddie O'Rourke had also taken notice of the youngster playing on a rough and bumpy pitch near the estate where he lived and couldn't help marvelling at his energy. Every time he saw Keane play he was impressed by his capacity to run and run. 'Never in my life had I seen anyone like him,' said Eddie. 'Up and down the field, defending then scoring goals.' Eddie was youth team manager for Cobh Ramblers, another local club made up of semi-professionals, and he reckoned that Keane's potential could be nurtured to mutual benefit with the Ramblers and that he would be a fine addition to the squad.

Cobh is a harbour town on an island reached by a single bridge some nine miles out of Cork. It would mean a bit of a trek for Keane to get out there to train and play but there was something about Eddie O'Rourke's genial, friendly approach that persuaded Keane that he should join the Ramblers.

Roy playing for Cobh Ramblers in 1989.

Since Keane had seemingly already pledged himself to Cork City, O'Rourke had to be quick off the mark to get the boy registered with the Football Association of Ireland. His forms were sent off straight away and landed in the FAI offices next day. Meanwhile a secretary at Cork City had decided to try to save money by waiting until a number of other pending registration forms could be added to Keane's before spending the price of a stamp to Dublin. Ultimately the outlay for one stamp cost Cork City the chance to recruit Roy Keane. The teenager who was to become captain of Manchester United and captain of the Republic of Ireland had slipped through Cork City's grasp. Keane was allowed to stay with Cobh only because they had registered him first.

It was just after his 17th birthday that Roy Keane became a Cobh Ramblers player and the timing of his joining the club could not have been better. In conjunction with the government, the Irish football authorities were planning to introduce a state-aided football training scheme for the most promising young players in Ireland's Premier League. Each Premier club in the League of Ireland was invited to nominate one player for the two-year course and when one club decided not take up its option, Cobh Ramblers from the First Division were asked to name their representative. They put forward the name of Roy Keane.

The FAS/FAI inaugural football academy course was to be held in Dublin, which meant Keane catching an early Monday-morning train from Cork's Kent station to Dublin. There he would spend the week in digs in Dublin before catching the return train to Cork on a Friday night ready for training with Cobh Ramblers and then a match for the club on the Saturday or Sunday.

For the young Roy Keane, it was a real adventure. He had never lived away from Cork before, had never been away from his family for any length of time, and it was with a mixture of apprehension and excitement that he boarded the train for Dublin one crisp September morning in 1989. At least he knew there would be a friendly face on the train and on the footballing course with him since Len Downey, his teammate from Rockmount who had now joined Cork City, had been put forward to the Irish football academy as City's representative. As the train pulled away from Cork the two youngsters chatted animatedly about what the weeks ahead might hold for them.

Keane and Downey were among 24 young football hopefuls who reported to the Leixlip Amenities Centre at Palmerstown, south-west Dublin, that day. As they checked in and the course was outlined to them it was apparent that they were in for a full week of strenuous activity – as well as some school lessons, which brought a nervous smile and a collective groan from the lads.

'WE'D PLAY LITTLE FIVE-A-SIDES AND SEVEN-A-SIDES AND HE'D BE SCORING GOALS. EVEN IN THOSE HE HAD THAT DESIRE TO WIN AND WOULD NEVER STOP RUNNING.'

Maurice Price, director at FAS/FAI inaugural football academy course

Inevitably among 24 youths with energy to burn brought together from different areas of Ireland, reputations to make and anxious to prove themselves, rivalries rapidly developed. Roy Keane's uncompromising attitude on the field resulted in an altercation early on with another young lad, named Richie Parsons, though it was quickly defused.

A typical day would begin at 10 a.m. with Keane and the others being put through a series of warm-up exercises followed by instruction and practice at improving a player's touch and control. Then they would split up into four sets of six youngsters to play three-against-three games before breaking for lunch. In the afternoon there would be coaching on shooting and midfield play, to which Keane paid particular attention, then talks.

'It was the first Irish soccer academy and every day of the week we'd train the boys from ten to twelve and then from two to four,' says Maurice Price, one of the directors of the course. 'On two half-days we had an education day, as we called it, where the lads had to go to school and learn a language. Roy didn't take to it much, but we taught him French, Spanish and Italian – just in case he made it as a footballer big time!

'At the start he wasn't very tall but when he came on the course he started to stretch a bit. The full-time physical-fitness training and weight training helped him fill out. He was dedicated to his training. Unbelievable! You couldn't give him enough. He loved it.

**WHEN THE BOYS WERE SENT OUT TO RUN LAPS OF THE FIELD, IT BECAME COMMONPLACE FOR KEANE TO SURGE 150 YARDS AHEAD OF THE OTHERS AND STAY THERE WHILE THE OTHERS PANTED ALONG BEHIND.**

'His attitude was superb. We'd play little five-a-sides and seven-a-sides and he'd be scoring goals and even in those he had that desire to win and would never stop running like he does now. He'd be here, there and everywhere. I thought he'd make it, but I wouldn't have said at that time he was going to be a world-class player. But with his attitude he was always going to get to the top. Some players have good skill but their attitude isn't right. Keane's was.

'He was always very skilful, always very professional and very good at working on the course. Keane and the other boys would

Keeping it in the family: with his younger brother, Pat, at the Cobh Ramblers home ground in Cork.

get a weekly wage but it wasn't much, maybe £30 if that, and then their clubs would put something towards their travelling expenses especially if they had a midweek game.'

At first Keane didn't take to life in Dublin. He missed his family and his friends and yearned for familiar surroundings. He was living in digs in Leixlip but didn't enjoy it. He preferred to spend his evenings with Len Downey round at the house where his friend was staying.

Whatever unease he may have felt about his new surroundings, there was no doubt in Keane's mind, however, that the course was helping him to improve greatly as a footballer. Importantly, it also brought home to him the extent to which dedicated training could help his game. He treated all the training exercises with such exemplary effort that he began to show up some of the others in terms of fitness. When the boys were sent out to run laps of the field, it became commonplace for Keane to surge 150 yards ahead of the others and stay there while the others panted along behind.

Back with Cobh Ramblers, his new teammates, club officials, staff and supporters were delighted he had joined them and enthused about his emerging talents and his courage. The First Division was no place for faint hearts or players who couldn't stand up for themselves and Keane remembers the advice his father used to give him before a game. Ignoring the finer technicalities of football he would urge his son, 'Just get stuck in.'

Ramblers groundsman John O'Driscoll knew Cobh had signed a decent player when he watched Keane in his first game for the club. 'I knew from the word go he was a good player,' he says. 'He had it in his head he was going to make it. In footballing terms he was head and shoulders above everybody. We knew we had a star here. Although he looked big on the pitch, muscular like, he was small. But you should have seen him jumping up for the ball from a corner. He was a wonderful header of the ball.

'Roy had devilment in him even then. He was a hard player. He wasn't a dirty player but he was fiery. He was a very good player but people weren't to know he was going to be the star player he is now so there'd only be about a thousand watching him play if we were lucky.

'It still sticks in the throat that we didn't put a clause in the contract when he later went to Nottingham Forest that Cobh would benefit if he was sold on. It was £3.75 million when he went to Manchester United and if we'd had 2 per cent at the time it would have set us right up.'

Roy's new teammates at Cobh Ramblers found the youngster desperately shy and quiet. It was a rare day when he said much in the dressing room. The truth was that Keane was rather in awe of the players around him, many of them hardened, seasoned semi-pros who had had to settle for the less glamorous reaches of football than the heights that Keane hoped to aspire to. They, in turn, soon learned to respect Keane's whole-hearted approach once he pulled on the claret-and-blue Cobh Ramblers shirt emblazoned across the chest with the name of sponsors South Coast Fisheries. There was never any doubting Keane's commitment when he was playing for Cobh Ramblers and gradually it was becoming noticeable, too, that he was starting to fill out physically. One Christmas he took a job over the holiday period with an off-licence helping to carry crates of beer up and down stairs, a job taken with the purpose of strengthening his legs.

Roy Keane got a special thrill playing for Cobh against a visiting team from West Bromwich Albion, an English club with a proud history, who were over in Ireland on a tour. For a young Roy Keane casting eyes on a career in English football, the West Brom fixture in 1989 was a very special occasion – how he wished he could play for a top club like that!

He couldn't help wondering why the scouts had so consistently overlooked him. Eddie O'Rourke always urged Keane to remain optimistic, however, telling him repeatedly, 'Your turn will come one day, Roy.' Within 12 months, Steve Coppell the former Manchester United and England star was able to say succinctly, 'Whoever it was who spotted Roy Keane should be made scout of the year.'

CHAPTER 2

# FROM COBH TO CLOUGH

ACE SOCCER SCOUT Noel McCabe could hardly believe his eyes. In the raw, urban setting of Dublin's Fairview Park the visitors from the beautiful countryside near Cork were completely overwhelmed by the more robust and sophisticated skills of the players from Belvedere Boys. The youth teams had drawn a bitterly contested cup game 1-1 with Roy Keane giving Cobh an early lead with a fearless diving header, only for Belvedere to equalise in the last minute of the game. Cobh knew they faced a difficult task in the replay. In fact, they were totally overrun – the replay was a very one-sided affair. The match in the bleak park on the north side of Dublin was just another game in the busy itinerary of scout McCabe who had come to run the rule over the highly rated Cobh goalkeeper Jamie Culliemore. But

**'WHOEVER IT WAS WHO SPOTTED ROY KEANE SHOULD BE MADE SCOUT OF THE YEAR.'**

Steve Coppell, former Manchester United and England star

by the time the hapless lad had picked the ball from the net four times McCabe's interest had been caught instead by the slight but valiant figure of one Roy Maurice Keane who that day was operating as virtually a one-man midfield division desperately trying to plug holes in a leaking defence.

In those days the laconic Mr McCabe was much better known for his motorcycle transport than for the footballers he had unearthed by his employers at Nottingham Forest, but he was very serious about his soccer and was about to be recognised for a scouting discovery of the highest quality. As soon as he saw lean, mean Roy Keane in energetic action he experienced that rare tingle down the spine that makes the lonely and frequently frustrating life of the dedicated soccer scout worthwhile. His heart leaped as he struggled to conceal his enthusiasm from other watchers. The rest of Keane's team might have been floundering to a disappointing defeat but

Keane holds a framed picture of Nottingham Forest in his old local, The Cotton Ball. His mother, Marie, is second from the left and father, Mossie, is in the back row, fourth from the left.

Roy's head never dropped for a moment. As the Cobh defence was overrun he still tackled like a terrier in midfield and struggled to generate counter-attacks with teammates who had long since accepted defeat. McCabe instantly recognised tremendous natural ability. Better still, he could see that this was talent married to astonishing energy, staggering workrate and a fighting spirit that McCabe instantly knew set the boy far apart from all the other players. Even if it was on the wrong end of a 4-0 thrashing. At half-time the scout quietly approached Cobh Ramblers' indefatigable vice-chairman John O'Rourke and, as casually as he could, asked for the name of the player in the number ten shirt.

Years later the day remained clear in Noel McCabe's encyclopaedic football memory. He reflected fondly, 'If players shine like Roy Keane did that day, it doesn't matter what the scoreline is. Roy Keane stood out in the game because he was head and shoulders above the rest as a player.' McCabe was deeply impressed by the relentless workrate and the high skill level of the slightly built youngster. 'His heading and his passing and his speed were all excellent. When he was on the ball he was really expressing himself in such a way that he looked special.'

Roy was already eighteen and a half years old on the day of the match, 18 February 1990, and well aware that this was old in terms of launching a professional career. Privately he was beginning to wonder if his chance of success as a footballer had passed him by. But he was still morosely smarting over the comprehensive defeat when he got the nod that a scout was watching. Despite his passionate ambition to make it as a professional player Roy refused to allow himself to get excited. Thinking back to that day later, he reflected, 'After the match John O'Rourke came up to me and said, "There's a Forest scout and I think he is interested in you." But I thought no more of it because I had heard that story hundreds of times. People were always saying, "There's somebody looking at you today so if you could do well you might get a trial," so I thought no more of it.'

But McCabe and Keane met and talked afterwards and the young player realised that this time could be different. Indeed, this could be his moment. Through his natural shyness and reserve Roy Keane somehow contrived to allow his dedication to his craft and his determination to succeed to show through and the shrewd Mr McCabe was heartened by the young man's drive and enthusiasm. The scout recalled later, 'We met in the Ashling Hotel beside Heuston Station afterwards and I was pleased with his attitude because he actually wanted to become a footballer. He was very shy and I was doing all the talking. But he gave me the firm impression that he would swim over to England to become a footballer, if that's what it took. So I set it in motion for him to visit Nottingham Forest shortly. It was a big thing to go on trial, as it still is. I travel a lot and the boys are usually keen and overanxious to get away. Roy was at the ideal age, approaching 19, and had never been capped at a senior level. He was mature and he had already been away from home on the FAS course so he was getting into that scheme of things, training full time on the course.'

**'WHEN HE WAS ON THE BALL HE WAS REALLY EXPRESSING HIMSELF IN SUCH A WAY THAT HE LOOKED SPECIAL.'**

**Noel McCabe, Nottingham Forest football scout**

The Cobh Ramblers youth team was then under the caring control of John O'Rourke's brother Eddie and he remembers Roy Keane's most important match very clearly. He is certain that even if it hadn't been for that all-important late equaliser that set up the crucial replay in the capital then his best player would still have been drafted to stardom somehow. But the match day began badly. Eddie recalls that as they were preparing for the long bus journey up to play Belvedere, Roy turned to him and asked plaintively, 'Will I ever make it?' And Eddie replied, 'This could be your day kid, you never know.' As it turned out, it was very much his day, although it certainly did not seem like it at the time.

Eddie O'Rourke says, 'We were hammered that day because the preparations were all at fault. We were just not tuned in on the day. The bus was late. We were late togging off. Everything went wrong but we didn't deserve to get hammered on the day. Roy was head and shoulders above everyone out there, even though we were beaten 4-0.' Eddie remembers the scout's post-match approach very clearly. They were over the road in a pub having sandwiches and McCabe was the only one of several spectating scouts who came in for the meal. 'I often ask myself what all the others were looking at,' he said later. Fervent Manchester United fan Eddie could perhaps have saved his favourite club a fortune if he had picked up the telephone to Old Trafford. But as he said some time afterwards, 'That's not my job, I'm a scout for Cobh Ramblers.'

The chance came at a pivotal time in the young life of Roy Keane. He was struggling with the frustration of seeing fellow players being given opportunities to make careers in the game and he desperately wanted his chance. He knew in his heart that he was a better player than many of those plucked to higher levels of the game, though he would never have voiced the view. Still, it was a very difficult time for the young man, who was just starting to wonder if his lifelong dream was ever going to come true. As Roy himself recalled later, 'At the time I was eighteen, unemployed and desperate to get a break. I knew if I did get a trial I would grab the chance. Some players are signed as apprentices when they are sixteen. I thought if Forest don't take me on now, I'm going to be eighteen and I might miss the boat.' With typical Keane modesty and understatement he added, 'Fortunately the trial went very well for me and they offered me a contract.'

In fact Noel McCabe had lined up three young Irish footballers for trials at Forest and Roy Keane arrived with two other fresh-faced hopefuls. Roy was nervous and even a little homesick but fortunately for him his time in Dublin had already introduced him to a big competitive world outside the cosy confines of his beloved Cork. It was still a nerve-wracking test for the young Irishman and fellow teammates remember him as a quiet and almost withdrawn visitor who was only transformed into life on the pitch. A fellow triallist recalls, 'Roy didn't really join in much of the joking and horseplay. We teased him a bit but not too much – he just had something about him that made us realise he could handle himself. Even as a youngster he had a strength and quietness about him that let you know he was not a man to be messed with.

'And on the pitch he was fantastic. Right from the very first time he played. I remember he tackled me in one five-a-side match and it felt like I had been hit by a bus. He was not a big guy but he was so fast and strong he wanted to be involved in every move. And he just hated to lose, even in a practice match. If he thought anyone wasn't pulling his weight he'd gee them up no danger. On the pitch he always had a confidence that even some of the established first-team players did not possess. He challenged for every high ball and was up and down the pitch like a demon. I've never seen anyone put so much into his game.'

Roy knew this might be the only chance he was going to get, so he was totally focused on making the most of every moment of his opportunity. He was certainly very much in awe of Brian Clough and his amazing achievements at Nottingham Forest. Today the Forest glory days have passed and the club has returned to its more familiar position, struggling just below the top division; Clough's impact is in danger of being forgotten. But his record at Forest, with inspirational assistant manager Peter Taylor, is still breathtaking. Today Manchester United's Alex Ferguson is arguably the most successful manager in English football, yet after 12 years in charge of the richest club in the land he

'AT THE TIME I WAS EIGHTEEN, UNEMPLOYED AND DESPERATE TO GET A BREAK. I KNEW IF I DID GET A TRIAL I WOULD GRAB THE CHANCE.'

**Roy Keane**

had still not won the European Cup. After five years at the helm of a comparatively poor club like Nottingham Forest, Brian Clough had won the European Cup twice. Nottingham was far and away the smallest city to ever claim the prize but Brian Clough and Peter Taylor made Forest think big, for perhaps the first time in the club's history.

This was the sort of success Roy Keane had seen on television as a young boy and so a trial with Forest was a fantastic chance. Millions of times as a youngster he had watched games on TV and imagined himself part of a stylish progressive outfit such as Forest. Roy was well aware of Clough and Taylor's hard-earned reputation for recognising talent that others could not see. Roy knew that it was Clough who had taken misfits and underachievers like John Robertson and Kenny Burns and turned them into European Cup winners who suddenly had glittering international careers before them instead of the scrapheap. At the end of the 1970s Nottingham Forest went a staggering 42 games without defeat.

Roy knew and admired the way Forest played attractive sweeping football and as soon as he arrived at the City Ground his mental resolve locked into place. He decided that this was his chance and he was going to take it. But his first trip over to Nottingham ended in disappointment. Keane remembers that no one seemed to take any notice of him at all. He was training with the youth team and the next thing he knew he was back on the plane to Cork. But coach Archie Gemmill had seen enough to offer Keane another trial.

Faithful long-serving Clough aide Alan Hill, then Forest's chief scout, said, 'We had him over and settled him into an hotel. We got him training for a couple of days and Roy was picked to play against Tranmere Rovers at Tranmere in a Midland Senior League game and Liam O'Kane and myself went to watch. Roy played in midfield and did very well. He broke forward, had shots at goal, headed the ball, stuck his foot in a little bit and we thought, "Well, this lad's got something."'

> 'HE JUST HATED TO LOSE, EVEN IN A PRACTICE MATCH. IF HE THOUGHT ANYONE WASN'T PULLING HIS WEIGHT HE'D GEE THEM UP NO DANGER.'
>
> **A fellow triallist at Nottingham Forest**

Forest's charismatic manager Brian Clough held back from too much day-to-day contact with triallists but he was quickly impressed by Roy Keane's remarkable fitness level and obvious dedication to his craft. There was something about the young Keane's cool confidence and the uncompromising venom and power of his tackling that reminded Clough of himself as a sublimely gifted young player perfectly well assured of his God-given talent. The decision was taken to take a chance on the shy youngster from Cork whom Brian Clough chose to refer to as 'the Irishman'.

'I knew it was make or break in that game,' Keane later reflected. 'I played well and they offered to buy me. It was a lot of luck because at that time I didn't think I was an awfully good player. I wasn't fit, my touch wasn't that good and I didn't really pass that well.'

Roy felt elated and could not wait to relay the good news to his family back in Ireland. Nottingham Forest had just won the League Cup and finished ninth in the First Division. The season before they had been third and with Brian Clough's towering presence influencing every corner of the club Roy Keane was in no doubt that he was joining one of the elite of the English game.

The dedicated but distinctly amateur management team of Cobh Ramblers arrived at the City Ground, Nottingham, home of the proud club that had twice captured the European Cup in the late 1970s, to discuss the sale of their prize asset. John O'Rourke, the Cobh chairman, recalls that Brian Clough came late into the negotiations in the oak-panelled boardroom in his green sweater. With him he brought his golden retriever and his first concern was not over Roy Keane's potential on the pitch but that the visitors from Ireland had not been provided with a drink. Assistant manager Ronnie Fenton was instructed to rectify this social oversight and then Clough turned to his deputy and asked almost casually, 'Is this lad any good?' And Ronnie Fenton replied prophetically, 'Oh yes, boss. His potential is the earth.'

Later, Cobh manager Liam McMahon reflected, 'Roy was a talented player and we sold him as raw talent. I think it would be fair to say that. We sold talent, but what value do you put on talent? Ireland had never had a £3.75 million player. He was a player who was going to make it but we didn't think he was going to make it that soon, or burst on the scene the way he did. I certainly didn't.'

But it was not all plain sailing for the amateur enthusiasts from across the water. John Meade, Cobh's vice chairman, said, 'Mr Clough came into the negotiations then and he asked, "Why did we want money?" and John said it was for the club and Brian Clough asked, "How am I to know that it's for the club? How am I to know that you won't put the extra money that you get into your pockets? It has happened with some of the players that I have got here." We told him we were doing it for the club, not for ourselves. And we pointed out that we had taken a day's holiday from work to come over and negotiate with him. But once Ron Fenton said Roy had the potential he said, "OK, pay him the money" and we made the agreement.'

The Cobh officials were grateful to rely for advice on negotiating at these dizzy heights from former Chelsea and England star John Hollins who had played an occasional game for the homely Irish club. Cobh received £47,000 for Roy Keane in all: £20,000 initially and then a further £10,000 after Roy had played ten first-team games, and another £10,000 after a second ten games. The final £7,000 came when he had won five international caps. By today's standards perhaps the money is rather less than astronomic, but it all arrived much more quickly than anyone on either side of the negotiating table could have imagined. And Forest also visited Cobh for a money-spinning friendly.

No one in the room could have dreamed that within three years the shy and frequently tongue-tied youngster would have blossomed into one of the world's most accomplished midfield players and be heading off to Manchester United for a multi-million pound fee. Sadly for Cobh Ramblers there was no clause in the contract to earn them another lucrative knock-on fee. Cobh didn't get another penny. 'That was the unfortunate part,' mused John O'Rourke. 'We had no knock-on clause, and that was the most regrettable thing. But at the time our big concern was the upfront money. When I think of the value of him today forty-seven grand is peanuts but it was very good for us at the time. I have no regrets. Sooner or later another club would have come in for him. I'm just amazed that only Forest did, even though there were rumours about Spurs and Brighton showing an interest.'

The famous Clough charisma played a huge part in clinching the deal. He told everyone to call him Brian except Roy Keane. Turning to the nervous young footballer he said gravely, 'You are to call me Mr Clough.' Roy Keane signed for Forest on 3 May 1990 and quickly warmed to the highly individual Clough brand of leadership. The manager once clouted striker Nigel Jemson in the dressing room at Derby after he failed to follow instructions in a match and because he felt the player 'Had as big a head as I have'. But Jemson's mother later wrote to thank him for applying just the sort of discipline her son needed.

John Meade was convinced that they had delivered their prized player into good hands and told Brian Clough he had done a very good piece of business before predicting, 'He will be in your first team inside a year.'

> **'AFTER KEANE WAS HOOKED THEY WERE OVER IN DROVES IN THIS TOWN, ALL THE SCOUTS, BUT THE HORSE HAD GONE, BOLTED!'**
> Eddie O'Rourke

Roy Keane remains by a large margin Noel McCabe's most important footballing find. And his share in the vast wealth since generated by the tremendous talent he unearthed is relatively modest. Nottingham Forest paid their motorcycling scout £500 when Roy signed professional forms with them and a further £1,000 when he made the first team. But he has no complaints: 'It is nice to be rewarded as many in this town are in schoolboy football on a voluntary basis. Ireland is a hotbed of talent. There were only about four or five of us scouting at that stage but it has boomed now.' As Eddie O'Rourke put it, 'After Keane was hooked they were over in droves in this town, all the scouts, but the horse had gone, bolted!'

In fact, Spurs scout John Fallon was also on the trail of Roy Keane but he was just too late to arrange a trial with the club that had been Roy's childhood favourite. John had already cleared the trip with Tottenham's youth development officer John Moncur. His tickets were ready but Cobh insisted on playing fair and explained that Forest's trial was already organised. John said, 'Roy went over the following Monday and on the Wednesday I got a phone call to say that Forest had made an offer and Roy's heart was set on signing for Brian Clough. We were close to getting him to Spurs and I am sure he would have done well there but I still don't think that anyone saw the talent that has since become so obvious for club and country.'

Nottingham Forest worked hard to protect their young signing from an undue early media pressure. Reporters searching for news from the City Ground were simply told by assistant manager Ron Fenton that they had signed a young lad from Ireland who was one for the future. 'Don't make a big thing about it,' wily Fenton advised the news-hungry local pressmen. Apart from a small picture recording the acquisition, the uneventful arrival of Roy Keane at Nottingham Forest was in complete contrast to his eventual headline-hitting departure.

Keane looked like a little boy lost in the photo, but then his early associates all remark on his shyness. 'Roy was incredibly quiet when I first met him,' said one Forest insider. 'He was quiet and withdrawn and you had to ask him a direct question if you ever wanted to hear him speak. He really missed his family at first and one night I remember after he'd had a drink he became quite misty eyed about Cork and everything he had left behind. He was never going to run off home because he was too desperate to make it as a footballer. But he told me how much he missed his family. He and his brothers were really close and he absolutely loved everything about his home back in Cork. The digs Forest found for him were fine and he got very friendly with Gary Bowyer, the son of the Forest player Ian Bowyer, when they shared together, and that helped him a lot. But you'd always have to persuade him to have more than the odd drink. He was just very concerned never to do anything which would affect his chances of making it as a footballer.

> **'HE LOVED TO TACKLE THE ESTABLISHED PLAYERS AND TRY TO TAKE THE BALL OFF THEM. IT GAVE HIM A BUZZ. HE USED TO REALLY COME ALIVE ON THE PITCH.'**
>
> **A Forest insider**

'He would never have that much to say. One of the first things I remember him saying to me was that he found conversations with older people difficult. But that playing football against older players was easy. He loved to tackle the established players and try to take the ball off them. It gave him a buzz. He used to really come alive on the pitch. Even in those early days I think it was what he really lived for.'

Roy Keane: 'I moved into a house with this lad called Gary [Bowyer] ... and we got on really well together, we enjoyed ourselves. Luckily I got into the first team pretty quickly and things just went on from there. It might have been different if I had been stuck in the reserves for a year, I might have got a bit homesick. But being in the first team the year just flew by because I was enjoying myself so much.'

The shrewd manager of men knew the young player's links with his happy home were important to him and allowed him as much freedom as possible for trips back to his beloved Cork. Roy noted warmly later, 'At least when I was at Forest I think Brian Clough understood I was a lot younger and obviously homesick at the time and he was very understanding.'

Roy Keane was quickly drafted in to the Forest squad for the prestigious annual Under-21 international tournament in Haarlem in Holland. Team boss Archie Gemmill was delighted with the way he fitted in to a line-up that included his own son Scott and other young hopefuls such as Philip Starbuck, Ian Woan and Steve Stone. Roy Keane was wide-eyed in amazement as the first game saw Forest sweep aside Sporting Lisbon of Portugal in an emphatic 2-0 win that saw Woan score two fine goals.

He was even more amazed as he found himself on the score sheet in the second game in an even more impressive 5-1 victory against PSV Eindhoven. Keane snatched an opportunist goal with Woan, Stone, Gemmill and Neil Lyne grabbing the other scores. Forest lost the next game against Haarlem 2-0 although they had dominated much of the play. This led to a semi-final meeting with wily Barcelona who busily employed the popular continental trick of diving to the floor as though struck by a sniper's bullet whenever a Forest player even threatened to make contact. One player said, 'Roy couldn't believe it. He had been used to the physical game in Ireland, where it's a matter of pride to stay on your feet unless you're just about out cold. He hated the feigning of injuries and I remember he kept muttering "Cheating bastards" all the way through the game.' Archie Gemmill was delighted with the restraint shown by all his young players. He said, 'It was a test of character for us as much as ability.'

And Forest passed the test with flying colours. Barcelona went ahead early on in the match but Forest equalised after Gemmill put Starbuck through only for the striker to be cynically fouled. Starbuck showed his own poise and promise by coolly getting up to score from the penalty spot. Lyne came on as substitute and scored two late goals and Barcelona conceded an own goal, which made the scoreline 3-1 to fairly reflect the run of play.

That meant a final against Haarlem, who had gone through the tournament ignoring the age qualifications and playing with what was virtually their first team. The match was a tense affair and score stood at 1-1 after 90 minutes. Starbuck got the equalising goal again from the penalty spot after the Dutch side had taken a 27th-minute lead and Forest were guilty of missing more than enough chances to have prevented the result being decided by the dreaded penalty shoot-out. It was left to a highly delighted Roy Keane to slam home the crucial penalty and win the game for Forest after Haarlem had twice missed. It was perhaps the most important moment in his young career and observers noted he blasted the ball into the corner of the net without so much as hint of nerves, as if it was a practice session.

Archie Gemmill was very pleased with his young players and said, 'It's always great to win a tournament but it also gave us the opportunity to look at a lot of the players who will be forming the backbone of our reserve side this season and I was very pleased with them.'

At first Roy had modest and down-to-earth hopes about the length of time it would take to make his name in England. 'They offered me a three-year contract,' he said, 'and I thought I'll sign the contract and use the time to try to settle in and hopefully maybe in that time possibly get a break in the first team and take it from there.'

But he underestimated himself. As the pre-season preparations got underway, the Nottingham Forest first team, studded with household names such as Nigel Clough, Stuart Pearce, Des Walker and Steve Hodge, and fresh from their Wembley triumph in the last Littlewood's Cup final, flew off on a sunshine tour of Italy. Roy found himself lining up as substitute for Nottingham Forest Reserves at the rather less glamorous location of Sutton in Ashfield. Alan Hill remembers that Brian Clough was very interested in seeing 'the Irishman' in action. And the boss was distinctly underwhelmed when told that Reserves boss Archie Gemmill had restricted Roy Keane to a place on the bench. Hill says, 'Archie's son Scott was playing in midfield where Roy would normally play. We waited until half-time and Brian said, "Archie, I would like to see the Irishman play, please." Archie ignored him so after five minutes Brian climbed over the fence, tapped Archie on the shoulder and said, "Son, get your son off and get the Irishman on." By the time he went on there were only 20 minutes to go and Roy didn't do anything that out of the ordinary.' But Cloughie had seen something in the closing minutes that convinced him Nottingham Forest had made a good investment.

Roy Keane was pleased to achieve his early target of a place in the Forest Reserves line-up and even happier when he starred in a hard-fought clash against local side Arnold Town. With 900 people packed into their tiny ground the game that really first revealed the potential of Roy Keane was played on 21 August. And the young professionals of Forest found the more experienced local league players eager to take them down a peg or two. Arnold swept into a 3-1 lead and it looked like an embarrassing defeat for the Forest second string. But Roy Keane gave a demonstration of his astonishing box-to-box stamina, galvanised his side into a furious fightback and scored both of the two goals that gave Forest a more respectable draw.

Brian Clough was just as enthusiastic, but he wisely kept his views to himself. Already a plan to thrust Roy Keane into the top level much earlier than anyone had first imagined was forming in his fertile football brain. The local papers only gave a minimal and grudging account of Roy Keane's arrival on the football scene. More important international events were dominating the papers at the time as the summer news pages were full of shocking details of Saddam Hussein's outrageous assault on Kuwait.

When the season spluttered to an indifferent start, no one knew that Roy Keane was very much in Brian Clough's immediate plans. Keane remembers, 'The first team played QPR on the Saturday and drew 1-1. Nigel Jemson got a penalty and on the Monday the Reserves were playing and I was named as substitute so I was delighted just to get involved as sub. I came on for the last ten minutes. The first team were playing Liverpool away the next day. I came in on the Tuesday morning to train because I'd only played for ten minutes and the assistant manager said, "Oh, you're going to Liverpool." I couldn't believe it.'

At the time Roy Keane was delighted to have established himself in the Reserves so quickly. He had quietly joined the rest of the team for a few drinks after the game and didn't get back to the hotel until about 2 a.m. and went straight to bed. But when he arrived for training the next morning he was told he was heading north. 'I thought there was something funny going on,' he remembers, ' because when I was getting on the coach somebody said, "Make sure you have your boots."'

Forest's stylish England international midfield star Steve Hodge went down with flu and with Stuart Pearce and Terry Wilson also unfit Clough was forced to shuffle his pack at the last minute, which meant a motorway dash to Merseyside. Keane travelled with striker Phil Starbuck but had no idea that he was to actually play until just an hour before kick-off. Clough the great psychologist wanted the youngster to be in doubt until the very last minute. Liverpool had swept aside the challenge of promoted Sheffield United in their first game and were riding high on confidence. In the historic Anfield dressing rooms Keane was helping Liam O'Kane to lay out the kit for the team who were still strangers to him before Clough gently but firmly pulled him aside and asked, 'Irishman, what are you doing?' Roy said, 'Helping to put the gear out, boss.' Cloughie said, 'Son, put the number seven shirt on. You're playing.'

Astonishingly, Roy had to be introduced to some of his new teammates. Until then he had only met the first team once when he signed for the club. He didn't even change in the same dressing room because Forest had such a big squad. 'We actually

> 'I CAME IN ON THE TUESDAY MORNING TO TRAIN BECAUSE I'D ONLY PLAYED FOR TEN MINUTES AND THE ASSISTANT MANAGER SAID, "OH, YOU'RE GOING TO LIVERPOOL." I COULDN'T BELIEVE IT.'
>
> **Roy Keane**

Scoring for Nottingham Forest against Oldham.

got on the pitch and the other Forest players were coming up and saying, "What's your name?" I said, "Roy," and they said, "Relax." But he didn't have time to worry if he was ready to face a glittering line-up that included international stars such as Peter Beardsley and John Barnes.

Long afterwards Roy reflected, 'Luckily enough it was just before kick-off. If I had been told on the Monday that I was playing at Anfield the next day I probably wouldn't have slept that well.'

Alan Hill noted, 'He went white when Brian told him he was playing, but once he got out on to the field he was unbelievable, it was as if he had been there years. He was so mature. When he came off the field he was drained. But what a performance.' It was a sensational night for young Roy Keane. The day after facing Rotherham Reserves at an empty City Ground he was hurled into Anfield with 33,000 fans mostly baying for their Merseyside heroes.

Keane strode on to the pitch as if he had been a first-team regular for seasons. But much of the evening was lost to memory in a torrent of exultant realised ambition. Though he did say afterwards, 'I remember at one stage I was running back and Steve McMahon was running forward next to me and I remember just looking at him and thinking, Is this really happening? It was a fantastic feeling. I'll never forget making my debut at Anfield.' Roy's only concern was that the debut arrived so fast that he hadn't had time to arrange for his father to come over to watch the game: 'It came right out of the blue otherwise my dad would have been over like a shot,' he said later. 'I rang him up to say that I was going up to Liverpool with the squad for a bit of experience. When I told my family that I was going to Liverpool with the team my dad was delighted – and he thought that I was just travelling with the Reserves. Little did I know at that stage that I would actually be playing in the first team. I had only been to Anfield once before to see a game and it was a dream come true to actually make my debut there.' And he noted, 'That day was amazing ... [the lads] gave me fabulous encouragement and told me what to expect and although we lost the game I thoroughly enjoyed myself.'

> **'WE ACTUALLY GOT ON THE PITCH AND THE OTHER FOREST PLAYERS WERE COMING UP AND SAYING, "WHAT'S YOUR NAME?"'**
>
> **Roy Keane**

League champions Liverpool won the game quite comfortably 2-0, with goals from Beardsley and Ian Rush, but Brian Clough was still delighted with his young protégé's debut. After the game the manager said, 'I was thrilled to bits with him. I know it's very difficult to judge a player on one performance, but he showed enough qualities in all aspects of his game to make me feel sure that I can't be wrong about him.' Later Clough reflected, 'People said I had flipped my lid when I picked Roy Keane for that match but he did well that night at Anfield ... after that I knew Roy Keane had the makings of a great player.'

Forest turned in a typically hard-tackling and workman-like display that night before Liverpool's class overwhelmed them. Roy Keane saw Des Walker and Steve Chettle hurling themselves into the fray and took his example. A full-blooded clash with Ray Houghton raised the eyebrows of the referee but inspired a nod of approval from the experienced and richly talented Walker. He said later that he knew then that Roy Keane was going to be a player to contend with.

Sitting high in the stand at Anfield that night was well-respected Manchester United scout Les Kershaw, who duly reported back to his demanding master Alex Ferguson that Forest's young Irish debutant had acquitted himself very well indeed.

As soon as the coach got back to Nottingham in the early hours of Wednesday morning the still-euphoric Roy Keane rang his parents: 'I'm not sure they believed me at first when I told them what had happened. Mind you, at the time I didn't believe it myself.'

Keane was quickly pulled out of Forest's youth team trip to

France to the eight-club Montetaire Tournament that Forest had won three years before in case he was needed in the first team. In fact, his days of junior soccer had ended that night at Anfield. From then on he was a first-team player. Privately, Brian Clough raved that Roy Keane had it all. He loved the young player's total commitment to the game and marvelled at his non-stop contribution to the game. 'The Irishman has everything he needs to go all the way,' he observed later. 'He can tackle, he can pass, he can head the ball, and he can score. And he can do it all with the impression he has plenty of time, which is always the indication of a top-class player. You didn't have to be a genius to see that he had something going for him – even my wife could have spotted it. He is one of the best headers of the ball I have ever come across. Blow me, I've not seen anyone jump so well since Red Rum called it a day.'

Clough was also highly enthused by the young player's temperament in his daunting debut match. He said at the time, 'For someone who is only nineteen he did incredibly well at Anfield. So I have absolutely no reservations about putting him in again when we play Coventry City at Highfield Road this weekend.'

Roy Keane duly found himself in the line-up and had a solid second game in Forest's 2-2 draw. He further established his all-action style of play, hurtling from one penalty area to the other with impressive energy and just missed a far-post header that would have given Forest their first win of the season.

Nottingham Forest were still without a victory as Roy Keane approached his home debut, against Southampton on 8 September. On this occasion there was time for Roy Keane's proud parents and two of his brothers to come over to see the big day. And also in the stand was Noel McCabe, who had come over for a fortunately timed scouts' meeting the night before. 'The scouts were all saying they were looking forward to seeing him play a home game.' They were not disappointed. Roy Keane turned in an all-action performance of such quality that the City Ground fans took him instantly to their hearts.

It was Roy Keane's relentless drive in midfield that inspired Forest's ascendancy after Rod Wallace had fired the visitors in front. Keane fed the ball through to rampaging winger Franz Carr who put over an accurate cross for Terry Wilson to head the equaliser. Nigel Jemson got the second with a beautifully judged chip

> **'BLOW ME, I'VE NOT SEEN ANYONE JUMP SO WELL SINCE RED RUM CALLED IT A DAY.'**
> Brian Clough, Keane's manager at Nottingham Forest

after he spotted Southampton goalkeeper Tim Flowers off his line and then added the third goal to make sure of the points. Keane was everywhere in the match and almost snatched his first Forest goal with a brave header that was saved on the line.

Brian Clough dragged Roy Keane off the field with just eight minutes of the match to go and the City Ground faithful responded with a spontaneous standing ovation. The young player was astonished and deeply moved by the accolade. He rushed off the pitch and went straight down to the dressing room, but Brian Clough sent Archie Gemmill to bring him back to the dugout and paid his own tribute to the young man who would become his most crucial players for the next three years by kissing Roy Keane firmly on the cheek. To say the young player was surprised is to say that he quite likes to win. He was shocked to his boots, embarrassed to be kissed by another man in front of his parents, let alone a packed City Ground. But he got over it. 'Afterwards he was thunderstruck,' said a member of the Forest coaching staff. 'At first he was angry at being substituted, even though Archie had told him it was only because the match was won and the Guvnor wanted to spare his young legs. But then being dragged out again and kissed publicly he didn't quite know what to think. But Brian charmed his parents so perfectly that he had the sense just to smile and say nothing about how he really felt.'

Roy Keane said after the match, 'I really enjoyed the game but I was absolutely shattered by the end so I was glad to come off. I was getting ready to have a shower when Archie Gemmill came to get me back again. I certainly didn't expect Mr Clough to react like that but then I didn't expect to make my debut at Anfield. It didn't embarrass me, I was just thrilled to be in the team.'

Roy Keane's first goal for Forest came in a 4-1 victory over Fourth Division Burnley in the second round of the Rumbelows' League Cup at the City Ground on 26 September. In fact, the scoreline flattered Forest and it was not until Burnley has seen their skipper Steve Davis sent off that First Division Forest made their superiority clear. Steve Chettle had grabbed an early lead for the home side but Burnley's Peter Mumby equalised just before half-time. Roy Keane altered the whole pattern of the game when he scored in the 72nd minute as he smoothly converted a Brian Laws cross. Then he set up Nigel Jemson for Forest's third goal with an accurate header before Stuart Pearce hammered home a trademark blockbuster to give Forest a healthy lead to take to the second leg at Turf Moor.

Roy was euphoric after the match: 'I was absolutely delighted to score. It was a fantastic feeling. When I jumped to meet the cross I was worried that I would miss, especially as we needed a goal at that time. But it was great when the ball hit the net because I wasn't really having a very good game until then. I thought I had scored in the first half after a one-two with Nigel Clough but their keeper made a good stop. I just hope I get a few more goals if I'm picked.' Neutral observers were impressed by Keane's remarkable determination and unflagging workrate. He was certainly the deciding difference between the two sides.

Forest hit a purple patch after the Burnley game, winning 1-0 against Manchester United at Old Trafford before hammering Everton 3-1 and beating Burnley again in the second leg. After the Manchester United match Roy Keane and Stuart Pearce were chosen for random drugs tests routinely organised by the Football Association. Brian Clough said, 'The way Stuart Pearce whacked in our goal I thought they might have stopped the game there and then to test Pearcy.'

Within a few games Roy Keane was transformed from an unknown into a first-team regular. It was an amazingly steep learning curve and a crucial part of that early education was an encounter with the acknowledged superstar of the moment, Paul Gascoigne. At the end of October Forest fought out a tense League battle with Tottenham Hotspur at the City Ground, which they narrowly lost by the odd goal in three. To make it worse the Spurs winner went in with the last kick of the game when the Forest players were sure they had secured at least a point against the stylish side then captained by England skipper Gary Lineker.

But even more memorable than the football was the 90-minute verbal onslaught that was sustained by Gascoigne on the young Irishman in the crowded midfield area. Roy said after the game, 'I tried to ignore him and get on with my own game, but it was difficult at times.' Despite the incessant provocation Roy managed to keep his temper in check throughout, but he was bitterly disappointed to be beaten at the death. 'Losing is awful at the best of times,' he said. 'But to be beaten by the very last kick of the game is sickening. All the lads were absolutely devastated in the dressing room after the match. I thought we deserved a draw and that would have been a fair result. Perhaps if we had taken our chances in the first half when we were on top things might have been different. But Tottenham are a good side and they really came at us in the second half. It just seems as if they never know when they are beaten. Every time we cleared our lines the ball just seemed to come straight back at us.'

Roy Keane's fine form with Forest had pundits insisting it was only a matter of time before the player received a call-up for his country and just before Christmas it arrived. Ireland manager Jack Charlton had received many messages suggesting he pick Keane and he named the player in the Eire Under-21 squad to take on Turkey in Dublin on 16 October. Roy Keane was determined to keep his feet on the ground and said, 'I know people are talking about the possibility of me playing for my country. But I have got to be realistic because it is only three months ago that I was in the Eire youth squad yet unable to get into the starting line-up. I would love to do well enough this season to get into the Eire Under-19 squad for the World Youth Cup in Portugal next summer. That is a target for me in international football, but what concerns me most at the moment is being picked for Forest.'

Roy Keane's remarkable arrival on the First Division scene was recognised on a wider scale than just among Forest fans as the player was named as the Barclays Young Eagle of the Month for the Midlands in October. He received the inscribed salver before the kick-off of the home match against Sunderland. Brian Clough enthused, 'It is no surprise to me that he is picking up awards and gaining recognition with his country Eire. He has done superbly well for us and maintained his form week in, week out.'

Nottingham Forest's long record of unbroken success in the League Cup came to a thrilling end in an astonishing encounter with Coventry City at Highfield Road at the end of November. Roy Keane was prominent in a high-scoring fourth-round meeting that began with the home side romping into a seemingly unassailable 4-0 lead, through a Kevin Gallagher hat-trick and a single goal from Steve Livingstone. But Forest were defending an unbeaten League Cup run of 22 games and were not about to concede defeat easily. With Roy Keane marshalling the fightback Nigel

**EVEN MORE MEMORABLE THAN THE FOOTBALL WAS THE 90-MINUTE VERBAL ONSLAUGHT THAT WAS SUSTAINED BY GASCOIGNE ON THE YOUNG IRISHMAN IN THE CROWDED MIDFIELD AREA.**

Clough hammered home a sensational eight-minute hat trick and Garry Parker supplied another score to leave the tie all square at 4-4. It was Coventry who snatched victory in the end, though, with another goal from Livingstone. Brian Clough was characteristically blunt after the final whistle, 'After that defensive performance our chairman would have every right to think about giving me the sack.'

After many near misses Roy Keane scored his first goal for Nottingham Forest in the visit to Sheffield United on 22 December, though the home side won the game 3-2. But when he headed home against Wimbledon it turned out to be the winner in a game that finished 2-1. Keane was much more pleased with the victory than with his own score: 'It is always nice to score goals but the most important thing is to win and after the disappointment at Sheffield it went our way against

Wimbledon. They are not an easy side to play against. They really do play to their strengths, and when they came at us in the second half we were just delighted to come away with a win.'

Assistant manager Ron Fenton compared Roy's powerful header to a classic Tommy Lawton effort from a previous era. It came within a minute of John Fashanu equalising Stuart Pearce's early Forest goal. Roy Keane might have got his chance in the first team thanks to an injury to Steve Hodge but within a few shorts weeks of the start of the season he had made the central midfield place his own. It was a remarkable achievement. Hodge was an established England international who had just returned, with Forest's other England stars Des Walker and Stuart Pearce, from a highly creditable showing in the World Cup in Italy. He had come back from a stint at Spurs to drive Forest to win the Littlewoods and the Simod cups.

Back in Ireland Keane's old manager Liam McMahon was watching his former star's remarkable progress that first season with interest: 'It's a monumental jump from playing for Cobh Ramblers to walking out at Anfield,' he reflected. But he was even more impressed that Roy sustained his form throughout the season. 'I thought he would tire at the back end of the season and they would rest him, but they never had to,' he remembered. Halfway through the season Roy Keane's impact won him wider recognition as a series of stirring performances in January secured him the Barclay's Young Eagle of the Month Award. McMahon paid tribute: 'I knew Roy would make the grade. The only thing that has taken me aback a bit is how rapidly it has happened for him and how he has managed to keep going through what must be a very tiring season. There must be tremendous pressure on him. But he has kept his consistency and I can tell you that when I saw him he was exactly the same old Roy who used to sit in our dressing room. He's quiet, level headed and he is crystal clear about his ambitions. He hasn't let the last six months affect his personality and I don't think he ever will. He comes from a lovely, supportive family who are football mad. They'll look after him for sure.'

In fact according to McMahon, Spurs and Aston Villa were already taking notice of Roy Keane's performances when Forest swooped. 'If he had gone to Spurs, I am sure he would still be in the Reserves and no one would have heard of him yet. But Brian Clough is not afraid to give youngsters a chance and Roy knew it. He told me he had been treated marvellously by everyone during his week's trial at Forest. He made his mind up there and then that he would move there straight away. As a club, we didn't push him in any direction. He made the choice himself and it was the right one.'

But the discovery of Roy Keane sparked a flurry of interest from scouts who had rarely previously ventured too far outside Dublin. McMahon said, 'Most of the scouts stayed in the Dublin area before Roy made his breakthrough. No one picked him up before because hardly anyone came down to see us.'

As the season progressed towards Christmas Roy Keane told friends he was still pinching himself to make sure that his Roy of the Rovers-style arrival in the Forest first team was really happening. Brian Clough told him to just keep doing what he was doing. And Keane said, 'I can't believe it really, but I'm enjoying every second of it. Last season I was only watching the likes of Liverpool and Manchester United on television. Now I am playing against them.

'When I signed a three-year contract my family were hoping

that by the end of three years I might get a chance to be a substitute but things have happened very quickly. The lads at Forest have helped me tremendously. Training with top players is an education for me and on match days they are carrying me through. The fact that I am in full-time training has helped too. Back in Ireland I was struggling to get through the 90 minutes but here the extra fitness has made a big difference to my game.'

Roy Keane was called into the Irish Under-21 squad for a Euro championships qualifier against Turkey. Maurice Setters, the Assistant Ireland Coach had this to say: 'The progress he's made is fantastic. He's got great control, he heads the ball well and he's clearly going to develop even more. The most important thing is that he keeps his feet on the floor. But with Brian Clough as his boss I don't think there's much danger of him getting carried away.'

Not for the last time in his career Roy Keane was denied more Ireland representative honours after being selected for the national Under-19 squad to play Algeria in Algiers at the end of January as part of Ireland's preparations for the FIFA World Youth Cup to be held that summer in Portugal. The dates clashed with Forest's Data Systems Cup tie against Barnsley at Oakwell. Keane was forced to withdraw and insisted he preferred to concentrate his thoughts on Forest rather than dwell on his ambitions to play for his country.

**'I JUST WISH ROY KEANE WAS ENGLISH.'**
Graham Taylor, then England manager

Keane scored a spectacular goal in the 6-2 away demolition of Norwich and was so elated he executed a somersault to celebrate. Afterwards he commented, 'People have talked to me a lot about the goal I scored at Norwich and although it is probably the best one to date it was fairly simple. I just saw the chance and hit it. Fortunately it flew in to the top corner.'

Brian Clough appreciated the goal, but not the acrobatics that followed. He threatened to sell Keane to a circus if he ever repeated the stunt. But while Clough was always keen to keep control over his young star, he couldn't stop Keane's reputation from growing steadily. He received the national Barclays Young Eagle of the Month Award for his achievements during December. And England manager Graham Taylor, who headed the judging panel, said, 'I just wish Roy Keane was English. Roy has done exceptionally well. I saw him make his debut at Liverpool and saw how easily he picked up the Forest style of play. It looks as though he has been at the club for two or three years and come right up through the youth team. He seems to be maturing and improving all the time. Breaking from midfield he can score goals and he has a very good engine.'

Former England manager Ron Greenwood was also on the judging panel and he echoed Taylor's opinion. Prophetically, Greenwood said, 'Playing central midfield Roy Keane shows a lot of confidence and makes some good telling runs à la Brian Robson.'

On 17 January 1991 Clough handed Keane a hefty pay rise and called him 'First Division find of the season'. Keane signed a four-year contract and Clough was reminded of a day way back in 1967 when he had signed Roy McFarland for Derby for less than £25,000 – McFarland helped Derby to take the League and was to win 28 England caps.

'The biggest compliment I can pay Roy Keane is that the impact he is making reminds me so much of what Roy McFarland did when Peter Taylor and I signed him for Derby County from Tranmere,' Clough commented. 'I know what I've said about the young Irishman since he got into our side against Liverpool last August but I didn't want to be found guilty of killing him with kindness. He's picked me up a time or two this season and it was only a matter of time before our board of directors considered giving him a new contract. It's a long time since I have been as excited by a young man – and he is still a stranger to me.'

Brian Clough was particularly impressed by Keane's versatility. In one game he pressed him into service as a stand-in central defender and Roy did so well the manager compared Keane to the great Franz Beckenbauer. Much to the young Irishman's embarrassment, the rest of the players took to addressing him in thick German accents.

The relationship between manager and player was one of mutual respect. Roy Keane might have been shy as a young arrival in Nottingham but he was not one to be overawed by his charismatic boss. Roy said, 'I got on very well with Brian. It baffled me the way some of the established stars at Forest got into a panic every time he was around the place. I was never afraid of him. I got on with him and if he said something I disagreed with I would tell him. He was a very nice man most of the time and was especially charming whenever he met my mother and father.'

Life was pretty good for Roy Keane as the New Year dawned, but in the third round of the FA Cup he was to experience the down side of soccer and learn that experience on the pitch is not always one success after another. Forest were drawn away against Crystal Palace – then riding high in the First Division – and after a dour 0-0 draw the replay was scheduled for the City Ground on 24 January. Palace grabbed a goal but scores from Stuart Pearce and Terry Wilson looked to be easing Forest through to the fourth round. Then an uncharacteristic error from Roy Keane led to the Palace equaliser. Keane slightly underhit a back pass while under pressure from Mark Bright, and Mark Crossley was forced to rush forward and boot the the ball clear. Unfortunately for the horrified Keane it went straight to the talented Nigerian-born player John Salako wide out near the touchline and close to the halfway line. Spotting that Crossley was well off his line after his panic dash, Salako smartly lobbed the ball into the top corner from some 50 yards out to level the scores with 30 minutes to go.

The City Ground faithful were stunned. Roy Keane making a mistake – whatever next! Goalkeeper Mark Crossley said afterwards, 'It was a terrible way to end a Cup tie, but we're still in the competition.' Indeed, it was soon business as usual: Forest won the toss over venue and duly dispatched Crystal Palace 3-0 thanks to two goals from Garry Parker and one from Gary Crosby.

The FA Cup presented Forest's best chance of honours from then on. And the players knew just as well as the media that this was the one competition Brian Clough had never won. 'There was a special tension before each Cup tie,' Keane remembered later. 'We were all desperate to win it for the boss.'

But Forest faced another difficult draw in the next round, away to Newcastle United. After just thirteen minutes of the game they were two goals down. Stuart Pearce snatched one back and Newcastle squandered an easy chance before Nigel Clough scored with just two minutes of the match left. Replay specialists Forest completely dominated the second meeting and won 3-0.

In the fifth round Forest survived another away draw, at Southampton, and another replay. They looked like going out of the competition after the home side scored early on and led for most of the match until Steve Hodge levelled the scores ten minutes from time. Forest started to believe that their name really might be on the FA Cup this year after Southampton's Rod Wallace hit the bar with a rasping shot just before the final whistle. Injury-prone Forest striker Nigel Jemson hammered home an excellent hat trick in the replay as Forest won the tie 3-1.

For their troubles Forest received yet another away draw, at Norwich. This time Roy Keane stepped forward to save the day. It was a tense and scrappy encounter with little to chose between the two teams until the young Irishman coolly grabbed an opportunist goal. Keane said afterwards, 'All goals are great when they go in but there's a special feeling when you manage to get the goal that wins the game. Everyone was desperate not to lose and I really enjoyed the match.'

**IN ONE GAME HE PRESSED HIM INTO SERVICE AS A STAND-IN CENTRAL DEFENDER AND ROY DID SO WELL THE MANAGER COMPARED KEANE TO THE GREAT FRANZ BECKENBAUER. MUCH TO THE YOUNG IRISHMAN'S EMBARRASSMENT, AS THE REST OF THE PLAYERS TOOK TO ADDRESSING HIM IN THICK GERMAN ACCENTS.**

The semi-final was at Villa Park against West Ham. It was the eighteenth time that Forest had played a game that gave them a chance to earn a place in an FA Cup final. And confirmed Forest fanatics knew that of those eighteen games their team had won precisely two. But this looked like being their year and a stirring performance from Roy Keane in midfield did much to inspire his side to a comfortable 4-0 win. Keane scored again and the other goals came from Gary Crosby, Stuart Pearce and Gary Charles. The game partly hinged on the sending-off of West Ham defender Tony Gale for a professional foul on Crosby after 25 minutes. And if an early West Ham effort had not struck the woodwork the result could have been very different. Spurs beat Arsenal in the other semi-final thanks to a memorable 30-yard free kick from one Paul Gascoigne and the scene was set for young star Roy Keane to lead Forest to capture the one trophy that had eluded the great Brian Clough. Things did not quite turn out like that, though.

Ironically the greatest challenge of Roy's young life so far was to come against the team he had followed fervently as a child, Tottenham Hotspur. 'I was a big Spurs fan when I was a kid,' said Roy on the eve of the big match. 'And when I watched them on television it was always in the back of my mind that I

> **'WHEN I WATCHED [SPURS] ON TELEVISION IT WAS ALWAYS IN THE BACK OF MY MIND THAT I WOULD LOVE TO PLAY FOR THEM ONE DAY. NOW ALL I AM DOING IS LOOKING FORWARD TO TRYING TO BEAT THEM.'**
> Roy Keane on the eve of Nottingham Forest's 1991 FA Cup final

Forest celebrate victory over West Ham in the FA Cup semi-final.

would love to play for them one day. Now all I am doing is looking forward to trying to beat them.'

The flagship Wembley finale became the highlight of Roy Keane's astonishing first season in English football. In the nervous days before the match Roy reflected on an amazing eight months, which had seen him move from part-time player with Cobh Ramblers to established Nottingham Forest midfielder. He said, 'This season has been a fairy-tale for me. To be truthful it has exceeded my wildest dreams. I was just happy to get a contract in English football. I seemed to be going nowhere in Ireland.'

The 1991 FA Cup final is remembered for all the wrong reasons. As a man and as a footballer the richly talented Paul Gascoigne has many wonderful qualities, but restraint is not one of them. Following his extraordinary goal in the semi-final the match became hyped up as Paul Gascoigne's big day. The London press preferred to concentrate on Gazza's mercurial skills and the platform that Wembley would surely provide for the Geordie midfield maestro at the expense of Forest and Brian Clough's chance to win the FA Cup.

**'I HAD DONE MY ANKLE LIGAMENTS ABOUT TWO WEEKS BEFORE THE GAME AGAINST SPURS. ALL THE TIME I WAS SITTING AROUND SEEING THE DAYS PASS BY AND I WONDERED IF I'D MAKE IT.'**

Roy Keane on the 1991 FA Cup final against Spurs

Keane had faced a desperate battle to get fit for the FA Cup final. He had only just made it, as assistant manager Ron Fenton admitted: 'Roy was our only doubt and had he not got through 90 minutes in the Reserves the other night he would not have been on our team coach.'

Roy remembered the nervous run-up to his first big game: 'I

**Sheringham and Keane celebrate another magnificent goal in 1991.**

had done my ankle ligaments about two weeks before the game against Spurs. All the time I was sitting around seeing the days pass by and I wondered if I'd make it. It was agony waiting to get a match in. When I knew that I was playing on Tuesday, I also realised that it was going to be all or nothing. If I had not come through that match without trouble then my chance of a place at Wembley would have been zero.'

Brian Clough was delighted that his star discovery was passed fit to play at Wembley. He paid tribute to Keane and stalwart Stuart Pearce for driving Forest's season on after a difficult start. 'I'm not forgetting the lift he gave us from the very first moment he grabbed his place in the first team,' said Clough.

By the time the teams reached the field, with Cloughie embarrassing Spurs manager Terry Venables by insisting on holding hands as they walked out on to the pitch, Paul Gascoigne's personal build-up to the game had got so out of control he was at boiling point. He stormed into the match like a man possessed. When he shook hands with the Prince of Wales before the kick-off commentator John Motson dredged up one of his most excruciating puns: 'The Prince of Wales meets the Prince of Wails.'

Within two minutes of kick-off Roy Keane could only watch in horror as Gascoigne hit Garry Parker with a tackle that looked like something out of a kick-boxing bout. With the ball nowhere near Gazza launched a high kick at the astonished Parker that hit him squarely in the chest. Even Terry Venables believed his best player was in deep trouble. But Roger Milford did not even reach for his book. It is a decision that ranks as one of the worst refereeing moments in FA Cup history. Worse was to come from the out-of-control Spurs star. After 12 minutes Forest's young right-back Gary Charles was kicked savagely on the right knee by Gascoigne long after the ball had gone. Again the forgiving Mr Milford did not see any need for a booking. Gascoigne was famously stretchered off to a backdrop of zero sympathy from the Forest faithful and Stuart Pearce drilled a splendid free kick into the top left-hand corner of the net.

Nayim replaced Gascoigne and Spurs rearranged their formation with Samways moving to cover Gascoigne's central midfield role and the new player taking over on the left. Spurs still had 11 players on the pitch and after Gary Crosby missed a relatively easy chance to increase Forest's lead it was increasingly Spurs who looked the stronger side.

Roy Keane strove manfully to stem the tide but he was not at his best that day. Gradually Spurs recovered from the Gascoigne hysteria and after 25 minutes Paul Allen put Gary Lineker through for the striker to score a typical opportunist goal, which was disallowed for offside, though endlessly examined television replays later proved beyond most people's doubt that Lineker was definitely onside when the ball was played. But when Lineker was again put through the Forest defence, this time by Paul Stewart, he was brought down by Forest goalkeeper Mark Crossley, who was lucky to stay on the pitch after the challenge. Lineker took the kick himself and struck the ball firmly towards the corner to the keeper's left. But Crossley guessed correctly and turned the ball to safety. This was only the second time a goalkeeper has saved a penalty in the FA Cup final. After this tumultuous first half Nottingham Forest were still 1-0 ahead.

In the second half Nayim equalised with a well-taken cross-shot goal and Forest, with playmaker Nigel Clough shackled by tight marking, scarcely managed a serious attempt on goal. In extra time Paul Stewart headed on a Nayim corner and the ultra-dependable Des Walker of all people headed it into his own net under pressure from Gary Mabbutt. It was a sad end to a day that had begun so brightly. Roy Keane had some robust skirmishes, notably with the combative Justin Edinburgh, but Spurs had won the FA Cup.

Roy Keane regretted afterwards that he had not been able to savour the moment. He reflected, 'On the day we didn't play well. And Tottenham beat us fair and square. Unfortunately, Des got an o.g. The day flew by me. People say you should take it in but I didn't. I was only a young player at the time. Obviously I would have loved to have won it but it wasn't to be. I was very disappointed. and I don't think I was 100 per cent fit. Luckily enough I was picked to play by Brian Clough but deep down I know I wasn't fully fit. I'm not making excuses but the day just passed me by. It's a pity because it should have been such a big day for me.'

FA Cup final drama against Spurs at Wembley, 18 May 1991.

But Roy Keane was not allowed to be down-hearted for long as his call-up to play for his country arrived and he made his international debut against Chile just after the FA Cup final. 'I was genuinely surprised to hear that I had been chosen,' he admitted. 'I have done fairly well for the Under-21s but looking at the team lately the way they have

FA Cup Final drama against Spurs at Wembley, 18 May 1991.

been playing I didn't think I would get a look in. There are a lot of experienced midfielders in the side and I thought I would be in for a long wait. So I'm delighted to be involved and even if I don't get on the field it will be a great experience for me.'

Not all of the countless headlines inspired by Roy Maurice Keane were for his footballing prowess. With success on the pitch came unwanted attention off it and Brian Clough became irritated by reports of trouble in night clubs involving the talented Irishman.

Alan Hill admitted frankly, 'Obviously when you're out of sight you get up to all sorts of things and Roy did. Roy was the typical young lad. If you're a genius as a football player then you do have things in your private life that aren't quite right that you get up to and you become a little bit arrogant and Roy was no different.'

Typically Roy Keane makes no excuses or apologies: 'I've obviously got involved in one or two scrapes over the years but I wouldn't change a thing. If someone is going to have a go at me then usually I'll have a go back,' he shrugs. 'You know, it's a fault but that's the way it goes.'

Roy Keane lived in the sleepy village of Scarrington just outside Nottingham, where the villagers grew to admire and feel protective of the fast-rising Forest star. His friendship with Gary Bowyer grew and both players were disappointed when it became clear that Gary was never going to have Keane's level of success in the game. Roy Keane was also very grateful for the support and advice he received from his manager. 'Brian Clough helped me greatly when I got myself into trouble off the field in incidents I should have avoided. I should have simply walked away from some of the night-club scenes in Nottingham. Cloughie was brilliant with me, though. He knew when to put his foot down and also when I didn't need a bollocking, but some friendly advice. He helped me to learn from my mistakes and I don't go where I could get into trouble now.

> **'IF SOMEONE IS GOING TO HAVE A GO AT ME THEN USUALLY I'LL HAVE A GO BACK.'**
> **Roy Keane**

'As a family we are still very close. My mum and dad come over here as often as possible. I got my tickets for the final, but it was difficult making 20 tickets go round 45 friends and relations. I don't particularly miss home, but it is great to go back now and again. Most of my friends slag me off or whatever and that is the way I want it to be, just treated the same as ever. But my dad Maurice is my biggest critic. When I go home and he sees me playing in a game on television he will let me know if I have played badly or not. And if he ever thinks I am getting too big for my boots then he will give me a kick up the backside. He often tells me he used to be a bit of a footballer himself, but I'm not sure whether I believe him or not! There are no better people in the world than the Irish. They are bubbly and outgoing. Not extrovert – that is too strong.'

Roy Keane was deeply grateful for the treatment he received at Nottingham Forest. 'The players and coaches have been fantastic in helping me settle down in Nottingham,' he acknowledged. 'Once you get to know people a bit better you can give a bit of stick back. I take enough of it from the lads.' Getting used to life in Britain was certainly greatly helped by his provincial surroundings. 'In many ways Nottingham is a lot like Cork,' he reflected. 'I love both cities. All my friends who come and stay remark on how similar they are. The pace of life is not that different in England. Mind you the pace of life is a little quicker at night. I've no girlfriends, no ties. At least not that I know of anyway.'

One of the most difficult things Roy Keane had to face in England was struggling to pass his driving test. 'Like I said, I would be on the dole if I wasn't here playing football, so I never dreamed that I would be able to buy a car when I signed. In the end I just had to take my driving test. I failed it miserably the first time and was determined that if I failed again I wouldn't bother with a car. As it happened I passed. But it tends to encourage the laid-back style of my nature, having a car to get around in all the time.'

Still happily living in digs, Roy was already looking ahead to trying to get himself a flat or a house of his own. But not too hard. He always preferred to concentrate on his football. 'I try not to to think too far ahead even though we young lads at the club are always being told to do more with our spare time,' he once said when he was still a new Nottingham Forest star. 'The trouble is I am a bit too laid-back for my own good. Although things have changed materially, I've got a car and maybe a house soon, at the moment I am not too bothered about possessions.'

After their grim disappointment in the FA Cup final, Forest and Roy Keane finished their first season together at eighth place in the First Division. Keane played in 35 games and contributed 8 goals. Only Nigel Clough and Des Walker player in more matches for Forest.

Keane was just beaten to the highly prized overall Young Eagle of the Year Award (which he was to win the following year) by Manchester United winger Lee Sharpe. The panel comprised then England team manager Graham Taylor, Irish boss Jack Charlton, and former stars Jimmy Armfield, Ron Greenwood, Bill Nicholson, Stan Cullis, Trevor Cherry and Terry Yorath. In words hardly likely to endear him to Forest fans, Taylor commented, 'Roy Keane is an exceptionally good player but what probably edges it for me is Lee Sharpe's ability to cope mentally with the demands of playing for a big club.' Roy Keane did not miss the significance of the remarks either.

**'I SHOULD HAVE SIMPLY WALKED AWAY FROM SOME OF THE NIGHT-CLUB SCENES IN NOTTINGHAM. CLOUGHIE WAS BRILLIANT WITH ME, THOUGH. HE KNEW WHEN TO PUT HIS FOOT DOWN AND ALSO WHEN I DIDN'T NEED A BOLLOCKING, BUT SOME FRIENDLY ADVICE.'**

**Roy Keane**

The prodigal star made an emotional return to Cobh Ramblers as the short summer break was ended by pre-season preparations. Nottingham Forest made the trip as part of the deal to take Roy Keane to the City Ground and in front of a packed house that included many members of his family and many friends who had watched his speedy progress from afar. Forest won the game comfortably 5-0 and of course Roy Keane was among the scorers.

But the whole Forest contingent was most impressed by the warmth of the Irish welcome they received. There was not a hint of feeling that they had sold their best player too cheaply. 'The only feeling I experienced from Cobh was friendliness,' said one Forest director. 'They could not have been more welcoming. And I think they were pleased to see that we were looking after young Roy.'

Roy Keane started the new season with a bang when he scored in the crushing 4-0 victory over local rivals Notts County. He followed that up with two goals in the 4-2 win over Wimbledon with new signing Kingsley Black also on the score sheet. Keane scored another two goals against Bolton at Forest's Rumbelows Cup campaign clicked into gear with a 5-2 win.

And most important to the deeply patriotic young Irishman was his call-up to play for the Republic of Ireland in the vital European Championship match against Poland in Poznan on 16 October. Roy Keane had already worn the famous green shirt twice in friendlies against Chile and Hungary but this was his competitive debut and it represented something of a turnaround by respected manager Jack Charlton. A couple of weeks earlier the uncompromising Charlton had insisted firmly that Roy Keane was 'not yet ready' for such a big game. But a string of injuries forced the manager to include Keane in his squad and when Ray Houghton joined Eire's casualty list the road was left open for him to win his first cap.

> **'MY DAD MAURICE IS MY BIGGEST CRITIC. WHEN I GO HOME AND HE SEES ME PLAYING IN A GAME ON TELEVISION HE WILL LET ME KNOW IF I HAVE PLAYED BADLY OR NOT. AND IF HE EVER THINKS I AM GETTING TOO BIG FOR MY BOOTS THEN HE WILL GIVE ME A KICK UP THE BACKSIDE.'**
> Roy Keane

On the eve of the game in Poland, Jack Charlton commented that Roy Keane, 'is a much better player than I thought he was. He gets better with every game.' Keane responded diplomatically: 'It is very nice of the manager to say things like that.' He was trying to remain cool about the situation but inside he was simply screaming for the chance to prove himself on the international stage. Keane had a good game in a fiercely contested game against the Poles that was eventually drawn 3-3.

**'I'VE NO GIRLFRIENDS, NO TIES. AT LEAST NOT THAT I KNOW OF ANYWAY.'**

**Roy Keane**

But the following week he came down to earth with a bang when he joined Forest's lengthening injury list after damaging an ankle in the 4-2 defeat at the hands of Sheffield United at Bramall Lane. Keane limped off sadly at half-time and was forced to miss the Zenith Data Cup tie against Leeds United at Elland Road the next week. Keane watched Darren Wassell come into his place and help Forest to an excellent 3-1 win. 'It is amazing how quickly your fortunes can change in football,' he reflected ruefully. 'One moment I was playing in an international and the next minute I was lying on the treatment table. It is frustrating but there is no use feeling sorry for yourself. I have just got to work hard to get myself fit again and take it from there. I am aware, though, that there are a lot of good players in contention for a place in the Republic's midfield and that I have got to keep doing well at club level.

'Hopefully once I am fit, I can pick up where I left off with Forest and get myself in contention for a place in the squad for next month's game against Turkey.'

Certainly his international manager seemed to have seen the light. 'Roy Keane is better than Gazza,' said outspoken Jack

Charlton. 'They are probably the best two midfielders operating in the country and worth millions of pounds. As an international manager it would be a dream to accommodate both of them in the same side. Gazza is magnificent on the ball. He has the superior first touch and brilliant vision to create things out of nothing. But at 21 Keane has an engine and a competitive instinct that are phenomenal. He certainly better suits the needs of an Irish side that expends an enormous amount of energy and sweat around the middle of the field. The lad is a marvel. He is only starting out as an Ireland player and already he is setting an example for the senior players around him. That kind of talent doesn't surface too often in football these days.'

The ankle injury was harder to shake off than Keane had thought and it was to keep him out of Ireland's match against Turkey. The Bolton performance brought Keane a surprise bonus, though. He was given a 21-inch TV set by sponsors Rumbelows as man of the match. 'I was a little bit down at the time,' he admitted, 'but it came as a big morale booster.'

Roy Keane came back into the side after four weeks out and almost immediately Liverpool made an attempt to sign him in a straight-swap deal for their striker Dean Saunders. Brian Clough firmly ruled out any such exchange, insisting that he valued Keane a great deal more highly than he rated Saunders.

The following year Graham Taylor commented, 'Jack Charlton is a very lucky man to have Keane. Not only is he good from box to box and an excellent passer of the ball, he also knows how to intercept and tackle. He scores more than his share of goals. In fact, I don't think you could ask much more of a player as young as him.'

Roy Keane won yet another Barclays Young Eagle of the Month award for February and donated his £250 prize to the

Anne Diamond Cot Death Appeal Fund. He received a warm letter of thanks from the TV presenter, who started her fund after tragically losing her own son to cot death.

This time Forest missed out in the final at Wembley as Manchester United won a dour match 1-0 with a goal from Brian McClair. But in spite of the two Wembley appearances Roy Keane's second season was much more one of consolidation.

> **'ROY KEANE IS BETTER THAN GAZZA ... THEY ARE PROBABLY THE BEST TWO MIDFIELDERS OPERATING IN THE COUNTRY.'**
>
> **Jack Charlton, then Republic of Ireland manager**

Nottingham Forest again finished 8th in the First Division and Roy Keane again scored 8 goals, this time from 39 games. But it was to be some time before Forest reached such dizzy heights again. The 1992–93 football season, the first of the new Premier League, proved difficult for Nottingham Forest as their charismatic manager Brian Clough moved towards the end of his long and controversial career. After a disappointing start to the campaign the season became a constant battle against the threat of relegation set against a sequence of disturbing headlines, both about Brian Clough and about Roy Keane's future with Forest.

On the opening day of the season Forest beat Liverpool 1-0 thanks to a fine goal by Teddy Sheringham in the first Premiership match to be televised live by Sky. But then they went on a run of seven straight defeats against Sheffield Wednesday, Oldham, Manchester United, Norwich City, Blackburn Rovers, Sheffield Wednesday again, and Derby County. It was a dreadful start from which they never recovered.

Roy Keane watched helplessly as newspapers speculated wildly about possible transfers. Early in November he was reported to be the subject of a £5 million bid from Blackburn Rovers. 'Keano just kept his head down and concentrated on his football,' one of his teammates commented. 'He knew that was the most important thing. But he hated the publicity. He kept saying, "It's just rubbish paper talk," if anyone asked him about it.

'Unfortunately it was happening at a time when the manager was coming to the end of his time at Forest. There was a lot of pressure on him as well, just when Roy could have used a strong shoulder to lean on.'

Brian Clough rejected Blackburn's approaches, determined to hang on to his young star. He brought Neil Webb back to the City Ground from Manchester United for £800,000 in the hope that he would form a useful alliance with Keane in the Forest midfield. Sadly it never really came off as Webb was past his best by then and played only nine games for Forest that season.

Despite the endless transfer rumours Roy Keane's form never faltered. Although Forest remained rooted to the bottom of the table there was the occasional highlight. On 5 December Forest ended Leeds United's proud run of 31 home matches without defeat with a thumping 4–1 victory, Keane scoring two of the goals.

It was not all football for Roy

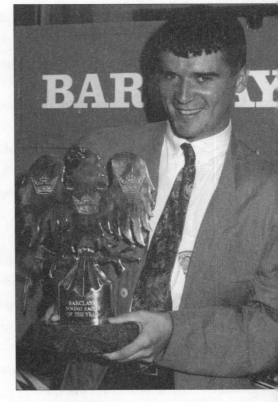

Flying high! Roy takes the Barclays Young Eagle of the Year award 1992.

Keane, though. The young Irishman again used his £250 award from Barclay for yet another Young Eagle of the Month Award for a good cause when he chose the Karen Seasman Trust Fund as his nominated charity. Baby Karen weighed just 1lb when she was born four months prematurely and she needed vital eye surgery at a special clinic in Michigan to save her sight. Keane was so moved by Karen's misfortune that he made a large personal donation himself. In fact, while at Forest Roy Keane began supporting a string of mainly children's charities with great enthusiasm. He privately told friends he never wanted this work to be made public and joked that, 'It would do my image on the pitch no good at all.'

Brian Clough was heartened by his young player's growing maturity. He traced this social awareness back to an unpublicised Forest visit to a home for handicapped children. Brian Clough said, 'The other day I took my son and Roy Keane to visit a children's spastics home. Some of the kids there can't talk, walk, or even move. We lit the place up but they lit us up too.' Roy Keane was deeply moved by the visit. He has a strong belief in the support of the underprivileged that shows itself in a constant quiet assistance for countless charities, sometimes by lending his name, at other times in more direct, more private ways. During the difficult months at the end of his three years with Forest he

**Champion!** With his Barclays Young Eagle of the Month award and Brian Clough with the Manager of the Month award. Both player and manager developed the utmost respect for each other.

found himself spending more of his time behind the scenes helping those less well off than himself. A friend said that Roy felt very deeply upset by any case of unnecessary suffering, particularly involving children and said that, 'Doing something to help a youngster who can't walk is a great way of stopping yourself getting worked up over which football club you happen to play for.'

On 29 January 1993 Brian Clough urged £5 million wanted man Keane to settle down with Nottingham Forest by getting married. The Forest manager had spent most of the season so far trying to persuade his brightest talent to sign a new contract. Suddenly, in a suitably Cloughie change of direction, he urged the signing of a marriage contract. As Forest prepared for a six-pointer relegation battle with fellow strugglers Oldham Athletic at the City Ground, Brian Clough admitted he was concerned by all the ceaseless speculation about Roy's Keane's future and told the Irishman that organising himself a more settled domestic life could be the answer to his problems: 'The best thing that Keany can do is get himself a steady girlfriend, have a courtship and think of settling down to married life. Believe it or not, that will help him as much as any other kind of assistance he can get from me.'

Roy clearly felt that the endless rumours linking him with Blackburn Rovers, Arsenal, Liverpool or Aston Villa were affecting his form. At the end of the year he asked for contract talks to be held over until the end of the season because he felt his game was suffering and his poor run reached a low point at Old Trafford when he was substituted by Brian Clough. The manager explained his decision: 'I took him off for two reasons. By his standards he was not having a particularly good game. I also thought he might get himself into trouble the way things were going. He is only 21 and still learning his trade and this is all part of his education. To an extent I could understand the way he was feeling because he was becoming frustrated. Now we all go through that, even me at 57. But in this game you have got to curb yourself. He'll learn. It's the same in life.'

Roy Keane bit his tongue over suggestions that he get married and settle down. He did not want the manger to know every detail of his private life because he had just met a beautiful young Nottingham girl from an Irish family called Theresa Doyle. He was instantly smitten and the couple were at the early stages of a passionate love affair that was to last, but the fiercely private young footballer did not want anyone to know that. Not even Brian Clough.

> **'THE BEST THING THAT KEANY CAN DO IS GET HIMSELF A STEADY GIRLFRIEND, HAVE A COURTSHIP AND THINK OF SETTLING DOWN TO MARRIED LIFE. BELIEVE IT OR NOT, THAT WILL HELP HIM AS MUCH AS ANY OTHER KIND OF ASSISTANCE HE CAN GET FROM ME.'**
>
> Brian Clough

As the wrangles over Roy Keane's departure from the City Ground intensified, Brian Clough chose more than once to criticise his favourite footballing son. In typically colourful language, on one occasion Clough accused Keane of behaving like 'a greedy child'. As Forest struggled to hang on to their best player Clough reacted angrily to contract demands that would have earned Keane £1 million over three years: 'He is a highly talented young man,' the manager acknowledged. 'Everything has come quickly for him and he is loved by everybody in football, particularly those at Forest. Keane is the hottest property in the game right now, but he is not going to bankrupt this club. We have made Keane an offer. He has his own ideas, but he is ours for eighteen months and the talks are on ice for now. I don't want to know about silly clauses, talking about what he'll do if we get relegated. I want him to sign a straight, no-nonsense contract that is within our budget.'

As the season drew on the results did not improve and the manager found himself under attack. A group of shareholders demanded the first extraordinary general meeting at Nottingham Forest for more than 20 years to question Brian Clough's running of the club. Negative stories about Clough added to the general unease at the City Ground.

These were difficult times for Roy Keane as well. As relegation loomed he seemed anxious to take the whole weight of keeping Forest up on to his young shoulders and sometimes it was a little too much. He grabbed a late equaliser at Arsenal to gain a point that gave Forest a chance of avoiding the drop on a night when tempers really boiled over. Keane was reported to police for swearing at supporters. Inspector Daniel Keogh of Holloway police said, 'Keane allegedly lifted his shirt and kissed it in front of a section of the crowd and then made abusive comments to those fans.' But common sense prevailed and no action was taken. Nottingham Forest announced that Roy Keane had signed a new three-and-a-half-year contract that would keep him at the club until a new wave of young players could arrive to revive the Forest fortunes. The club did not announce that the contract contained a clause that gave Keane the chance to leave should Nottingham Forest be relegated.

At the time Keane was forced to defend himself against some fans who felt he was behaving greedily. 'Money isn't everything,' he insisted. 'People seem to think all I'm interested in is money. They've seen stories calling me a greedy child and claiming I want £6,500 a week. They can believe it if they like. I know the financial side of the deal is all sorted out and I'm happy with it. And I've told Forest I would like to stay for four or five years. I've never been to the club and demanded more money or demanded anything.

'I feel over the past two or three months I haven't given my best and all the rumours have not helped,' he confessed. 'Now I feel I can get back to concentrating on keeping Forest in the Premier League. Forest were the club that gave me a break three years ago and I would like to repay them a little bit. The manager is brilliant, the coaching staff are brilliant and I feel I can get better with Forest.' Assistant manager Ronnie Fenton told the local newspaper, 'Obviously we are over the moon.'

At the same time, Roy revealed the relegation clause in his contract that meant he would definitely be leaving Forest if the club went down. The publicity and growing furore over his future at Forest grew hard to bear towards the end of the 1992–93 season and the player was upset when some of the stories resulted in his family being pestered by the press at home in Mayfield. On 24 April, the Saturday before Ireland's crucial World Cup qualifier against European champions Denmark in Dublin the following Wednesday, he opened his heart to his local newspaper, the *Cork Examiner*.

**'KEANE IS THE HOTTEST PROPERTY IN THE GAME RIGHT NOW, BUT HE IS NOT GOING TO BANKRUPT THIS CLUB.'**
Brian Clough

'Over the last couple of months I have had some bad publicity but when I moved to England I got some good advice,' he revealed. 'I was told the press will build you up only to knock you down. And the person who said that to me was true to his word. Because over the last few months everything I could do off the pitch has been in the press. People who know me know that I have not changed. I am still the same

Roy receives the Forest club team award in March 1993.

person, but the problem is that the press in England can write what they want. I know I am in the right, even though I know that I am no angel.'

Roy found himself pursued by the press even in his home town. He said, 'I can recognise the difference between the news and the sports reporters. But I think the sports lads are more understanding about what is happening in football. They know and recognise the sort of pressure a player might be under but the news boys don't. Any scrap of news and they will go for it and they are ready to write news for people to read and they believe it if it is in the papers.'

To make matters worse, the young star increasingly found himself the target for every intoxicated hardman keen to make a name for himself in front of his mates. Most of the time Roy and his teammates were able to deflect the aggression, but there was always a side of Roy Keane that found it hard not to give aggressive louts the sort of lesson they so richly deserved. 'People just want to have a go at me wherever I go and I just have to be careful,' he admitted. 'I suppose I haven't helped myself sometimes but it is quite difficult. Even when I come back home to Cork it's hard but my family and friends know that I am the same person as I was when I left three years ago. People can write what they want but they don't know me. I don't go round looking for trouble and provoking people in dance halls and that's a fact … All I am doing is trying to become a professional footballer to the best of my ability.'

> **'IF THEY GET AN OFFER THEY CAN'T REFUSE THEY WILL PROBABLY SELL ME, BUT THAT'S FOOTBALL FOR YOU. IT'S A BUSINESS, IT'S AN INDUSTRY. IF THE CLUB DOES GO DOWN IT WILL BE UP TO MYSELF WHERE I GO.'**
>
> Roy Keane, on rumours about his leaving Nottingham Forest if the club were to be relegated

Another trademark run brings another goal for Forest against West Ham.

Roy was less than delighted when the clause in his contract providing him with an escape route should Forest be relegated became public knowledge. 'Forest released the fact that I had an escape clause,' he stated, when the news broke. 'That was up to them, I do have a clause in my contract but that was not for the press. What I am more interested in over the next three weeks are the three biggest games of my career. We play Sheffield United on Saturday, Ipswich Town away the week after and of course Denmark in the World Cup next Wednesday. It is all happening for me at once. I have to be concentrating on now and that is what is important to me.

'I want Forest to stay up, obviously, because I have signed a three-and-a-half-year contract, but if we get relegated I will have to sit down with the club and discuss my future. If they don't go down I am under contract and I could be there for the next three years ... if they get an offer they can't refuse they will probably sell me, but that's football for you. It's a business, it's an industry. If the club does go down it will be up to myself where I go. Money is not the be all and end all of it. What is important to me is that I make the best career move I can. I will look after my best interest, that's the bottom line and then I can decide which is the best club to go to.'

The club was understood to have valued Roy Keane at £3 million if he was to be sold to a British club and £5 million if he were to go abroad. Roy said prophetically, 'I don't know if these figures are quite true to be honest. They could be more! But the thing is that I do have a clause in my contract and I was only looking after my own interests … I have to be clued in, especially with the World Cup next year. I have to look after my own career … at the same time I am trying as hard as anybody to keep Forest in the the Premier League, and why wouldn't I –

Shielding the ball from Geoff Thomas of Crystal Palace.

they pay my wages every week. If Forest go down at the end of the month I will know I have done my best to keep them in the top flight. But if they do go down then I will have to look after myself and concentrate on my international future, especially as it's World Cup year. I don't think First Division football would be in my best interests.'

Roy paid tribute to Brian Clough for giving him his big chance in the game, but at the same time it was clear that he would not be willing to commit himself to a long-term future at Forest: 'I am not sure yet what I want to do. For God's sake, I won't be 22 until August!'

On 26 April, with relegation almost inevitable, Brian Clough announced his decision to retire at the end of the season. The last home game, a 2-0 defeat by fellow strugglers Sheffield United, presented the bizarre spectacle of a departing manager who had just led his club into relegation receiving a standing ovation from a packed crowd.

> 'IF FOREST GO DOWN AT THE END OF THE MONTH I WILL KNOW I HAVE DONE MY BEST TO KEEP THEM IN THE TOP FLIGHT. BUT IF THEY DO GO DOWN THEN I WILL HAVE TO LOOK AFTER MYSELF AND CONCENTRATE ON MY INTERNATIONAL FUTURE, ESPECIALLY AS IT'S WORLD CUP YEAR. I DON'T THINK FIRST DIVISION FOOTBALL WOULD BE IN MY BEST INTERESTS.'
> Roy Keane

Roy Keane was hit harder than most by Brian Clough's departure. The charismatic manager had been like a father to the young player during three exhilarating years at the City Ground. But Keane had grown up in that time and now without his mentor at the helm he knew his future lay elsewhere. 'He was the one who gave me the chance in the first place and I was banking on him being with us for quite a bit longer,' he admitted. 'I've still

Keane, Lee Glover and Daren Wassall celebrate a goal against Spurs in the Rumbelows Cup.

**Team mates Keane and Sherringham.**

got a lot to learn and I was planning on him helping me out. I was with the Ireland team when I heard the news of his retirement so obviously it was a *major* shock. I was absolutely shattered.' At the same time Keane firmly denied that plans for him to leave were already in motion. He said, 'I don't know where those stories came from but they were not true. I had no part in them at all. I never spoke to anyone but I'm getting used to all the rumours and speculation.'

Frank Clark took over the manager's job from Brian Clough with high hopes of persuading Roy Keane to stay at Forest. But as soon as he saw the terms of his contract he knew there was no chance. According to the clause in Keane's contract, if another club were prepared to pay £3 million for him, Forest would have to release Keane. Not only that but the player would receive more than £600,000 from any such deal. It meant that Roy Keane was leaving and Frank Clark knew it. He was amazed that Keane had ever been given such a contract but he knew he had no chance of keeping the player.

Clark did point out that 'It was a tribute to Keane's professionalism that he still played his heart out to keep Forest in the Premier League.' When Clark became manager he was given a folder listing all the clubs interested in buying Roy Keane. 'There were so many it took me twenty minutes to read through it. Keane considered offers from a number of clubs including Arsenal and Blackburn before choosing Manchester United. He continued training with Forest while the negotiations were taking place. You might have expected him to take it easy and not bother, but you would have been wrong. He was giving it everything even then, running and chasing and tackling as if his life depended on it.'

And the fans certainly believed Roy Keane always gave 100 per cent on the pitch. The Nottingham Forest Supporters Club annual Player of the Year poll showed how highly they regarded Roy Keane. Stuart Pearce had taken the title for the previous two seasons and had high hopes for a hat trick until it became clear that Keane had scooped 31.5 per cent of the votes. He was well ahead of Carl Tiler on 13.5 per cent and Ian Woan on 12 per cent.

The chance to sign Roy Keane had all of the big clubs circling the City Ground. But it was Alex Ferguson at Manchester United who was to eventually land the influential midfielder.

> **'HE CONTINUED TRAINING WITH FOREST WHILE THE NEGOTIATIONS WERE TAKING PLACE. YOU MIGHT HAVE EXPECTED HIM TO TAKE IT EASY AND NOT BOTHER, BUT YOU WOULD HAVE BEEN WRONG. HE WAS GIVING IT EVERYTHING EVEN THEN, RUNNING AND CHASING AND TACKLING AS IF HIS LIFE DEPENDED ON IT.'**
>
> Frank Clark, Brian Clough's successor as manager of Nottingham Forest, on Roy Keane's final days at the club

## CHAPTER 3

# 'ALEX, GET HIM BOUGHT!'

AT PRECISELY 5.45 p.m. on Sunday, 2 May 1993, lowly Oldham Athletic did United an unexpected favour by beating the Reds' title-chasing rivals Aston Villa. And with that win, Manchester United became League champions for the first time since 1967. Villa's defeat meant that United were uncatchable in the Premiership. They were champions again, at last.

For the Old Trafford supporters it had been far too long a wait but now, after 26 years, they could at last look forward once more to seeing the trophy draped in the red-and-white ribbons of Manchester United's colours. After being pipped by Leeds United for the title the year before, Alex Ferguson's team had triumphed and had finally laid to rest the ghost that had lingered for more than a quarter of a century.

Old Trafford witnessed unprecedented scenes of celebration when Steve Bruce and Bryan Robson jointly lifted the trophy the following night after United had defeated Blackburn Rovers

3-1 in their last home game of the season. The players set off on a lap of honour greeted with euphoria by the fans and watched with pride from the Directors Box by Sir Matt Busby, architect of the last United League-winning team, who later went down to the dressing rooms to seek out the players and Alex Ferguson to offer his congratulations in person.

Winning the Premiership in 1993 is something that the Manchester United players involved will never forget as it brought to an end a lengthy period for the club without the domestic trophy footballers treasured most. They could look back on a season of wonderful achievement but, as Steve Bruce can testify, Alex Ferguson was not prepared just to sit back and enjoy the moment of success; he was already looking ahead. 'To celebrate, Alex Ferguson produced a white envelope and told us it contained six of our names,' Bruce recalled. 'He said the names were big-time Charlies who thought they had cracked it by winning the title but added that they should think again. He said if we hadn't won the title the following season, he would open the envelope and reveal the six names.'

Ferguson was determined not to rest on his laurels and, with Bryan Robson having made only five starts in the League all season because of injury and nearing the end of his fabulous

> **'ALEX FERGUSON PRODUCED A WHITE ENVELOPE AND TOLD US IT CONTAINED SIX OF OUR NAMES. HE SAID THE NAMES WERE BIG-TIME CHARLIES WHO THOUGHT THEY HAD CRACKED IT BY WINNING THE TITLE BUT ADDED THAT THEY SHOULD THINK AGAIN. HE SAID IF WE HADN'T WON THE TITLE THE FOLLOWING SEASON, HE WOULD OPEN THE ENVELOPE AND REVEAL THE SIX NAMES.'**
>
> Steve Bruce, ex-Manchester United star

career, the manager was looking to strengthen his squad in the crucial midfield area. And he knew just the player he was looking for.

Alex Ferguson had first heard of Roy Keane from Manchester United scout Les Kershaw who had been in the stands at Anfield on the night a 19-year-old untried, untested Irishman called Keane made his debut for Nottingham Forest against Liverpool. Kershaw reported back that the young lad looked very promising and it was agreed that Keane should be watched in his next game against Aston Villa. Keane's performance wasn't quite as impressive this time but it was felt that he may have been feeling the pressure of playing at home for the first time.

It was some weeks later that Alex Ferguson first set eyes in person on Roy Keane when he slipped into Manchester City's ground at Maine Road to watch United's arch rivals play at home to Nottingham Forest in a midweek match. Ferguson was there to assess the Forest team who would be visiting Old Trafford for a League fixture just over two weeks later. It was a routine reconnaissance on upcoming opponents for Ferguson but by now he was also aware of the reputation Keane had already begun to build for himself at Forest in his very first season and he was interested to see for himself if the good reports were justified. Keane gave a typically energetic performance and Ferguson came away from the Maine Road match suitably impressed.

When Forest visited Old Trafford a fortnight later on 29 September 1990, Ferguson did not have to wait long for his estimation of Keane to rise several degrees higher, even if his initial reaction was one of sheer indignation. The game was just seconds old when Ferguson witnessed the young upstart Keane, playing only his fourth top-flight match, brazenly clattering into his great talisman Bryan Robson with a crunching tackle. Keane's challenge was forceful and fearless, bristling with determination and aggression. It was impudent, too, so early in the game and sent out the message to Manchester United and the crowd of more than 46,000 that he was not going to be intimidated by any player, not even by one of Robson's outstanding reputation as a magnificent footballer and the toughest of competitors.

**THE ONE CLUB THE YOUNG KEANE HADN'T WRITTEN TO WAS MANCHESTER UNITED. HE FELT HE SIMPLY WASN'T GOOD ENOUGH FOR THEM.**

The impact on Robson may have been physical, and considerable, but Keane's tackle on the United skipper also left its mark – though much less painfully – on Alex Ferguson. 'I always remember the kick-off,' said Ferguson. 'The ball went back to Robson and Roy absolutely cemented him! I said, "Bloody cheek of him! How dare he come to Old Trafford and tackle like that!"' Beneath Ferguson's indignation, however, was a measure of grudging regard for a player so young to have had the nerve to confront Bryan Robson in such an uncompromising manner on his own turf. Nottingham Forest beat Manchester United 1-0 that day with a goal from Stuart Pearce. Keane played his full part in the victory and Alex Ferguson told himself that Manchester United must sign him. In fact, he called Forest the very next day to enquire about him.

Not long afterwards Ferguson was to read in a newspaper article that Keane had once written to every single club in England hoping to get a trial. Aghast, and not best pleased that Keane therefore must somehow have slipped through the United scouting net, Ferguson asked his scouting office to find

Keane's letter of application. Fortunately for the scouting staff they did not have to endure Ferguson's wrath at a missed opportunity since it later emerged that the one club Keane hadn't written to was Manchester United. He felt he simply wasn't good enough for them.

Throughout the remainder of the season Ferguson kept track of Keane's progress with Forest and at the end of that campaign, the United manager made his first moves to bring Roy Keane to Old Trafford. Ferguson had been anxious to build up his squad and go for the League championship after winning the European Cup Winners' Cup in 1991 and once he had seen Roy Keane in action, the Irishman came increasingly to mind. An opportunity for Ferguson to add Keane to his squad appeared to present itself when Brian Clough sought to bring Neil Webb back from Old Trafford to Nottingham Forest, for whom Webb had previously been a star performer. Ferguson considered Webb had fallen back somewhat as a player and, since he felt Webb would not be figuring in his grand plans for the future, he informed Clough that the player was indeed available. But he added the important rider that he would like Keane as part of the deal. Clough dismissed this suggestion instantly. He would not hear of it.

Prolonged negotiations followed intermittently without any real progress and Ferguson's pursuit of Keane was not ultimately resolved until Nottingham Forest's poor showing in the League in the season of 1992–93. That season Manchester United tried once again to sign Keane before the transfer deadline but Frank Clark, who had now become Clough's successor at Forest, was understandably loth to allow Keane to leave when the club was still fighting hard to stave off the threat of relegation. Manchester United, however, knew there was some sort of clause in Keane's contract with Forest that would allow him to leave the club if Forest were relegated. So, while they had made no secret of their wish to make Keane a Manchester United player, they were prepared to wait till the time was right for Forest to part with him. 'Once they were relegated we moved in quickly,' said Ferguson. But almost not quickly enough.

Inevitably, Manchester United had not been alone in casting covetous eyes over Roy Keane. George Graham, then manager of Arsenal, had closely tracked Keane for much of his last season with Forest, and Kenny Dalglish, then in charge of Blackburn Rovers, was another prominent manager who was also chasing Keane's signature.

One bright Saturday morning during the close season events took a dramatic turn. Over breakfast Alex Ferguson was greatly disturbed to discover from a newspaper report that the player he had tracked for so long was now apparently about to slip through his grasp. The gist of the newspaper story, which made him almost choke on his toast with shock, was that Keane was on the very brink of joining Blackburn Rovers, the latest big signing for a club whose chairman Jack Walker was in the process of spending many millions of pounds assembling an impressive team at Ewood Park. The report that Keane had had a meeting with Dalglish, that agreement had been reached and that player and manager had shaken hands, all came as a severe jolt to Ferguson who was preparing that morning to travel to Macclesfield to pay a visit to a girl he knew who was ill in hospital.

Alarmed by what he was reading, Ferguson immediately telephoned Forest's manager Frank Clark at home to check if the story was true. Clark was furious at the news. 'He was astonished that this meeting had taken place,' said Ferguson, 'and he said, "Well, you have my permission to speak to Roy."'

Keane, it transpired, had indeed spoken to Blackburn the day before. Not only had he spoken to them, he had agreed a contract with the club and decided that he would go home to Cork for the weekend to think things over. Crucially for Alex Ferguson, Keane had not signed Blackburn's contract.

The following day was a Sunday and Keane was both surprised and not a little pleased to receive a telephone call from Ferguson who asked him to take a plane to Manchester the very next day to meet Ferguson at his home. How could he say no?

> **'IT WASN'T JUST ONLY ME TRYING TO IMPRESS ROY. I WANTED TO BE IMPRESSED BY HIM IN TERMS OF CHARACTER AND TEMPERAMENT TO COME AND PLAY AT OUR PLACE.'**
>
> **Alex Ferguson on his initial talk with Keane about him becoming a Manchester United player**

Over lunch and a game of snooker at Ferguson's home, the two men sowed the seeds of what was eventually to become a mutual admiration. Ferguson used the meeting to let Keane know just how anxious he was to bring him to Old Trafford and to impress upon him the exciting future he could have as a United player. But the manager was also mindful to appraise Keane of what Manchester United was like to play for. That may sound trite, but as Ferguson spoke to Keane about his becoming a Manchester United player, he was probing for some sort of instinctive reaction as to whether the 21-year-old Irishman could handle coming to a club with such an illustrious history as Manchester United's. He was right to be wary and it was a genuine concern because other fine players had in the past arrived at Old Trafford and had struggled to come to terms with just how big the club was. They had found the weight of a big transfer fee, the pressure to perform at the highest level week in and week out, and the expectations of its supporters all just too much for them. 'It was a two-way thing,' Ferguson said of that first meeting with Keane. 'It wasn't just only me trying to impress Roy. I wanted to be impressed by him in terms of character and temperament to come and play at our place.'

Keane came away from the meeting with a high regard for Ferguson and his ambitions. Ferguson, for his part, was left in little doubt that Keane had the qualities required to become a Manchester United player and would wear the shirt with pride. He had taken to him the minute they first shook hands; with genuine feeling, Keane had told Ferguson how pleased he was to meet him. Keane's firm handshake showed he meant it and the manager noted that in front of him was a fully developed man, which wasn't always the case with players of Keane's age.

Intriguingly, the subject of money and terms did not come into the conversation between the two men. That in itself was a pointer to Ferguson that Keane's ambitions lay with joining a team to win trophies rather than to get rich. The manager was able to count himself fortunate that Keane had gone straight into Nottingham Forest's first team at such a young age. It would mean that if he did come to Old Trafford he would already have enjoyed two years of top-class football, including three appearances in Wembley finals. It was invaluable experience and yet Keane was still only 21.

**'ALEX, GET HIM BOUGHT!'**

Jack Charlton's advice to Alex Ferguson

Ferguson had never imagined he would be able to find anyone good enough to replace Bryan Robson. But now he genuinely felt Keane could do it with his fantastic engine, his speed over the ground, his power, his ability to hold things up and his competitive nature. Any wavering doubts in Ferguson's mind were dispelled by a telephone conversation Ferguson had with

Jack Charlton, who had been in charge of Keane in his capacity as manager of the Republic of Ireland's national squad.

'Alex, get him bought!' was Charlton's enthusiastic and blunt reply to Ferguson's queries about whether he should go out and buy Keane. According to the 1966 England World Cup hero, Ferguson was initially concerned at the size of the transfer fee, which would easily top £3 million. But Charlton assured Ferguson that Keane would be worth every penny. 'You'll never regret it,' said Charlton. 'He's got a great engine and if you want to sell him on in a couple of years you'll probably get six or seven million out of Europe for him.'

Keane's mind was made up after his meeting with Ferguson and his decision was reinforced when he returned to Cork. Although he had already loosely agreed terms with Blackburn, back home in Cork his friends and family, who nearly all followed United, urged him to sign for the Red Devils. By now he didn't need much persuading.

Once he had spoken to Manchester United there was no other club for Roy Keane. Arsenal were offering the biggest transfer fee at £4 million, Blackburn Rovers were able to offer him significantly more than he could expect at United, but the lure of joining what his family and friends kept telling him was the most famous football club in the world, the chance to become part of Alex Ferguson's avowed assault on football's greatest club trophies, was too appealing to resist. With the help of Brendon Batson of the Professional Footballers Association and Keane's adviser, solicitor Michael Kennedy, negotiations quickly came to a satisfactory conclusion and the deal was done.

Alex Ferguson was delighted with his capture of Keane at last. Roy Keane would leave Nottingham Forest for Manchester United on 22 July 1993 for a fee of £3.75 million, a British transfer record at the time. His wages would be some £2,000 a week short of the £10,000 a week Blackburn were offering but bonuses and sponsorship deals would allow him to recoup the balance. Most of all, he wanted to play for the best club in Britain and Manchester United were League champions.

Roy Keane was disappointed that some Nottingham Forest fans felt let down by his departure. He said, 'Some people have a bad opinion of me for leaving the club but I made a statement that when I signed my new contract if we got relegated I was going to leave the club. Simple as that. Nottingham forest made £3.75 million out of me and they only paid £15,000. The season Forest were relegated Brian Clough made me player of the year. It's not as if I threw the towel in, I just thought, well, I'm going to get my move no matter what happens. I tried as hard as anybody. But it just wasn't to be, we just weren't good enough in that season.'

Keane appealed for understanding from fans he was leaving behind: 'The fans have been brilliant and I just hope they understand my decision. In a World Cup season I could not afford to be playing Division One football. The best thing is just to forget about me. I'm only one player and the club is bigger than anyone. If Forest come straight back up they can stick their fingers up to me and say we did it without you. I hope they do. I'll still probably spend my weekends in Nottingham wherever I end up. I've just bought a house here and it's my home away from home. I don't think anywhere else will be the same.'

That said, there was no doubt that Roy Keane was happy with his decision: 'I signed for Manchester United because they have got the best stadium, the best team and the greatest supporters in the country,' he asserted. 'Blackburn Rovers made me a fabulous offer but as soon as United declared an interest there was only one outcome. This is a career move. To come to a club of this size is a good thing for my future. I just want to be a part of it all. Now the new demand for me is to get into the United team. That will be hard enough, they have some fantastic players.'

In Cork, Tony Maher could hardly believe his eyes when his newspaper dropped through the letterbox and, as usual, he turned straight to the back-page sports stories. 'Keane signs for Manchester United for £3.75 million! I just couldn't believe it,' said Tony, who soon made his way up to the Temple Acre Tavern. 'As I came up to the pub, who was in front of me but Roy Keane and his brothers Denis and Johnston and I walked over and shook his hand and said, "Roy, you've made my day."'

Naturally Keane's transfer and the record-breaking fee was not the talk just of the Temple Acre Tavern but of all the many bars in and around Cork, especially O'Flaherty's, a well-known meeting place for Manchester United fans. On that red-letter day for Keane it was uncanny as the Guinness went down just how many people managed to lay claim to having played with or against Britain's most expensive player or to having felt the weight of Keane's right hook in the boxing ring. But, like Tony Maher, everyone who had observed or been associated with Keane's progress from a nine-year-old at Rockmount was genuinely thrilled for him. At home, Keane's parents could hardly contain their excitement as they fielded telephone calls from family, friends and well-wishers all wanting to pass on messages of congratulations and good luck.

Cork's rejoicing was all the more celebratory for the fact that Keane was carrying on a long-cherished tradition. He was by no means the first Corkman to make his mark with Manchester United. Cork was proud of its long-established links with the illustrious club and down the years several Leesiders had famously given Manchester United great service in one capacity or another, most notably Noel Cantwell, Frank O'Farrell and Denis Irwin – the latter was soon to become Keane's Manchester United roommate, close friend and Republic of Ireland international colleague.

Older members of Cork's footballing fraternity remembered how Noel Cantwell had begun his footballing career with Western Rovers and Cork Athletic before joining West Ham in 1952 and then moving on to Manchester United in 1960 for £29,500, a record fee for a full-back at the time. Cantwell was captain of Manchester United for five years and represented Ireland at both cricket and soccer.

Frank O'Farrell had found his way to Old Trafford not as a player but as manager. O'Farrell had taken a roundabout route. Since his first ambitions had been to follow in his father's footsteps and drive the express train from Cork to Dublin. He started his working life shovelling coal on Irish railways before pursuing his footballing ambitions with Western Rovers and Cork United. He was among a crop of promising young football managers when he joined United from Leicester in 1971 but was sacked 18 months later after finding it almost impossible to live in the shadow of the great Sir Matt Busby.

There were other Irishmen, too, who had made significant contributions to Manchester United's history down the years. Johnny Carey, signed as a 17-year-old from Irish team St James' Gate, went on to become captain of the first great Matt Busby team. There was Shay Brennan, a classy right-back capped at 19 and thrown into Manchester United action early after the Munich air crash. Harry Gregg was a commanding goalkeeper who became a hero of the crash, helping survivors to safety.

Then, of course, there was the legendary George Best, Sammy McIlroy – sometimes described as 'the last Busby Babe' – Norman Whiteside, who in 1983 became the youngest player to score in the FA and League Cup finals, Kevin Moran and Paul McGrath. The impending arrival of Roy Keane at Old Trafford was simply a continuation of Manchester United's links with players from across the Irish Sea.

Keane's transfer was the talk of the soccer world and while some wondered whether the huge fee was justified and whether Keane could cope with the burden of a £3.75 million tag on his back, Ferguson had no doubts. He saw Keane as the eventual successor to Bryan Robson.

Keane put his signature to the Manchester United contract on the Monday and the following day he found himself on a plane bound for South Africa for a pre-season ten-day tour with the rest of the United squad, which Keane later said had been the ten best days of his life to date. That said, his first introduction

**Fergie's boys: Alex with Eric Cantana and Roy Keane.**

to his new colleagues was not exactly cordial. The story that famously circulated among United fans is that Keane's first greeting to them was, 'Right, you don't like me and I don't like you, now let's get on with it.' Keane swears it isn't strictly true but he does say, 'I'll never forget the first time I met the players because I'd had a lot of run-ins with them from my days at Nottingham Forest especially Paul Ince, Gary Pallister and Peter Schmeichel. It was quite difficult for me to get to know them.'

**'RIGHT, YOU DON'T LIKE ME AND I DON'T LIKE YOU, NOW LET'S GET ON WITH IT.'**

Roy Keane's first words to his new Manchester United teammates, according to legend

Keane's reputation had preceded him. Long before he arrived at Old Trafford, the United players knew all about Roy Keane. They knew how eager Alex Ferguson was to sign him because he'd openly told them so. Whenever United had played Forest, Keane was the only player from the opposition whom Ferguson singled out in his pre-match team talk. He was the only player in the Forest side whom the United boss felt it was essential to counter, the only one it was necessary to stop.

It made for some fiery confrontations between Keane and various United players – even with Lee Sharpe, who had rarely had a run-in with anyone. So relations were initially far from harmonious. Keane thought back to the games he had played for Nottingham Forest against Manchester United and worked out that he'd probably argued with every one of United's players. In fact, in Keane's last match as a Forest player against Manchester United at Old Trafford on 27 January, he had been substituted by Brian Clough in a 2-0 defeat for Forest and had left the pitch exchanging frank opinions with Paul Ince.

Keane and Ince had tangled in midfield more than once during the match and next day when Keane was called to

Clough's office, the Forest manager asked him if he knew why he had been substituted. When he replied that he didn't, Clough explained it was because he had been fighting. Keane was somewhat bemused by this assessment because he felt he had had one of his quieter games with only a couple of on-field arguments with Ince. He reminded Clough that in other Forest games he had had many more flare-ups and not been taken off but Clough maintained he had been a bad lad. It was Clough's way of teaching him a lesson and punishing him in front of the Old Trafford crowd.

At least there was one friendly face waiting for Roy Keane in the United ranks: that of Denis Irwin. In South Africa Keane was happy to room with his fellow Corkonian and Republic of Ireland international with whom he also roomed when on international duty. Gradually he was able to get acquainted with his new colleagues, acclimatise himself to United's training and playing methods and ease his way into the squad largely away from the glare of the British media. He was also put through a rigorous pre-season fitness training programme under an unforgiving South African sun that rose every day to fry the sky.

What struck Keane very early on was the wealth of footballing talent around him. In early training sessions surrounded by the likes of Cantona, Giggs and Sharpe, he sometimes found he couldn't get a kick. All he could do was run around and chase the others and he found it little different when he dropped down a level to try and shore up his confidence by playing with United's kids. They were, he was alarmed to find, quicker and sharper than he was.

The South African visit left Keane in no doubt that he had joined the most famous football club in the world. There was a crowd of many thousands at the airport waiting to see the team arrive. Everywhere the players went, thousands more clamoured for just a glimpse of them and Keane found the visits to the black townships of Tembisa and Soweta outside Johannesburg especially moving, as the children he met there proved so well mannered and appreciative.

Over the coming months Keane was to find out just what it was like to be a United player: the standards Alex Ferguson expected of him and the other players, the expectations of the fans, the attentions of the media, and playing what amounts to a Cup final every game with every opposition side seemingly raising their game to play Manchester United. For every footballer there is pressure to win; at United there was pressure on the team to win every single match.

In every way it was a major change for Keane. He found the training was twice as hard as anything he'd known before and that he hardly ever got a day off. But he found the care with which United looked after his fitness and health was exemplary. After trips abroad on international duty to countries like Macedonia and Romania, for example, he was often whisked home by a private jet specially laid on by United to get him and Irish colleague Irwin home more quickly if it was felt they might need treatment and to allow them more time to rest between games. It was drummed into him that he should be proud to represent Manchester United and that pride should be reflected not just on the field but off it as well. A smart club blazer and tie was required, whereas at Forest Keane and the other players had travelled in tracksuits.

For Keane, there was no doubting Ferguson's hunger and drive for success, his determination and his own pride in the club. Manchester United and Ferguson had their eyes on greater achievement. Having outgrown the Cliff, the club was buying 100 acres for a new training ground and Ferguson dreamed of the day Manchester United would emulate the triumph of 1968, win the European Cup once more and play in an 80,000-seater stadium. Keane was happy to think he was involved in these dreams.

Roy Keane's first significant appearance for Manchester United on British soil came on a sunny afternoon at Wembley on 7 August 1993 against Arsenal in the Charity Shield curtain-raiser to the season. The match is soccer's summer showpiece but with the rivalry between the two teams it was always going to be a competitive game. As he walked out on to the famous Wembley turf Keane was able straight away to sample the fervent support and excitement that surrounds Manchester United wherever they play.

A spectacular volley from Mark Hughes, fully horizontal in mid-air when he struck the ball, put United ahead after only eight minutes but his strike was later matched by another goal of equal individual brilliance and flair by Ian Wright, a snap shot from distance that arrowed in an arc at pace into the top right corner of Schmeichel's net.

When the game ended in a 1-1 draw and went to penalties, Wright had the chance to win it for Arsenal but drove his spot kick wide. Instead it was Schmeichel who won it for United when David Seaman surprisingly stepped up for Arsenal with United leading 5-4 on the penalty count. The Arsenal goalkeeper shot low to the big Dane's left but Schmeichel saved it with some ease. Roy Keane left Wembley that day as a Manchester United winner for the first time.

The first game of the League programme was away to Norwich and Keane made an auspicious start, his cross leading to United's first goal of the campaign from Ryan Giggs in a 2-0 win. Old Trafford had to wait until the second game on Wednesday, 18 August to see their big new summer signing in action at home to Sheffield United and typically Keane produced a performance worthy of the occasion.

Britain's most expensive player was given a rapturous reception by a crowd of nearly 42,000 as he ran out wearing the famous red Manchester United shirt at Old Trafford in a major match for the very first time. The team, the crowd and Martin Edwards didn't have to wait long before he started to repay some of the big money United had paid out for him.

Ince, with his back to goal, contrived to produce an optimistic overhead kick in midfield and it found the head of Giggs, who nodded it on into space behind Sheffield's defence. There was Keane accelerating powerfully on to the ball to ram it home before turning away and sliding joyfully on his knees for several yards in celebration of his first United goal. He was to add a second after a move involving Kanchelskis and Ince that ended with Hughes rolling an inviting pass into his path for him to drive gleefully into the net from close range.

Two goals on his home debut was an encouraging start to his Manchester United career. Keane followed up his bright debut by scoring twice against Honved in Budapest the following month in the European Champions Cup with United winning 3-2. He had dreamed all his footballing life of playing for the European Cup and now he had delivered two priceless goals on his first European foray. Keane's goals went some way to ensuring that Manchester's first European Cup tie for 24 years staged at Old Trafford two weeks later would almost make it a formality for United to go through to the next round.

But it would take some time before Keane felt thoroughly

settled and established in the team. He had joined a fine team, a winning team, but he was young and still had much to learn. He was fortunate, however, to have become a member of a United side buoyed by the confidence that comes with being champions and there were times on the domestic front during his first season when they looked unstoppable.

United had searing pace down the flanks from Andre Kanchelskis and Ryan Giggs who also had a productive season as a goalscorer when he moved inside to allow Lee Sharpe to play on the left. Up front, Mark Hughes, always one of football's greatest big-game players, proved as strong and reliable a target man as ever while Eric Cantona orchestrated all United's creativity with his own magic, vision, skill, audacity, composure and eye for goal. In midfield Robson and Paul Ince were powerful and at the back were the duo known as 'Daisy and Dolly' – Steve Bruce and Gary Pallister – who with the dependable Denis Irwin, Paul Parker and Peter Schmeichel (then widely coming to be regarded as the greatest goalkeeper in the world) formed a formidable defensive rock. For good measure, United also had Brian 'Choccy' McClair, whose wealth of experience, willingness to run non-stop and ability to score goals proved invaluable. Surrounded by such a wealth of footballing talent, particularly in midfield, Keane knew he had no divine right to walk straight into the team despite the record fee but he was prepared to fight for his place and with Robson now aged 36 it was likely that he would get his big chance before long.

Typically Robson wasn't willing to give way to Keane just yet. In pre-season friendlies Keane and Robson took it in turns to anchor the midfield but when they played together against Glasgow Celtic early in August it was noticeable that the veteran at one point virtually shoved his would-be successor off the ball in order to direct operations. With Ince, never short of self-confidence, also the kind of player who never gave an inch, it was apparent that Keane would have to assert himself if he wanted to be a regular in the team.

Importantly, the Old Trafford faithful took to Roy Keane from the start. While some critics argued that £3.75 million was an awful lot of money to gamble on a young player's potential, Manchester United's fans were prepared to let Keane ease his way into the team in his own way. Keane, by his own admission, wasn't the sort of player to catch the eye with flamboyant on-the-ball artistry or party tricks and he hoped that the fans understood that he was essentially a solid midfield team man. His strength was not dribbling past people and unleashing thunderbolts from 25 yards. He also asked for the fans not to judge him too quickly in a team brimming with talent. The fans paid heed: they were content to support him with patience and without overloading him with expectations of instant miracles. They sensed that what United's manager had seen in Keane would eventually come good.

There is no question that Keane himself initially found the tag of being Britain's costliest player difficult to live up to and he felt his best way of trying to justify the transfer fee was to score goals. It was, he later conceded, perhaps not the ideal solution. At Nottingham Forest he was used to getting forward to snatch goals and he was trying to do the same at United in his first season until Bryan Robson eventually advised him that if he was going to play in midfield for Manchester United then he'd have to get the ball from the back four more, become more of an all-rounder and start getting more involved in the build-up play as a playmaker. Keane conceded Robson had made a good point and reacted accordingly.

Off the pitch the transition from Nottingham to Manchester was not easy either. For the first three months at United Keane was in a city he did not know and was living something of a nomadic existence basing himself in an out-of-town hotel while he looked for a permanent home. Years before, he had read stories of soccer stars recounting that it took them a couple of months before they could settle at a new club and he hadn't been able to fully comprehend it. Now he was finding out for himself exactly what they meant and what a change of club entailed.

**BRYAN ROBSON EVENTUALLY ADVISED KEANE THAT IF HE WAS GOING TO PLAY IN MIDFIELD FOR MANCHESTER UNITED THEN HE'D HAVE TO GET THE BALL FROM THE BACK FOUR MORE, BECOME MORE OF AN ALL-ROUNDER AND START GETTING MORE INVOLVED IN THE BUILD-UP PLAY AND AS A PLAYMAKER.**

Keane's routine consisted of picking up his hotel key after training and going to his room, whereupon he would order up room service and eat alone. To eat in the hotel restaurant would constantly invite stares, idle chat and requests for autographs. After some salacious headlines in the more lurid tabloids about his off-field adventures while a Forest player, he had learned to keep his head below the parapet. As Britain's costliest player at a high-profile club, he decided it was best to keep a low profile. Manchester city centre was a good half-hour from where he was living and he tended to avoid it, preferring instead to restrict himself to just two nights out a week on Wednesdays and Saturdays after a game for a few drinks with Lee Sharpe who lived close by.

To complicate his living arrangements, he also still had his house in Nottingham and was often going backwards and forwards, occasionally staying overnight and then driving back to Manchester the following day for training. It was far from ideal and, in retrospect, Keane felt that he was probably not doing himself full justice because in order to play well it was necessary to train well.

Eventually Keane moved out of the hotel and spent a further three months in a luxury rented flat in a Victorian house in the Cheshire stockbroker belt of Bowdon, where his curtains were kept drawn for days on end to avoid prying eyes from inquisitive neighbours wanting to catch a glimpse of Britain's most expensive footballer. Finally he was able to move himself and his favourite Madness records into a house nearby at Christmas and only then did he start to feel settled. 'I found that putting down roots is really important,' he confided. Buying a home was, he reckons, a major turning point and the difference showed out on the pitch.

Keane's new £500,000 abode was a home that befitted football's hottest young star, who was reputed to be earning around £8,000 a week. It was a luxury, architect-designed house built in 1988 overlooking a cricket ground on millionaire's row in the highly sought-after area of Bowdon. It comprised Italian marble floors, seven bedrooms, a comfortably spacious snooker room, sitting room, television room, dining room, a kitchen-cum-breakfast room as well as a laundry room, a freezer room and another room for wine storage. For good measure, the house also boasted a remote-controlled double garage, a built-in floodlit barbecue and mature, well laid-out gardens.

After United's good start to the 1993–94 season, two goals from Sharpe in a magnificent 2-1 win away to Aston Villa, United's close rivals of the previous season, served notice that United were not going to sit back and bask in the glory they had earned the year before. Under Steve Bruce they were determined to keep their standards up and bring more silverware to the club.

They were not going to surrender their championship status easily and, moving into September, United were top of the League with thirteen points from five games and were already eleven points ahead of the chasing pack by the end of October. Possibly the month's most important contribution from Keane was a goal in the 2-1 win against Spurs, a volley struck with precision with the outside of the foot from the edge of the box. It was Keane who would also provide the near-post cross for Hughes to score at White Hart Lane in the 1-0 return fixture against the club Keane had supported as a young boy.

If there had been any doubts that the Old Trafford faithful would take Roy Keane to their hearts they were totally and gleefully dismissed when United played Manchester City at Maine Road on 7 November. This was Keane's first experience of a Manchester derby and the build-up to the game left him in no doubt as to how both teams viewed the fixture. Any United–City match really was something special, a match where local pride was at stake, where both teams were compelled to fight extra hard for every ball.

By half-time Manchester City were able to walk off to deafening applause from the Maine Road crowd with a 2-0 lead from two precise headers by Niall Quinn, although Keane might have scored one for United when he found himself clean through only to have his shot saved by City's goalkeeper Tony Coton. Things looked ominous for United at the break, although 2-0 can sometimes be a deceiving scoreline. The game's next goal would prove crucial. If City scored it they would wrap up the match but a goal for United would bring them right back into the game.

Typically Eric Cantona rose to the occasion and two second-half goals from the Frenchman brought the game level and poised for a pulsating climax. United's tremendous fightback was not yet complete. Having looked on their way to defeat at half-time, now they were out to win the match in the closing stages and when Irwin surged down the left and sent over a deep cross, there was Keane sprinting late into the box to meet it on the half-volley with a powerful right foot shot low into the corner to make it 3-2 to United.

City's 35,000 fans were numbed and they could only look on in dejection and dismay as Keane flung himself full length on the Maine Road turf in a sliding dive of sheer jubilation before rising to his feet to be mobbed by his teammates. It was a marvellous moment for United's newcomer to savour.

In that instant Roy Keane was a hero to one half of Manchester. To the other half he was the villain, the man who had arrived late and spoiled their party horribly. If Roy Keane needed one special moment, one deed by which to endear himself to United fans, then this was it. He had scored a late winner against deadly rivals City, and on their own patch too. All the more difficult for City fans to swallow was that until Keane's strike they had been unbeaten since Brian Horton had taken over as manager of their club from Peter Reid. Now United had brought that fine run to an end. 'That late match-winner in my first Manchester derby really meant something to me,' he reflected modestly afterwards.

The magnificent fightback against Manchester City gave United added impetus to their season and an unbeaten November saw United climb 14 points ahead in the championship and they held the same margin over second-placed Blackburn by the end of the year.

At Christmas Keane was at last able to move into the home he could really call his own and his well-being improved both on and off the field. Even shopping for his own food became a pleasure after months of simply lifting a phone to order room service. Now, too, he could invite his mother and father, his brothers, and other members of his family over from Cork to stay. Since his big summer signing he had managed to get home to Cork only twice to see his mum and dad and each time it had been a welcome break. He could feel fully relaxed in their company and there was always a special greeting for him from Ben, the family's Scottish terrier, which had always really been Roy's dog. Somehow Ben always seemed to know when Roy was coming home. Now he looked forward to gatherings of the Keane clan at his new home and when he proudly showed his parents round his magnificent home they were wide-eyed. They could hardly believe their Roy lived in a home as sumptuous as this.

Roy Keane's £500,000 house in Bowden that he bought after settling at Manchester United.

A special welcome was also reserved for John Delea, now chairman of Keane's old club Rockmount, who frequently travelled over to Manchester with a group of friends, including Keane's uncle Michael Lynch, to see his former protégé play. John was tickled pink to be given his own bedroom in the Keane mansion and even his own key to the house so he could let himself in and out and come and go as he pleased.

On the field, too, Keane felt he made noticeable progress once he had a house he could call his own home. 'Everything else seemed to click into place then,' he said. 'I don't think I really began playing to my potential until Christmas. The lads used to rib me about this, saying that they thought I'd actually only signed at Christmas. Definitely, once I'd settled in, I felt much happier about my performance from then until the end of the season.'

Keane acknowledged he had not exactly set Old Trafford alight in his first few months but he received great encouragement from the other players, the coaching staff, Alex Ferguson and his assistant manager Brian Kidd, and he moved up a gear when there were suggestions in the sports pages from some commentators that he would be dropped to make way for Bryan Robson, who had worked his way back to full fitness. Keane felt that the speculation wasn't justified and was both heartened and relieved that Ferguson thought the same way. 'I'm not sure if I felt deep down I had something extra to prove but, from that moment on, my form improved.'

In his first couple of months as a Manchester United player Keane had also been hampered by a slight hamstring strain, which he didn't really tell anyone about as he was so desperately anxious to do well and make an impression at his new club. There was, however, to be an injury setback that was far more serious. During the magnificent 2-0 defeat of Rapid Vienna away, Keane was chasing a lost ball and made a great tackle but managed to catch the full force of his opponent's studs and needed 19 stitches in a leg injury that put him out for a month.

In January came the death of Sir Matt Busby, the man who had rebuilt Manchester United from the ravages of war into a great modern football club. Old Trafford was still engulfed in sadness at his passing two days later when Everton were the visitors for a game that Alex Ferguson would have preferred to have been postponed as a mark of respect to Sir Matt.

When it went ahead it was always going to be a difficult match from the moment a lone Scots piper led out the two teams and there was a one-minute silence observed in the memory of Sir Matt. It would be a game in which the players would find it hard to express themselves. United struggled for much of the time to impose their superiority on Everton, ultimately winning by the only goal of the game from a Giggs header after an incisive run and cross by Keane.

By the end of January, United's lead in the Premiership had stretched to 16 points and appeared deceptively unassailable. But they had played three more games than Blackburn Rovers and by the end of March that lead had been whittled down to just six points. It might have been closer still but for Keane heading a goal to earn a much-needed away point at Swindon. Despite a 2-0 defeat by Blackburn in what was effectively a six-point, crunch match at Ewood Park with two goals from Alan Shearer, wins against Oldham, Manchester City again and, crucially, victory away at Leeds, kept United's noses in front.

It was Coventry who helped ensure United would be champions again by beating Blackburn on 2 May and fittingly it was Coventry who were at Old Trafford for United's last home game of the season played in a party atmosphere with United already assured of the championship. Keane almost finished his first League season with the club in the very best possible style when he put the ball into the net – though it was subsequently ruled offside. The game finished in a goalless draw before Steve Bruce and Bryan Robson went up together to collect the League trophy for the second successive year.

That final League home fixture of the 1993–94 season against Coventry was to prove a turning point in Roy Keane's footballing career. It was Bryan Robson's last match after thirteen years of outstanding service in a red shirt. He had made 345 appearances and scored 74 goals for Manchester United but, dogged by injury which saw him make just ten starts in the League in 1993–94 season, now he was leaving Old Trafford for Middlesbrough as player–manager. Inevitably the game was tinged with sadness for the fans who were watching one of their great heroes bestride the Old Trafford pitch for the last time and wondering who could possibly step into Robson's boots. Many thought Robson was irreplaceable.

For Roy Keane the silverware United collected that season was vindication of his decision to sign for the club rather than for the others who had courted him. He not only won a League Championship medal in his very first year but an FA Cup winner's medal as well, when United went on to become only the fifth club to do the Double.

They comprehensively beat Chelsea 4-0 on 14 May 1994, in the Cup final at Wembley. Chelsea had beaten United twice in the League and for an hour they played with purpose and promise. But United won with the help of two clinically dispatched penalty goals from Eric Cantona. The second was still billowing the net when an exuberant Keane leaped on to Cantona's back in delight. There was no way back for Chelsea from there. As United paraded the Cup around Wembley there was no prouder member of the Manchester United team than Roy Keane. It was his first FA Cup final as a Manchester United player and for the opposing team his boyhood idol Glenn Hoddle had made a late appearance in a vain attempt to salvage the match. The medal around Keane's neck was proof of a remarkable first season in which he was so nearly a Treble winner, United losing somewhat unluckily to Ron Atkinson's Aston Villa in the Coca-Cola Cup final.

Such was the team's success and general commitment that Steve Bruce and the other players never did get to know the names of the 'big-time Charlies' Alex Ferguson had put into his envelope after the winning of the 1993 League Championship. 'He never opened his envelope because we won the Premiership and the FA Cup!' said Bruce.

Keane could feel well satisfied when he reflected upon his first season at United. He had been an automatic choice in United's starting line-up and he would have racked up more than his eventual 34 League appearances, the same number as Eric Cantona, but for injury taking him out of action for a four matches during November. Gradually he had become used to playing with the other United regulars and they had got used to him. He had joined Manchester United to improve, he was happy to learn as he played, and could sense and feel he was already becoming a better player. Keane also felt that the pressure had largely been taken off him by playing within a team that numbered a lot of bigger stars than himself, players such as Eric Cantona, Ryan Giggs and Paul Ince; the latter liked to be called 'The Guvnor'. Keane's general feeling of Old

Trafford as home during his first season was helped by getting to know all the staff at the club as well.

Alex Ferguson was more than happy with Keane's contribution to the team's continued success and with the player's performances in general. Ferguson was particularly pleased by the development of Keane's vision, something that usually came with experience but which Keane seemed to possess naturally. The manager's only major concern was when Keane and Robson were playing together and both were at times itching to get forward into the penalty box at the same time. Ferguson knew they couldn't both be doing that if the team was to keep its balance and discipline.

Of one thing both Ferguson and assistant Brian Kidd were certain. They had seen enough to know that Keane possessed the qualities in relation to players around him that would eventually make him a major influence on the team in midfield. They were confident he was the kind of player who would have even more of an influence when the going got tougher. They recognised in him the resilience, the stamina and the character to cope in games when United might be losing and needed to dig deep and produce something special to snatch a win. Ferguson also believed Keane had all the basic assets to become a really top player and went so far as to say that he felt he was going to be one of the best players the club had ever had. It was praise indeed and Ferguson needed to be confident in his assessment. It would take an outstanding player to fill Bryan Robson's boots. The stage was set for his replacement.

By the time he reported back for training at Old Trafford for the 1994–95 season, Roy Keane had been named as soccer's youngest millionaire, at the age of 22, in the May 1994 issue of *Business Age* magazine.

To those within the game of football, it was no real surprise. In addition to his Manchester United pay packet, Keane's wealth had been boosted by signing what was then thought to have been the largest boot sponsorship deal in English football history. His three-year boot contract with sports firm Hi-Tec was his first major commercial venture since his record-breaking transfer and was reputed to be worth a handsome £110,000.

Keane was fortunate that he was making a big name for himself at a time when football was becoming increasingly fashionable, when more money than ever before was coming into the game from TV and sponsorship and rewards for the top players were becoming correspondingly lucrative. According to *Business Age*, television – particularly the millions poured into the game by Sky Sports – had enabled leading footballers such as Roy Keane to double their earnings in two years.

For Roy Keane, it wasn't just his bank balance that was improving. So, too, was the quality of his football. With the departure of Robson, Keane assumed greater responsibility at the heart of United's midfield and he made up a powerful duo in harness with Paul Ince. But after the heady excitement of the Double the previous year, it proved ultimately to be a season of disappointment and heated controversy, both for Keane and for Manchester United.

By the end of the night of 7 December, United were out of the Champions League having come third in their group and in the process suffering a crushing 4-0 defeat by Barcelona at the Nou Camp. Those Barcelona goals were to be crucial, eventually allowing the Spanish club to go through from the group to the knockout stages by virtue of conceding overall three goals less in their six games than United had in their six matches.

It was an unhappy exit for United but the experience of

Signing a lucrative boot deal with Hi-Tec in 1994.

competing against some of Europe's best players had whetted
Keane's ambitions still further for the club to succeed in Europe
and he could at least look back with some satisfaction on his
own personal contribution to United's European cause.

At Old Trafford against Barcelona it was Keane who provided
the cross for Sharpe to score with a cheeky backheel and ensure
a 2-2 draw on a thrilling night of action. And Keane showed
great composure to control a cross and beat two men before
calmly stroking in a left-foot shot for United's third goal in the
4-0 defeat of Turkish club Galatasaray.

In the League, Keane was flourishing, laying on a goal for
Mark Hughes in the 5-0 thrashing of Manchester City, scoring
against Queens Park Rangers after a storming run, and giving
an eye-catching Boxing Day power show against Chelsea. One
surging, determined Keane charge into the Chelsea penalty area
ended in a trip and the resulting spot kick was despatched by
Cantona with his customary aplomb. Another similar foray
created a chance for McClair.

Against Ipswich Keane struck the opening goal in a 9-0 demolition of the East Anglian strugglers that included an astonishing six from Andy Cole, who had been transferred from Newcastle for £7 million. It was Cole, not Roy Keane, who now had the burden of carrying the tag of being Manchester United's most expensive player.

But Cole would have traded all six against Ipswich for just one goal against West Ham at Upton Park on the last day of the season. Just one chance taken from several that presented themselves in the last 20 minutes of a fraught afternoon for United would have clinched the Premiership. But, instead, it was Blackburn Rovers, the club that had so nearly added Keane to its squad two years earlier, who won the title by a single point. Nottingham Forest, the club he had left, came third. Having come so close, it was a desperately disappointing end to United's campaign. Disappointingly for Keane, he was the possessor of not one but two runners-up medals that year.

By the end of the 1994–95 season Alex Ferguson had formed the view that Keane was starting to outshine Ince as a player in many ways. It was apparent to the manager, and to Brian Kidd, that their combative Irishman was really starting to blossom and showing positive signs of coming to maturity. They both felt Keane was destined to become a major influence in the club and it was a timely burgeoning of his talent, strength and tactical awareness because Ferguson was planning to give him more responsibility and make Roy Keane, not Paul Ince, his midfield anchorman. He had, most controversially, made up his mind to sell Ince.

Ferguson's primary motivation was that he had begun to feel that Ince was not maintaining his discipline. But it still came as a considerable shock to the Manchester United fans when Ince was sold to Internazionale, especially as Mark Hughes was departing for Chelsea and Andre Kanchelskis for Everton and there were no big signings to replace them – although after serving his long suspension, Eric Cantona would be back.

Keane had mixed feelings about Ince's departure. The two players may have had their run-ins when Keane was at Forest but since they had become colleagues in the same team they had developed a mutual respect for each other's spirit and abilities. Together on the field they had formed a powerful midfield duo for United and now Ince was vacating his self-styled 'Guvnor' role it would mean greater pressure on Keane to become the midfield motivator for United.

Even some of United's most loyal supporters questioned whether Ferguson was doing the right thing in allowing three outstanding players such as Hughes, Kanchelskis and Ince to leave, but the manager knew that in midfield he had a youngster called David Beckham waiting in the wings as well as a lad of superb ability called Paul Scholes and a combative player in the Keane/Ince mould called Nicky Butt. There were a pair of brothers, Gary and Philip Neville, who were more than promising too.

So it was that Keane at the relatively tender age of 24 found himself beginning the 1995–96 season as one of the older hands in the Manchester United team in only his third season with the club. Incredibly, against Aston Villa on the opening day of the season United fielded no less than seven players who were 21 or under, which made Roy Keane feel like a veteran. United suffered a 3-1 defeat that day and it seemed that Keane's drive and energy would be much needed if United were realistically to contest for honours. And the former Liverpool and Scotland stalwart Alan Hansen was moved by such a parade of footballing youth to declare on BBC TV's *Match of the Day* that 'You don't win anything with kids.' It was a remark that United fans would not let him forget and spurred Keane and the team on to prove him wrong.

**'ALAN HANSEN WAS MOVED BY SUCH A PARADE OF FOOTBALLING YOUTH TO DECLARE ON BBC TV'S MATCH OF THE DAY THAT 'YOU DON'T WIN ANYTHING WITH KIDS.'**

It was a remark that United fans would not let him forget and spurred Keane and the team on to prove him wrong.

The opening-day defeat and Hansen's assessment was like a red rag to a bull for Keane and 'Fergie's Fledglings' as his young players were being dubbed. Typically Keane was very much the catalyst in the very next game at Old Trafford against West Ham and scored a vital goal in the 2-1 victory over the Hammers. As he turned away after gliding the ball into the net he was swamped by United's rising young stars all wanting to congratulate him. It was, remarked one observer, like a favourite uncle being pursued gleefully by his young nephews because he had just produced a bag of sweets.

Keane again showed the youngsters the way in the following game by scoring twice in a 3-1 victory over Wimbledon and two days later it was his sheer determination to win a 50-50 ball at Blackburn Rovers that led to the ball breaking for David Beckham to curl in an opportunist and crucial winner.

But the match at Ewood Park was to end amid more controversy for Keane when he was sent off for a second bookable offence, the referee believing he had dived in the penalty area. Keane was bearing down swiftly on goal when he was tripped by Colin Hendry and was sent sprawling. Television replays showed Keane had reason to feel hard done by.

Keane made further unwanted headlines when he was sent off

against Middlesbrough but there was something of a silver lining in that he was able to serve his suspension while recovering from another hernia operation. In all he was out for six League matches but was back in time for two crucial League games around the Christmas period against Leeds and Newcastle.

Losing to Leeds placed even more importance on the Old Trafford clash with high-flying Newcastle and after Andy Cole had given United the lead against his old club with a powerful first-time shot, Keane showed wonderful composure to score United's second, which effectively wrapped up the points. He made a darting run to the back post with a wave to Beckham who picked him out with a perfect cross. Keane controlled the ball neatly and coolly drilled it low past Pavel Srnicek into the bottom right-hand corner.

No less vital was the goal Keane scored with similar composure in the championship run-in against a ten-man Leeds after their goalkeeper had been sent off for handling the ball outside his area. Lucas Radebe took over as keeper but, try as they might, United could not find a way past him until Keane cleverly worked some room for himself slipping past two defenders on the edge of the box and again drove a perfectly placed shot of pace and accuracy low into the corner of the net.

It was a goal that earned a priceless three points and, with Cantona scoring in seven of the last ten games of their League programme, United powered their way to the Premiership title, in the process surging past Newcastle who had seen the twelve-point lead they had at one point held gradually drain away.

It was another League champions medal for Roy Keane but he reserved his finest performance of the season, and one of the finest he has ever produced in a Manchester United shirt, for the FA Cup final.

When Manchester United arrived at Wembley on 11 May 1996, for their third FA Cup final in succession, they were just 90 minutes away from creating football history. No English team had ever achieved two Doubles – League and FA Cup winners in the same season – and now only Liverpool stood between them and unprecedented glory. To call their opponents 'only Liverpool' would be to do them a gross disservice for this was a team that had developed into a formidable, well-knit unit under the tutelage of their coach Roy Evans.

Liverpool had an able shot-stopper of a goalkeeper in the towering David James, a central defender of vast experience in England's Mark Wright, midfield men who could provide penetrative passes and score goals in Jamie Redknapp and the skilful John Barnes, and Steve McManaman who, on his day, could destroy teams with his mazy, dribbling runs. Up front there was the power and strength of Stan Collymore and the predatory eye for goal of Robbie Fowler whom Keane and his teammates needed no reminding had already put four past United that season. If need be, available to Roy Evans on the bench was Ian Rush, one of the most prolific goalscorers of his generation.

Undoubtedly this was a Liverpool team to be duly respected if not feared, a team that, if sparked into life, could be devastating with all cylinders firing. Alex Ferguson was anxious to ensure that the Liverpool machine as an attacking force should only splutter at the very most. Ideally he would like it never even to get into first gear and he knew just the man to effect exactly that.

All week United prepared with great dedication with Ferguson talking over tactics with his key players. Roy Keane, it was decided, should play a crucial role just in front of the back four with three men in midfield in front of him. This, it was hoped, would nullify Collymore's dangerous runs and also deny

Liverpool space in which to create their attacks. The tactics worked like a charm.

The outcome of the match was still in the balance with five minutes to go, with Liverpool having never looked threatening, when United won a corner on the right. As it came over, goalkeeper James weakly punched it clear but straight on to the shoulder of Ian Rush from whence it bounced towards Eric Cantona on the edge of the penalty area. The ball was almost past him and at an awkward hip height when the Frenchman, displaying not only incredible ability to shift his balance in a trice but marvellous sleight of foot, managed from the shortest of backlifts to deliver a shot of great power that screamed through a mass of players into the net. It was a goal worthy of winning any Cup final, and one worthy, too, of creating an historic double Double.

That final will be remembered for Cantona's incredible goal, the only one in what was a dismally dour game played out in front of a crowd of around 79,000 who had come to Wembley hoping for fireworks from United and silky passing and sharp shooting from Liverpool. Instead they sat through a dreadful game of football until Cantona's moment of genius won United the Cup for a record ninth time.

That the Merseysiders failed to show any sort of spark was down very largely to Roy Keane's incredible performance. Given responsibility in holding the deep-lying midfield role, Keane carried out Ferguson's instructions to the letter and completely stifled the life out of Liverpool. It was evident from his crunching tackles in the opening few minutes that he was out to run the show and he proceeded to run up and down Wembley winning tackle after tackle. Operating almost as a third centre-half denying Liverpool space, he tackled, he harried, he ran and tackled some more, seemingly covering every blade of Wembley.

Most players found the Wembley to be an energy-sapping surface to play on. Not Roy Keane. He was quick to snuff out every hint of threat from McManaman, suffocated Redknapp's attempts to get Liverpool moving, shackled Collymore, forced Barnes so deep he became ineffectual, and tirelessly patrolled the midfield at his masterful best. It was fully an hour before McManaman was finally really able to have a go at United. But when he did get to beat two men on the right, Keane was there to win the ball and stop the attack.

If you were a Liverpool fan it wasn't pretty to watch Keane's total destruction of Liverpool's beautiful game. But from United's point of view and, as football's cognoscenti acknowledged, Keane's was a Herculean performance that, despite Cantona's astonishing effort, won him the Man of the Match vote from the BBC. It was richly deserved – and Cantona knew it. At the final whistle the Frenchman, who had broached the idea to Ferguson that Keane should occupy a position in front of the back four, ran straight towards Keane flourishing a fist-clenched salute to United's enforcer before wrapping his arms around him in a grateful hug.

After the disappointment of losing to Everton the previous year, Alex Ferguson was thrilled with the win and paid enthusiastic tribute to Keane's blunting of Liverpool. 'For all of their possession, they didn't open us up once,' he said. 'Keane must take the credit for that. He carried out our tactical plan to perfection. Roy is capable of doing that because he understands the game as well as anyone. We made sure McManaman had no room to damage us. Keane protected that space.'

In an astonishingly short space of time, and against stiff competition from his talented teammates, Roy Keane had made himself an indispensable part of Manchester United. The future was indeed looking rosy for Fergy's Fledglings.

## CHAPTER 4

# FROM INJURY TIME TO AWARDS TIME

ON TUESDAY, 20 August, Roy Keane gave Alex Ferguson the news his manager had been desperately hoping to hear. After due deliberation, Keane had decided to pledge his future to Manchester United for a further four years and signed a new contract worth around £1.2 million a season, which would keep him at Old Trafford until he was 28. It was a fillip for Keane's and Ferguson's start to the new 1996–97 season.

After weighing up all the options, in the end it was a relatively easy decision for Keane to make. He could have left United on a free transfer and the playing fields of Italy, Spain and Germany beckoned invitingly. Had he been a single man, Keane believes he might well have taken the option to move abroad. But now he had ties, a family, a fine house and friends in Manchester.

The sole incentive to move to a foreign club would therefore have been money. A tax-free fortune in the region of £10 million could have come his way from offers laid in front of him by AC Milan and Bobby Robson's Barcelona. There was even talk of the possibility of Keane skippering a new Dublin team shaped around Wimbledon's mooted ambitions to move to the Republic of Ireland. But, not for the first time and not for the last, Keane decided financial reward on its own was not the be-all and end-all. Money was not the main motivation.

There was no question that financially Keane could have set himself up handsomely for life and Keane believes that if he had been with any other club he would have left. But a close scrutiny of European clubs made him realise there were actually very few as big as United and, with the advances the team was making, all the signs were that United would be very seriously competing in the Champions League for the next few seasons. He based his decision to stay on the chance to win the European Cup and that ambition was always in his mind during the negotiations.

Keane was conscious, however, of the need to make the most of his position. He was a top player and he could leave the club without Manchester United receiving a penny for him. He was therefore able to tell the club, 'Give me the right deal and I'll stay.' They did, to the tune of a reported salary rising to above £20,000 a week.

Having pledged his allegiance to United, Keane doubted now that he would ever move abroad unless United chose to sell him. Interestingly, he felt he could not see himself playing at the top level much beyond the age of 30. His own particular high-action midfield role was one that inevitably took a physical toll and the thought of dropping down to play football in lower divisions did not appeal to him in the slightest.

With his immediate future secure, Keane generously splashed out £150,000 on a new home for his parents in rural

**The £150,000 home that Roy bought for his parents in Cork.**

Whitechurch just beyond Cork city's Northside boundaries off the old Mallow road. He had always wanted to buy his mum and dad a dream home as a way of thanking them for their love and unflagging support and he could hardly have chosen better. The house included a bathroom with built-in sauna, a Jacuzzi bath, and five bedrooms, two with en suite bathrooms. A first-floor verandah with white railings ran the whole width of the house, with colonial-style columns underneath, affording views back into Cork's Northside. 'Probably the most attractive house on the northern outskirts of the city ... a truly charming residence,' ran the estate agents' blurb.

Ferguson was genuinely delighted that Keane was remaining at Old Trafford. 'It will secure the heart of Manchester United for the next four years,' said the manager, who was looking forward to Keane reaching his peak over the next few seasons.

But Ferguson's relief and Keane's willingness to go out and demonstrate once again his worth was soon clouded by the need for the player to have a knee operation that would keep him out for a month. Keane had scored a beautifully worked goal at Wembley in the 4-0 drubbing of Newcastle in the Charity Shield and played the following week in the 3-0 win at Wimbledon. Now, frustratingly for Keane, he would be sidelined for a period that would include five League matches and United's opening game away against Juventus in the Champions League. He was sorely missed, especially in Turin, where Juventus won 1-0.

Worryingly for Keane, no sooner had he returned to action than he was sidelined again. Drafted back into the side against Aston Villa away in a 0-0 draw, he then missed a further three League games. The troublesome start to the season was compounded by a red card when he was restored to the United team against Southampton at the Dell on 26 October. His return should have been all the more welcome for United since they had shown a rare vulnerability against Kevin Keegan's Newcastle United the week before and had taken a 5-0 hiding. But at the Dell Keane was promptly sent off for a second booking in an extraordinary match that United contrived to lose by an incredible six goals to three.

**KEANE FELT HE COULD NOT SEE HIMSELF PLAYING AT THE TOP LEVEL MUCH BEYOND THE AGE OF 30. HIS OWN PARTICULAR HIGH-ACTION MIDFIELD ROLE INEVITABLY TOOK A PHYSICAL TOLL AND THE THOUGHT OF DROPPING DOWN TO PLAY FOOTBALL IN LOWER DIVISIONS DID NOT APPEAL TO HIM IN THE SLIGHTEST.**

Worse was to come when Keane suffered a horrifying injury against Rapid Vienna in a game where he nullified Rapid's danger man Kuhbauer in an excellent 2-0 away win. It was while making yet another tackle on Kuhbauer that Keane sustained a deep gash just below the knee when his opponent's studs ripped painfully into his flesh. United colleagues quickly waved for a stretcher amid immediate fears that Keane had broken his leg. Mercifully that did not prove to be the case but, after going to hospital the following day for an examination on the leg injury, the diagnosis was still gloomy. He would be out for a further four games.

Keane's season of misfortune took another twist in February after an incident in the vital 2-1 League win at Arsenal. The game was always going to be keenly contested by two teams with designs on the title but it was inflamed by Ian Wright jumping in at Peter Schmeichel with a fierce tackle. Words were exchanged and the bad feeling between the players continued over the incident in the tunnel after the game with Wright claiming he was the victim of a racist remark while Schmeichel claimed he merely told Wright as the game finished, 'You tried to do me.' While this rumpus was going on, Alex Ferguson certainly heard a racist remark – from an Arsenal player who called Roy Keane an Irish bastard. Ferguson could hardly believe his ears and quickly called for calm. Keane and United had the last laugh over Arsenal by winning the League with the Gunners seven points adrift and finishing third behind Newcastle.

United were knocked out of the FA Cup by Wimbledon and Keane's burning European ambitions foundered at the semi-final stage when both ties were lost to Borussia Dortmund. At least United could say they lost to the eventual champions – Dortmund beat Juventus in the final held in Munich. Alex Ferguson was in Munich for the final and was shown to a seat for the game in the front row of the Directors' Box. From there he could see the magnificent Champions League trophy and was almost close enough to touch it. One day, he thought to himself, he would get his hands on it – by winning it.

For Roy Keane, the 1997–98 season could hardly have begun on a more encouraging note, with Alex Ferguson naming him as his new captain after Eric Cantona had said an abrupt *au revoir* to Manchester United. Cantona's decision to retire from football had come as a supreme shock to everyone in the game, and yet in its own way it was typically Cantona, a man who had always been something of a law unto himself. On 9 May 1997, two days after United had become League Champions, Cantona had quietly informed Alex Ferguson that he wanted to quit football. Strenuous efforts were made to persuade him to change his mind, but Eric was not for turning. On 11 May Cantona lifted the Premiership trophy at Old Trafford after the game against West Ham and then turned his back on football for good.

**SOME EXPERTS QUESTIONED WHETHER KEANE HAD THE TEMPERAMENT FOR THE CAPTAINCY GIVEN HIS VOLATILE NATURE, ESPECIALLY WHEN KEANE VENTURED THE OPINION THAT HE WAS NOT GOING TO CHANGE HIS GAME JUST BECAUSE HE WAS CAPTAIN.**

His departure not only left United with a huge gap to fill on the pitch but also with the need for a new captain. Looking round his team, Alex Ferguson had three main candidates to succeed Cantona: Peter Schmeichel, Gary Neville – although Neville was very much viewed as a captain for the future rather than the present – and Roy Keane. Keane had acquitted himself creditably when twice handed the captain's armband during 1997 in tough League matches at Arsenal and Chelsea when Cantona had been suspended.

Ferguson's eventual choice of Roy Keane to succeed the mercurial Frenchman was, however, a controversial one, and there were more than a few raised eyebrows in footballing circles at his appointment. Some experts questioned whether Keane had the temperament for the captaincy given his volatile nature, especially when Keane ventured the opinion that he was not going to change his game just because he was captain.

Cantona had been an excellent skipper for Ferguson. He had proved an inspirational player and a captain who had quietly commanded great respect from his teammates, not least from Roy Keane, who considered Cantona the best player he had ever played with. Robson, Bruce and Pallister were also great players in Keane's opinion but he

'WHAT ERIC [CANTONA] DID WITH REGARD TO WINNING TROPHIES AND THE KNACK OF SCORING IMPORTANT GOALS STANDS OUT ... AS AN INDIVIDUAL HE WAS A LEGEND.'

Roy Keane

regarded Cantona's individual contributions as phenomenal. 'What Eric did with regard to winning trophies and the knack of scoring important goals stands out,' he said. 'He scored so

many goals to win the Double. That goal against Liverpool at Wembley in 1996 – I just don't think anyone would have been capable of scoring that goal. So as an individual he was a legend.'

Ferguson felt Keane would not only lead by example and become the catalyst of the team in the mould of Cantona but he also believed Keane had now started to acquire a real authority on the pitch and could take everything in his stride.

Keane's determination and fierce will to win reflected Ferguson's own character traits. Importantly, too, even if his own form was below par, Keane would still not flinch from giving a colleague a rollicking if he felt he needed it. Keane was not a man who cared about reputations and if a player was not pulling his weight he would not hesitate to let him know, even if – as had been the case in the past – it was the great Eric Cantona.

Ferguson stated that his new captain was a great competitor and a tremendous footballing talent, insisting that assuming the role of skipper would add a further dimension to his game. Ferguson saw nothing wrong with Keane's aggression and felt that making him captain would encourage him to channel it more effectively. He believed he could have a big influence on the other players very much in the way Bryan Robson had done. From the outset Ferguson had admired that special trait in Keane that makes him a winner and a major factor in his decision to make him skipper was the feeling that Keane would spread this spirit throughout the team. Ferguson was confident he now had the maturity to make a fine leader.

There was no doubt that Roy Keane's recently acquired on-field maturity reflected his settled circumstances and stable home life away from football. At the end of May, Keane had returned to Cork to wed his sweetheart Theresa in a quiet ceremony attended only by close relatives, all of whom respected his wishes that the press should not be alerted in advance about the wedding. There were fears that if word had leaked out the church in his hometown area of Mayfield would be besieged by Manchester United fans.

Only a handful of Keane's nearest and dearest, including his daughters Shannon and Caragh, were ushered by Keane's groomsmen brothers Denis and Pat into The Church of Our Lady Crowned for the five o'clock ceremony on Thursday, 29 May. It made for a largely empty church but it was nonetheless a delightful family occasion for Keane and Theresa, who was given away by her father. Keane's display of family loyalties was completed by having his sister Hilary as Theresa's bridesmaid and, standing by his side as best man as he took his vows, was his eldest brother Johnson.

Marriage to Theresa cemented the couple's relationship in the most positive of ways and Keane's life as a husband and father took on a much calmer and contented balance, quite different from the nightclubbing and champagne lifestyle most people imagined he enjoyed. 'I actually live quite a boring life,' he said, confessing that, quite apart from anything else, he didn't like champagne because it gave him a headache.

As a footballer of such high profile, invitations to all manner of functions regularly came Keane's way and, if he'd had a mind to do so, he could have been out being feted almost

Roy and his wife Theresa leaving the Keane family home in Mayfield.

A cut above the rest: Roy opens a Virgin Megastore in Cork in 1997.

any night of the week — with all the temptations that could entail. But Keane chose to turn them all down, preferring to spend time with his young family. As a general rule, he never went out during the week and reserved outings for the weekend with his family. In his more restless youth he might have switched off by enjoying a drink in a bar or a nightclub. Now he found the perfect mental relaxation by walking his three dogs in a public park close to his Cheshire mansion. Being Roy Keane it was rarely a short walk, his natural energy taking him on foot for mile after mile as he unwound.

It was not at Old Trafford or at Wembley that Roy Keane lifted his first trophies as Manchester United captain. It was on a pre-season tour of the Far East when Jordi Cruyff gave United a 1-0 victory over South China in a match played in Hong Kong before an excited crowd of 36,000. Two Solskjaer goals then secured victory over the Japanese J-League team Urawa Red Diamonds in Tokyo. Keane and the rest of the players had flown first to Thailand, where they had been amazed to find 2,000 Thai Manchester United fans waiting for them to arrive at Bangkok airport. Even a training session at Thailand's national stadium attracted an enthusiastic crowd of 4,000.

The oriental hospitality in Thailand, Hong Kong and Japan provided a pleasant way for Keane and his team to start inching their way into the new season. They were accorded the warmest of welcomes wherever they went, swamped with gifts ranging from flowers to lucky string bracelets, and treated to displays of traditional Thai dancing and kick-boxing.

Back in England once more, Keane got United's season off on the right foot by leading the side to victory against Chelsea on 3 August at Wembley in the Charity Shield. The match ended in a 1-1 draw but United went on to win 4-2 on penalties with Keane comfortably tucking away his own spot-kick before Nicky Butt's clincher. It was United's first silverware of the season, but few could have foreseen the chain of events that would also make it the season's last.

After that Wembley showpiece it was down to the serious business of the League and it was a proud moment for Keane when he celebrated his 26th birthday on August 10 by leading out Manchester United in the Premiership for the first time against Tottenham at White Hart Lane. In the next few weeks Keane got on the scoresheet in the 3-0 win over Coventry and also in the 2-1 victory over West Ham. Then United travelled to Elland Road on 27 September for the League fixture with Leeds United, always a tense affair, and met with disaster.

**'ROY IS A GREAT PLAYER BUT YOU CAN'T GO ON LIKE THAT. YOU HAVE SEEN IT BEFORE. SOMETIMES HE GETS TOO HYPED UP AND LOSES CONTROL. HE NEEDS TO STOP, THINK AND CONTROL HIMSELF MORE.'**

**Alf-Inge Haaland on a wild tackle that saw Keane seriously injured**

To lose 1-0 against their dreaded rivals was bad enough for United, especially as it brought to an end an unbeaten run in defence of the Premiership title. But the goal they conceded, a header from David Weatherall that condemned United to defeat, was nothing compared with an incident towards the end of the game that became a sickening turning point in United's season and in the footballing career of Roy Keane.

Thirteen minutes before the end of a game in which United had not played well, Keane chased a through ball and made a despairing, crunching, lunging tackle for it with Leeds' Norwegian international Alf-Inge Haaland. It was a reckless challenge and suddenly Keane's studs seemed to catch in the turf and he staggered before collapsing full length, writhing in agony, just inside the Leeds penalty box.

Even in the baying cauldron of a packed Elland Road crowd of nearly 40,000 Keane had actually been able to hear something snap as he went for the ball and he knew it wasn't his shinpad. He lay prone on the turf while Haaland leaned over him and mouthed his anger at Keane's challenge while Weatherall also closed in to remonstrate before Beckham pushed everyone away and bent to aid his stricken colleague. Later Haaland was to reflect, 'Roy is a great player but you can't go on like that. You have seen it before. Sometimes he gets too hyped up and loses control. He needs to stop, think and control himself more.'

Keane was at once aware that whatever injury he had suffered it was most certainly serious. He received prolonged attention on the pitch but, with United having used up their substitutes, going off the field would have meant his team would be down to ten men. Gamely he therefore resolved to continue even though, once back on his feet again, Keane found the referee adding punishment to injury by booking him for his despairing challenge on Haaland. He carried on, clearly suffering, before eventually hobbling off to jeers of derision from the Leeds fans, who revelled in his obvious pain and discomfort.

Once off the field, the full severity of Keane's injury quickly became ominously apparent. 'I knew as soon as it happened that the injury was very serious,' he said. 'I actually heard the ligament tear as I went down and I told our physio Dave Fevre it was bad.'

Nonetheless, Keane kept his immediate thoughts positive and even harboured hopes that he would still be fit for the European Cup game against Juventus, which was just four days away. Deep down, however, he feared the worst and when Fevre was able to take a closer look at the knee, Keane asked him to tell him straight just how bad it was. 'He just said, "The knee is knackered." But I already knew,' said Keane, who left Elland Road on crutches.

This was by no means the first time Keane had suffered knee damage. In 1996 he had sustained a deep gash in his leg that required 17 surface stitches and micro-stitches under the skin to hold the flesh together. But now Keane had suffered the injury that footballers dread most – ruptured cruciate ligament damage.

Within minutes of Dave Fevre's accurate early diagnosis, arrangements were being made for Keane to be taken to hospital for an examination by Jonathan Noble, Manchester United's orthopaedic surgeon. Next day Noble confirmed, as suspected, that Keane had indeed sustained cruciate ligament damage and the following day the player underwent orthoscopic treatment to determine just how badly the knee had been injured. Noble decided he would operate once the swelling on the knee had been given time to go down. After just nine matches of the League programme and one European tie against Kosice in Slovakia, Keane's season was most definitely over.

It was a cruel and bitter blow for Keane, who could now expect to be out of action for eight to ten months, and for Manchester United, who would lose the services of their most dynamic player for the rest of the season.

The sports pages of the Sunday papers were full of the irony that Keane had needlessly injured himself while clattering into another player. It was poetic justice, said some commentators, who castigated Keane because they considered the injury was essentially self-inflicted.

Once the severity of Keane's condition was established, Alex Ferguson concerned himself with the question of when to pick the right moment to break the bad news – not just to Keane and his family, but to the fans, the press and Juventus. The Italian club would, of course, be most interested to know there was no hope of Keane facing them in the Champions League. But despite strenuous efforts to keep the seriousness of Keane's injury shrouded in secrecy, it was inevitable that the whispers should start and by the time the Juventus game came around on 1 October it appeared to be almost an open secret.

The club was naturally anxious that such depressing news, although not yet officially confirmed, should affect neither the players nor the Old Trafford fans for the Juventus match. But although Manchester United have never been nor will ever be a one-man team, the absence of Roy Keane on the teamsheet that night was undeniably a huge blow and the gloom was compounded when United found themselves a goal down before many of the 53,428 fans had settled in their seats, Del Piero racing away to put Juventus 1-0 up with a smart finish after just 24 seconds.

But, even without Keane to haul them up by their bootlaces from this setback, United managed to find the collective will to fight back to win 3-2 with goals from Sheringham, Scholes and Giggs on what turned out to be one of those greats nights of European football at Old Trafford. It was a match Roy Keane would have relished and would have been proud to have played in, though in the end he could only watch it on television.

Next day the general euphoria at the club over the defeat of Juventus was clouded by United's gloomy announcement that Keane would be out for the rest of the season. The club said that Keane would be admitted to hospital some time within the following month for a cruciate ligament operation. 'Roy Keane had an exploratory operation on Monday,' it was announced. 'A small piece of cartilage was removed and it was also discovered that he would require a cruciate ligament operation. That will be performed in approximately four weeks when the swelling has gone down. He will be out for the rest of the season.'

The official bad news, though softened by United's win over Juventus without their most important player, was seen in footballing circles as a terrible blow for United's hopes of fending off domestic challenges as well as for their ambitions of winning the European Cup. 'It is a great disappointment to lose such an important player for such a long time,' said Alex Ferguson. 'But we have no fears about the long-term situation. We have absolutely no doubt that Roy Keane will be back for the start of next season.'

**'I KNEW AS SOON AS IT HAPPENED THAT THE INJURY WAS VERY SERIOUS. I ACTUALLY HEARD THE LIGAMENT TEAR AS I WENT DOWN AND I TOLD OUR PHYSIO DAVE FEVRE IT WAS BAD.'**

**Roy Keane, on the same injury**

Once the full extent of the damage to Keane's knee was clear, the long healing process began virtually straight away with Keane and Terry Cooke, one of United's young players who had also suffered a similar sort of injury, sitting down together to watch a starkly detailed video that pulled no punches about the operation they were soon to undergo to repair their knees. Gruesome as this might sound, it was all part of the psychological process of helping Keane come to terms with the injury. 'That certainly opened my eyes,' Keane said of the video. 'I saw the whole thing. It was a little frightening but now we know what lies ahead and the more you know about this injury the better.'

Playing to win. The captain of the world's greatest ever team.

On top of his game.

*Above:* A pause during one of Man U's training sessions.

*Below:* Keane on one of his trademark runs.

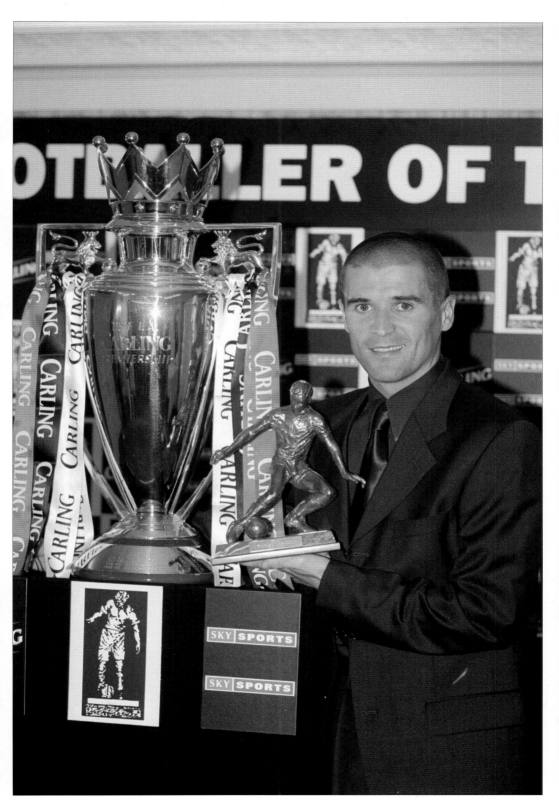

A true champion. Keane accepts the Football Writers Player of the Year Award 2000.

Proud to captain his country.

The fight for fitness stretched for months in front of him and winning the mental battle would be just as important as the physical one. Mentally it had been a terrible shock. One moment he had been captain of the world's most famous football club, the next his season was over and he was facing an uncertain future.

There was a time not so long ago when the type of injury Keane had sustained almost certainly spelled the end of a player's career. Major strides had been made in recent years in the treatment of torn cruciate ligament, but all sorts of questions inevitably still raced through Keane's mind – not least whether he would ever play again. Was his career over at 27? If the operation was a success, would he be able to recover fully? Would

**KEANE COULD NOW EXPECT TO BE OUT OF ACTION FOR EIGHT TO TEN MONTHS; AND MANCHESTER UNITED WOULD LOSE THE SERVICES OF THEIR MOST DYNAMIC PLAYER FOR THE REST OF THE SEASON.**

he still be as determined, strong and committed in the tackle? Could he get back to being the player he was? How would he cope if he couldn't? The road back from cruciate ligament damage is a long, hazardous and often lonely one and it was impressed upon him that infinite patience would be needed over the coming months. But patience was not something that many would readily associate with Roy Keane, a man who was obsessed with football and who never stopped running.

At the back of Keane's mind was a return to football in time for the European Cup Final in May 1998 or the World Cup in France in 1998. 'I spoke to Dave the physio and of course the World Cup was at the back of my mind,' he said. 'But I cannot set myself any targets. That's pointless. If I was a betting man I wouldn't put much money on myself recovering for France but you should never say never. Either way I've been told it's just better to get on with the day-to-day business of recovery and let the future take care of itself.'

Keane was realistic enough to admit to himself and to others that cruciate ligament damage could be a career-ending injury.

**ONE MOMENT HE HAD BEEN CAPTAIN OF THE WORLD'S MOST FAMOUS FOOTBALL CLUB, THE NEXT HIS SEASON WAS OVER AND HE WAS FACING AN UNCERTAIN FUTURE.**

For every Alan Shearer and Paul Gascoigne who had come back from it, there were other lesser-known players down the other divisions who had not. He also counted himself lucky that at Old Trafford he would receive the best possible treatment. 'I know it's going to be hard but if anyone can get me back, I know it will be Dave and United,' he said. 'It looks as if I will miss an exciting year on the club and international front but that's life. There's nothing I can do about it and there's no point in dwelling on it.'

Understandably it felt strange for Keane to be at home with his wife and children on 4 October, the first Saturday since his injury, when United kicked off against Crystal Palace without him. It was something he was going to have to get used to though, even if only temporarily. Pointedly he largely stayed away from the club after the injury while awaiting his operation. 'I'm not a good spectator when it comes to football,' he explained, 'and I don't like the idea of going down to the club and hanging around. I feel I'd almost be making a nuisance of myself.'

In fact, during his recuperation period Keane went to just a handful of matches at Old Trafford and a few away games. He preferred not to travel to away matches with the United team as he felt he would be a distraction for them. Instead he watched from the crowd although such distancing of himself from his team made him feel like the forgotten man.

Quite apart from Keane, his family, his teammates, Alex Ferguson and everyone at Manchester United, there were others ruing the fact he had collected an injury that would sideline him for so long. Diadora, the boot manufacturers, had just signed a new distribution contract for Ireland with Glentawn Sports and Leisure, a subsidiary of Dubarry Shoemakers of Athlone, and Roy Keane was the centre of their promotion. When they took him over to Dublin on 10 October just two weeks after his injury at Elland Road, Diadora introduced Keane as the star of the Diadora posters, which brazenly featured the whites of the United skipper's eyes painted red accompanied by a slogan that read: 'We sold our soul to the devil.'

The irony of the suggestion that Keane viewed things through a red mist was not lost on anyone, but Andrew Ronnie, general manager of Diadora,

**'I'M NOT A GOOD SPECTATOR WHEN IT COMES TO FOOTBALL AND I DON'T LIKE THE IDEA OF GOING DOWN TO THE CLUB AND HANGING AROUND. I FEEL I'D ALMOST BE MAKING A NUISANCE OF MYSELF.'**
**Roy Keane**

England, commented, 'The red eyes and the slogan refer to the Red Devils, the fact that he is a player with Manchester United and the type of player Roy is – a very hard, committed player.

'From a business point of view I was disappointed when he was injured but as a Manchester United fan I was gutted for the club and for him personally. This was going to be a very big year for Roy and United. Of the many players who endorse our boots, he is one of the easiest to deal with. He's a shy guy and very genuine with it.'

By November Keane had undergone his cruciate ligament

operation and it went well enough for everyone to assure him that there was no reason why he should not make a complete recovery. It was heartening news for Keane and for Alex Ferguson although Keane admitted, 'After I'd had the operation all I could think about was whether I would walk again, let alone play football again.' But he gave an immediate post-operation indication of his determination to fight back to fitness. Although he was, of course, on crutches the day after the operation, it still did not stop him hobbling into the gym to work on the weights, mindful of advice that although it was his knee that had required surgery his body should not be neglected.

It showed admirable spirit from Keane and this post-op bravado impressed everyone. But Alex Ferguson was at pains to stress to the club's physio staff that the player's rehabilitation must not be rushed or put in jeopardy in any way. The manager was as anxious as anybody to have him back playing again but he was looking to Keane's prospects as a long-term player at the club, not as a player to be hurried back to fitness in case he might need him. There would be no quick fix at the expense of proper, measured, programmed rehabilitation with the aim of re-establishing him as good as new for many more seasons to come. Ferguson wanted the Roy Keane he knew, admired and valued so hugely in his team and, not for the first time, he was prepared to wait till he got him.

> **'OF THE MANY PLAYERS WHO ENDORSE OUR BOOTS, HE IS ONE OF THE EASIEST TO DEAL WITH. HE'S A SHY GUY AND VERY GENUINE WITH IT.'**
> Andrew Ronnie, general manager of boot manufacturers Diadora

> **'AFTER I'D HAD THE OPERATION ALL I COULD THINK ABOUT WAS WHETHER I WOULD WALK AGAIN, LET ALONE PLAY FOOTBALL AGAIN.'**
> Roy Keane

# CHAPTER 4

Once Keane was able to abandon his crutches after the operation the physical rebuilding process could begin. Eventually he was able to start going in to the gym daily but it was far from easy. The gym was not the most cheerful and uplifting of places – it had no windows and Keane found himself staring at the same four blank walls every single day. Right from his earliest days Keane had been a good trainer and he was no less conscientious during his recuperation. If ever there had been a temptation to drown his sorrows in a beer glass, it was quickly dismissed by the knowledge that he had to look after his body. If he put on extra weight it would make recovery that much harder for him.

He knew, too, he could cut corners with the exercise routines but if even the merest inclination to do so entered his mind it was quickly banished by the surgeon's warning ringing in his brain to the effect that it was like building a house and if he didn't get his foundations right then he would have problems later on. However

> **'OBVIOUSLY THERE ARE QUITE A LOT OF PEOPLE, THE SO-CALLED BEGRUDGERS, WHO WERE HAPPY TO SEE ME INJURED BUT THEY JUST KEPT ME GOING. THEIR ATTITUDE JUST MADE ME HUNGRY TO GET BETTER.'**
> **Roy Keane**

expert the surgeon and the physio staff were, once the specialists had discharged him Keane knew full well that now it was down to him to battle back to fitness.

Often it was a lonely process pedalling away on a bicycle machine or swimming solitary lengths of the pool but always he was spurred on by the 'begrudgers', as he termed those he felt were glad he had injured himself. 'I don't think I deserved the injury because I nearly lost my career for trying to trip a bloke up,' he said. 'Obviously there are quite a lot of people, the so-called begrudgers, who were happy to see me injured but they just kept me going. Their attitude just made me hungry to get better.'

Like any sidelined athlete the temptation was always to press on for fitness quicker than was perhaps good for him. His young body and limbs responded well but mentally Keane went through a whole range of emotions from impatience to frustration to restlessness tinged with depression to envy of his teammates, just as everyone told him he would.

Sports psychologists have expressed the view that an athlete's reaction to a serious injury can be compared with the grieving process experienced following the loss of a loved one. The victim will experience denial, doubt, anger and depression and there was no reason to suppose that Keane, facing such a long period out of the game he lived for, would react any differently.

'I haven't forgotten how low I was at times at home,' he later reflected. 'I tried to put on a brave face to the press but there were times when it was so hard.' Barely a day or even an hour went by without Keane wondering if he would get his footballing career back. But he knew that football was his life, what he had always wanted to do, and ultimately his determination was unshakeable. 'There was no other way than to come back strongly,' he said. 'What was I to do? Sit back and think, "Well, that's the end of it"? I was only 27. I had no choice but to battle back.'

The mental frustration of being out of the reckoning for team selection and day-to-day involvement with the players was one of the most difficult hurdles Roy Keane had to face. Naturally he felt distanced from the team despite the wise counselling and cheerful banter he regularly received from assistant manager Brian Kidd to lift his spirits. Alex Ferguson, too, of course, regularly visited Keane in the treatment room but the player understood and accepted that as he was injured and not involved Ferguson had more important things on his mind. There were football matches to be won for Manchester United and Keane could play no part. He was out of the picture and that was desperately hard to take for a player used to being a team regular.

There were times when he would watch the other players going through their paces in training and the sad knowledge that he had not a hope of joining them for many months gnawed away at him. How he envied those other players. The footballing fraternity are notorious for ribbing each other but questions posed in jest like 'Have you joined the ex-players association yet?' and 'You're still here, are you?', although only jokingly intended, can sound frighteningly loaded when you are full of self-doubt and feeling isolated. There were occasions when Keane simply felt awkward and almost embarrassed to go into the ground knowing he was still being handsomely paid by the club and yet not able to go out on the pitch to do what he was paid to do. And always there was someone to ask the same question: 'How's your knee?' The enquiries were nearly always warm and genuine but Keane would not have been human if he had not got sick of being asked the same question over and over when so many months of recuperation stretched in front of him and progress was slow. In the end he frequently opted to stay away from Old Trafford. That way he could avoid the feeling that he was just getting in the way. His choice was to miss a lot of Old Trafford matches and simply stay at home.

But that in itself was a consolation that Keane came to value enormously. He was able to spend a great deal more time with his young family and months into the treatment he was able to reflect on what a wonderful silver lining this had turned out to be. 'When you get an injury like this you realise how important your family are to you,' he said. 'Before it was football, football, football, but over the last few months I've spent a lot of time with my two girls. It was harder for my wife Theresa than for anybody else with me hanging around the place at weekends. I couldn't say I'm the easiest person to live with. She's had to bite her tongue a few times and realised that I was so bored not playing football for ten months.'

Much later, when his restoration to the team was complete and he had at last made his comeback, Keane was able to reflect that overall the experience had been good for him. He returned refreshed with a much deeper appreciation of being a footballer. He realised how lucky he had been to get his career back on track and his place back in such a fine team and to play a part in its success.

Having previously taken for granted that football was his way of life, now he also discovered that he enjoyed training a lot more. He only had to cast his mind back to the days he spent on the treatment table gazing out of the window at the players in training to remember why. His feelings, he remembered then, were of utter envy. 'I would have given anything, absolutely anything to be out with them,' he said. 'So now, even in five-a-sides I enjoy it a lot more than maybe I did a few years ago.

'Things happen for a reason,' he said philosophically. 'I believe a lot in fate and I know for a fact that what's happened to me has made me appreciate the game a lot more. I hope I'm that little bit wiser. So no regrets ... but of course I wish it hadn't bloody happened.'

For a man with such a fierce will to win Keane interestingly confided that his attitude had changed slightly since his injury. He stressed that he was still upset if his team lost a game but that now he felt the good had to be taken with the bad. His attitude had always been not to get too carried away if you were winning and not to get too upset if you lost. 'But after my injury,' he concluded, 'I realised there's a lot more than football.'

For the rest of the 1997–98 season Manchester United had to find out the hard way if there was a lot more to their team than Roy Keane. Alex Ferguson could have moved into the transfer market to buy a replacement but decided against it, admitting

> **'WHEN YOU GET AN INJURY LIKE THIS YOU REALISE HOW IMPORTANT YOUR FAMILY ARE TO YOU ... BEFORE IT WAS FOOTBALL, FOOTBALL, FOOTBALL, BUT OVER THE LAST FEW MONTHS I'VE SPENT A LOT OF TIME WITH MY TWO GIRLS.'**
>
> **Roy Keane**

that Keane was such a great player that there weren't many who could take over from him. Instead Ferguson used Nicky Butt and Paul Scholes in midfield and they responded with some gritty performances.

In fact, United did manage to ride the loss of Keane with some aplomb at times, memorably with a drubbing of Chelsea in the FA Cup. United's electrifying performance saw the London side losing 0-5 at one point in front of their own supporters at Stamford Bridge, quite a number of whom could bear to watch the torture no longer and started for home before Chelsea made the final score 3-5 after United took their foot off the pedal.

While United continued to get good results Keane had to put up with regular ribbing that the team were doing quite well enough without him, that they weren't missing him. But his riposte to such joshing was to say, 'We'll see at the end of the season.'

He was right to warn the jesters to be wary. As the season wore on, injuries to Pallister, Giggs and Schmeichel cost United dear in all competitions. With Keane also out, the spine of the side was missing and Arsenal, with a late run of ten consecutive victories, deservedly won the Premiership. But when John Giles commented, 'Keane's injury cost Manchester United the title,' there were few prepared to disagree with him.

It was on 27 July 1998 that Roy Keane was at last able to make his return to senior football. He played for 45 minutes in a friendly in Oslo on Manchester United's pre-season Scandinavian tour and happily for Keane his knee came safely through the test. Significantly, the long lay-off had apparently not blunted his competitive spirit – he collected a yellow card. He followed up by playing his first full game on 31 July in a 6-0 thrashing of Bronby, Peter Schmeichel's old club. But the sterner tests were still to come. By his own admission, Keane's combative spirit and will to win is 90 per cent of his game. Now everyone, not least Roy Keane himself, was wondering whether he really could resume his career and be the forceful player he had once been.

> **'THINGS HAPPEN FOR A REASON,' HE SAID PHILOSOPHICALLY. 'I BELIEVE A LOT IN FATE AND I KNOW FOR A FACT THAT WHAT'S HAPPENED TO ME HAS MADE ME APPRECIATE THE GAME A LOT MORE. I HOPE I'M THAT LITTLE BIT WISER.'**
>
> **Roy Keane**

Roy Keane was finally officially able to leave the darkest days of his football career behind him on 9 August 1998, when he led out Manchester United against Arsenal at Wembley in the Charity Shield. For his family, his friends, the club, the team, the Manchester United supporters, the medical staff who had supervised his comeback, it was a heartening sight to see him emerging from the famous Wembley tunnel, shaven-headed, determination and focus written all over his face as usual, but noticeably less heavy than many of United's fans were accustomed to seeing him. During his recuperation Keane had worked hard on improving and maintaining his upper body strength and he had shed a lot of body fat. He looked lean and fit and obviously he was relieved and delighted to be back. Messages wishing him good luck on his return flowed steadily in and he was able to reflect on how far he had come since that fateful moment against Leeds 316 days before. 'Playing again seemed a million miles away,' he said. 'To have had to have finished at such a young age would have been very hard to take.'

A 3-0 win for Arsenal in the Charity Shield was not the outcome Keane would have wished for on his return. But he had come through the match without undue concern and now he could look ahead. Keane knew perfectly well that after such a long lay-off it would take time for him to regain match sharpness and to get back to somewhere approaching his best. He wasn't expecting simply to slip back into peak form. At the start of the season he had sat down with Alex Ferguson and Brian Kidd and together they had looked to October, when he would have a dozen games under his belt, as the time when he could expect to be playing something like his old self. Around that time Keane could also look forward to having become a father again, as his wife Theresa was expecting their third child in September.

Inevitably, once he was back in a United shirt Keane's natural inclination was to try and prove himself as quickly as possible. For the first six weeks his performances fell short of his best. He knew he was not doing himself full justice but in reality it was only to be expected. Predictably fans, opponents, and football writers were all scrutinising his performances each week to see if he was launching as whole-heartedly into tackles as he had before, what progress he was making and whether the injury would permanently hamper his naturally energetic, aggressive game.

Keane was spurred on by his teammates, for whom the very sight of their skipper restored to the centre of the spine of their side once more was enormously reassuring, even if it meant that their ears were occasionally left burning by a withering blast from the captain calling for more effort.

**THE SIGHT OF THEIR SKIPPER RESTORED TO THE CENTRE OF THE SPINE OF THEIR SIDE ONCE MORE WAS ENORMOUSLY REASSURING FOR HIS TEAMMATES, EVEN IF IT MEANT THAT THEIR EARS WERE OCCASIONALLY LEFT BURNING BY A WITHERING BLAST FROM THE CAPTAIN CALLING FOR MORE EFFORT.**

It was, however, of undoubted help to Keane as he strove for match fitness that the team was generally performing well, strengthened both at the back by the arrival of Dutch defender Jaap Stam and up front by the transfer from Aston Villa of striker Dwight Yorke and Swedish winger Jesper Blomqvist; the combined cost for the three newcomers came to £27.7 million. While the team were playing well, Keane could blend in more easily. Had United been struggling then the finger could all too easily have been pointed at any failure by Keane to reach a decent level of form.

Seven wins in the first dozen League games and only one defeat – albeit another pride-denting 3-0 loss to Arsenal at Highbury – meant that by mid-November there were glimpses of the momentous season to come. As Keane grew both in strength and confidence he began to produce regularly a level of performance with which he could feel quietly satisfied.

On a personal note, he was also thrilled by the arrival of a baby boy he and Theresa named Aiden. Everyone was delighted for him that the baby had been a boy, as he already had two beautiful little daughters. It wasn't long before the Keane clan flew over from Cork to see the new addition to the family and there were heartfelt congratulations, too, from John Delea on one of his regular trips over from Cork with his friends. Keane was always delighted to see them all and went to great lengths to make each stay memorable. He personally drove out to the airport to pick them up, transported them to the hotel he had booked for them in advance, and handed them each tickets for the weekend's game and tickets for the players' lounge afterwards. By the end of the Treble year, Delea was able to claim with pride that he now had a photograph of himself with every Manchester United player. After a convivial sojourn in the players' lounge, it was back to Keane's house for something to eat and then a drink at his local. On Sunday morning, Delea and his pals would find Keane waiting for them outside their hotel to drive them in his Jeep to United's training ground. Keane would join the other players for training while they stayed and watched from the Jeep. Delea was thrilled to the core when one morning Keane brought Alex Ferguson over to meet him.

Keane's hospitality didn't stop there. On the Monday it was his wont to take Delea and his pals off to one of the best restaurants in Manchester for a pre-booked slap-up lunch, paid for in advance, before dropping the party off at the airport for the flight back to Cork. 'Unbelievable what he does for us,' said Delea after one such trip. 'When I go back to the brewery where I work, the people there just don't believe me.'

It was always a memorable few days for Delea and his friends, never more so than after they had flown over to see United play Liverpool one year. Keane rounded off their stay by pressing an envelope into Delea's hand with the quiet explanation that it was 'Something for the club'. Just before he boarded the plane, the Rockmount chairman opened the envelope to discover a cheque to his club for £5,000.

At the end of November came an event that was particularly pleasing for Roy Keane: his first Premiership goal for 14 months. Fittingly, having sustained his cruciate injury at Elland Road against Leeds United, it came against the same club at Old Trafford in a vital 3-2 win. Keane's face was wreathed in smiles as he recorded his first goal since his strike against West Ham at Old Trafford on 6 September the previous year.

This time Keane scored with a left-foot shot and the joy with which his teammates greeted his strike spoke volumes for their genuine delight that he was now well and truly back. They mobbed him and a beaming Andy Cole, impressed that the skipper had scored with his left foot, went across to Keane and light-heartedly lifted up his skipper's left leg, presenting Keane's foot for inspection to a chortling Yorke.

Keane had also got on the scoresheet in October against Bronby in a 2-6 victory over the Danish club in the Champions League. He played a neat one-two with Yorke and showed his old familiar acceleration to take the return pass and fire home with a powerful drive. The goal and the manner of its scoring was a great boost to his confidence.

After coming safely through against LKS Lodz in the qualifying round of the Champions League, United had been drawn in Group D, ominously nicknamed 'The Group of Death' because apart from Bronby it also contained Spanish giants Barcelona and mighty Bayern Munich. In the event, United drew home and away with both Barcelona and with Bayern in matches that thrilled Europe, Keane scoring a vital goal against Bayern in the 1-1 draw at Old Trafford on 9 December. Keane's effort was enough to enable Manchester United to look forward to resuming their European ambitions in March 1999 after the competition's traditional winter break.

Soon it became apparent that Manchester United would be challenging for honours on three fronts – the Premiership, the Champions League and the FA Cup. In the League, Cole and Yorke were proving a formidable duo. Good friends off the pitch, they forged an exciting and penetrative partnership up front that was to result in 35 goals between them for the season while the young Norwegian Ole Gunnar Solskjaer was to add 12 of his own despite starting just 14 games. Coming on as a substitute he proved invaluable, always likely to score one goal – or even four! Against Keane's old club Nottingham Forest, Solskjaer came off the subs' bench to score a staggering 4 goals in just 20 minutes in an 8-1 demolition.

At the back, Peter Schmeichel, after a couple of un-characteristic mistakes that had the experts questioning whether he was still the great goalie of old, was again proving himself a massive figure as the last line of defence. In front of him Jaap Stam, who had taken a little time to acclimatise to English football and integrate himself into the team, was also proving a towering, reliable presence and by the turn of the year Roy Keane was in full flow once more. The engine that had always enabled him to be a box-to-box player appeared to be ticking over nicely. His presence as a tireless, driving force in midfield was becoming more conspicuous in almost every game. Once

Alex Ferguson had got to grips with his team's defence after a shock 2-3 defeat by Middlesbrough at Old Trafford on 19 December, United's general all-round air or superiority began to have the fans talking optimistically of a Treble.

In the FA Cup, a third-round win over Middlesbrough paired United with Liverpool for a fourth-round tie at Old Trafford. After United went behind early to an Owen goal, Keane urged United forward with renewed purpose … only for it to appear that it was not to be their day. Chances went begging and Keane himself came frustratingly within a whisker of an equaliser when he hit the post. In a dramatic finish, a Beckham free kick

Roy shows why he's known as 'human dynamo' by some of the top people in football as he charges past Scott Parker of Charlton Athletic.

conjured a simple tap-in equaliser for Yorke and Solskjaer then produced a marvellous winner in the dying moments, shooting through a packed penalty area to leave Liverpool on their knees.

It was not to be the last time that the Norwegian striker would have the final say in a big game.

Fulham's spirited performance at Old Trafford was overcome in the fifth round and two Yorke goals secured victory over Chelsea in the sixth-round replay after the first game had ended in a goalless draw. Another goalless draw against Arsenal in the semi-final should have resulted in a victory for United after a wonderful half-volley from Keane struck with power and precision screamed into Arsenal's net. Keane had wheeled away in joy when the goal was ruled out by referee David Elleray after a referee's assistant flagged for offside. The official had apparently spotted Yorke encroaching – though no one else did. Television replays indicated it was a decision that could be hotly disputed and Keane could feel genuinely aggrieved that he had been robbed of a perfectly legitimate goal.

Salt was rubbed into Keane's wounds when he was sent off in the replay at Villa Park during a game that will live long in the memories of everyone who saw it and millions more watching on TV. From the start Keane and Butt had battled manfully to gain the upper hand in the midfield against Arsenal's Patrick Vieira and Emmanuel Petit. No quarter was asked or given as four of the most combative of midfielders in the game clashed for supremacy. In the process Keane picked up a yellow card and when he brought down Marc Overmars in the 75th minute he feared it would become a red card for a second bookable

> **'ROY KEANE EPITOMISES EVERYTHING I BELIEVE IN IN FOOTBALLERS – HIS DETERMINATION, HIS WILL TO WIN, HIS HUNGER.'**
> Alex Ferguson

transgression and he left the pitch with barely a backward glance of confirmation at David Elleray, the referee who had so controversially ruled out his 'goal' against Arsenal in the first game. There was much sympathy for Keane and a reminder that football can be a cruel game.

Keane stalked briskly off the pitch and watched the remainder of a pulsating game from the bar. Ironically he had done the same thing when he had been sent off four years earlier in another Cup semi-final against Crystal Palace.

Keane was entitled to curse his misfortune as he left the tie when it was delicately poised. David Beckham had given United the lead in the first half with a marvellous curling shot from 25 yards that arced at pace past Seaman's outstretched right hand. Then Arsenal had got back on level terms in the 69th minute with a shot from Bergkamp that deflected past the unlucky Schmeichel. Keane's sending off came six minutes later and, with United losing their lead and their captain and having to battle on with only ten men, Arsenal gained renewed momentum. When soon afterwards Philip Neville tripped Ray Parlour in the box for a palpable penalty it looked all over for United. Bergkamp stepped up to take the spot-kick but the Dutchman struck his penalty with too little power and Schmeichel leaping to his left was able to palm it away.

As every Manchester United fan remembers with relish, Ryan Giggs won the match for United with one of the greatest goals ever seen in the modern game. In the context of the importance of the match, the fact that his team were down to ten men and that a gruelling game had reached eighteen minutes of extra time, Giggs's wonder goal must rank among the very best. Picking up a sloppy crossfield pass from Vieira well inside his own half, the Welsh winger drove at the Arsenal defence, swaying and weaving past no less than four international defenders, slipping the ball from one foot to the other with stunning control, before blasting a left-foot shot into the roof of Seaman's net. It was a winner worthy of gracing any occasion, including this thrilling roller-coaster of a match, and although it would have been impossible for anyone to top Giggs's ecstatic shirt-whirling display of elation, there was no more relieved man at Villa Park than Roy Keane. Now he and his teammates could look forward to a Wembley Cup final against Newcastle.

While Arsenal attempted to argue that their elimination from the FA Cup would allow them to concentrate on their League challenge, United were able to travel to Turin in good heart to meet mighty Juventus in the Champions League having drawn 1-1 with them in the first leg.

Previously United had disposed of Inter Milan in the quarter-final with a 2-0 win at home and a 1-1 draw in Milan with Paul Scholes calmly slotting the goal in the 88th minute that would take United through to the semi-final against Juventus. In Milan, Keane proved himself human after all when he failed to control a difficult bouncing ball in front of goal, thereby allowing Ventola to give Inter the lead on the night. But ultimately of far greater consequence to the team was the booking that Keane picked up in the home leg against Inter, leaving him one yellow card away from missing the Champions League final should United get through. Keane was suitably annoyed with himself because the booking was for dissent.

In Turin, United looked down and out after just 11 minutes by which time, incredibly, they were already 2-0 down to Juventus. Inzaghi had stolen in at the far post to put the Italian team one up after just six minutes and five minutes later he scored a second goal helped by a deflection off Stam that cruelly looped up and over a helpless Schmeichel.

But, as if stung by the injustice of it all, United hit back with some stunning football inspired by a moment of power, skill and sheer determination from Roy Keane. With a Turin crowd of some 60,800 still revelling in Juve's early 2-0 advantage, Keane leaped high to meet a Beckham corner from the left with a perfectly directed header guiding the ball fiercely into the top right corner of the Juventus goal. It was a fabulous riposte, a priceless away goal, a true captain's effort and a moment of glorious individual Roy Keane defiance. The way in which Keane almost immediately turned away to run purposefully back to the halfway line for the restart sent out a message to the Juventus players that he intended his goal to be just the start of United's fightback and that there was much more to come. It signalled to his colleagues that Keane felt the game was anything but lost.

**KEANE LEAPED HIGH TO MEET A BECKHAM CORNER FROM THE LEFT WITH A PERFECTLY DIRECTED HEADER GUIDING THE BALL FIERCELY INTO THE TOP RIGHT CORNER OF THE JUVENTUS GOAL.**

By reducing the deficit to 2-1, Keane galvanised the United players around him. Now just one more goal would see United ahead on the away-goal ruling. But eight minutes later came the moment that would rob Keane of the chance of ultimate glory. A sloppy pass from Blomqvist led to Keane being cautioned for a tackle on Zidane and that meant that if United were to get through to the final in Barcelona, Roy Keane would not be leading his team out on to the Nou Camp pitch.

It may have been a bitter personal blow to Roy Keane as his name went into Swiss referee Urs Meier's book but his reaction was exemplary in the extreme. Keane simply intensified his efforts to get his team to the final although he knew he would play no part in it, raising his game, running the extra yard, urging his colleagues forward.

Keane's drive and energy that night rubbed off on the team in spectacular fashion. In harness with Nicky Butt, Keane won the midfield battle with Edgar Davids and Didier Deschamps and allowed United to push forward in search of what would be a precious equaliser. It duly arrived two minutes after Keane's yellow card when Cole put over a cross that Yorke rose athletically to head home. At 2-2 United were now in the driving seat, ahead on aggregate by virtue of two away goals.

During the second half Keane continued to be an inspiration, helping to snuff out Juventus's attacks as they probed for a winner then turning defence into attack. Irwin hit an upright, Cole squandered a chance then finally, as the game was drawing to a close, United got their just reward when Yorke sped through only to be pulled down by the Juventus goalkeeper. It would almost certainly have been a penalty but for the referee allowing play to continue – Cole latched on to the loose ball and slid it into the net from an acute angle. United were in the final – but Keane would not be there. Back in Whitechurch, Cork, his mother Marie watching the drama unfold on television expressed the family's personal disappointment for her son. 'My heart is cracking over Roy,' said Marie. 'It's always been my dream that Roy would lift the

> **'MY HEART IS CRACKING OVER ROY. IT'S ALWAYS BEEN MY DREAM THAT ROY WOULD LIFT THE EUROPEAN CUP ONE DAY. I THOUGHT THERE WERE A LOT WORSE THINGS HAPPENING ON THE PITCH THAT WENT UNPUNISHED.'**
>
> Marie Keane, Roy's mother, on the yellow card that kept her son out of the European Cup final

European Cup one day. I thought there were a lot worse things happening on the pitch that went unpunished.'

Even at the final whistle, no trace of dejection showed on Keane's face. On the field he shared the elation of the rest of the team as the Juventus players hung their heads and set off despondently for the dressing room. It was only when he was leaving the arena where he had showed the heart of a true warrior that Keane's face betrayed the personal misfortune he was feeling, his downcast expression contrasting so poignantly with the broad grin of Dwight Yorke, who draped a consoling arm around his sad skipper.

Alex Ferguson described the performance as the finest he had ever seen from his team. They had given mighty Juventus a two-goal start then whipped them on their own territory. It was a magnificent victory but there was no denying some of the gloss was taken off it by the fact that Keane and Paul Scholes, who had also picked up a booking after being sent on as a sub in the second half, would miss the final. Ferguson said on the night he would appeal on behalf of his players but Keane gamely said it did not matter.

Of course, both players knew their fate as soon as the referee reached into his pocket for a yellow card. It was a bitter disappointment for them both and it only really sank in well after the game was over. Quite apart from losing two vital players from his Nou Camp line-up against finalists Bayern Munich, Alex Ferguson was desperately sorry for them to be missing out. The names of Roy Keane and Paul Scholes would, he said, most definitely be the first two on his teamsheet for the FA Cup final.

Keane bravely dismissed his booking as just one of those things, but that was a real understatement. He had been absent, through injury and suspension, on each of the last two of Manchester United's big European clashes in previous seasons – against Borussia Dortmund in the 1997 semi-final and against Monaco, one stage earlier, in 1998. Now he would miss the biggest night of all.

Obviously, he revealed afterwards, he was mindful before the Juventus game that another booking would cost him a place in the final; of the actual incident he remembered it wasn't a great pass from Jesper Blomqvist that led to it but in retrospect felt that that maybe he should have taken it in his stride rather than let it run across him. 'It was just a mistimed tackle,' said Keane philosophically. 'I've had thousands of them, hundreds of thousands of them. Some people said it was a silly booking but we had pushed forward and were trying to hit them on the break and if Zidane had got away from me ...'

When asked how he felt about missing the final Keane was equally forthright in his reply: 'I wasn't emotionally upset,' he said, 'just annoyed with myself because what really cost me was the booking I received against Inter Milan in the quarter-final. Coley or Yorkie was arguing with Simeone and I ended up, believe it or not, tying to break it up. Then Zamarano came over and we started having an argument and the referee booked the two of us. Ultimately you can't help getting booked for tackles but I was annoyed I got booked for arguing.'

It was Denis Irwin who put into perspective just what Keane's absence would mean against Bayern Munich. 'Roy will be sorely missed in Barcelona,' Irwin conceded. 'He's been outstanding for us all season, a huge influence, especially in the big games and I'm disappointed on a professional and personal level. It was typical of Roy that he didn't let the second yellow card get to him. If anything it spurred him on. He got us back into the game with a brave header and never stopped driving the team on.'

There was a word of comfort from Denis Law. The legendary quicksilver goal-poacher of United's great team of the 1960s had also had to sit out his team's greatest night, the 1968 European Cup final at Wembley, after a season blighted by injury. 'Keane is young. I'm sure he'll get another shot at the final,' said Law encouragingly.

> **'IT WAS TYPICAL OF ROY THAT HE DIDN'T LET THE SECOND YELLOW CARD GET TO HIM. IF ANYTHING IT SPURRED HIM ON. HE GOT US BACK INTO THE GAME WITH A BRAVE HEADER AND NEVER STOPPED DRIVING THE TEAM ON.'**
>
> **Denis Irwin, on Keane's performance in the European Cup semi-final**

Favourites to land the Premiership title, favourites to beat Newcastle in the Cup final, favourites – just – for the Champions League. Talk of a unique Manchester United Treble was inevitable and with just three games of their season left it became more than just a distinct possibility. But football has a habit of delivering the occasional nasty surprise and Keane and Alex Ferguson could not emphasise too strongly to their team that they had won nothing yet and there were no guarantees.

The first trophy to come within United's grasp was the Carling Premiership. The 1999–2000 campaign had gone down to the wire, with everything depending on the outcome of United's and Arsenal's respective last games on 16 May. Just the one point ahead of the Gunners, United could not afford to slip up. Arsenal, who were playing Aston Villa, were looking to their north London rivals Spurs, by now managed by former Arsenal favourite George Graham, to do them a favour by beating United at Old Trafford.

It looked as though a sensational upset could be on the cards when Les Ferdinand scored first for Spurs with a freakish goal from a speculative cross-cum-shot from the outside of his boot, which looped high over the unlucky Schmeichel as the goalkeeper advanced. But by half-time Beckham had imperiously swept in an equaliser across Ian Walker's goal and into the top corner from wide on the right.

It was Andy Cole coming on as a substitute after half-time who clinched the title soon after the restart. He showed great skill to control a pass then produced a deft lob over Tottenham's advancing goalkeeper Walker to send the crowd of around 55,180 delirious with joy. United had to endure a nervous half-hour, the crowd baying and praying for the final whistle, before the game ended with United confirmed as champions. The 2-1 win left United triumphant on 79 points with Arsenal still just a point behind. United had deservedly won the Premiership. They had remained unbeaten in their last 20 League games following the 2-3 defeat by Middlesbrough on 19 December.

Referee Graham Poll's final whistle was greeted with scenes of unbridled jubilation around Old Trafford and an exultant Alex Ferguson rushed on to the pitch and made straight for his captain to give him a grateful hug of congratulation. It was a public show of thanks from the manager to Keane for his superb contributions all season. His pats on the back for Keane as they embraced were well merited. Ferguson knew just how important Keane's efforts were to the team, not least that very day. At one point Keane had been doubtful for the Spurs game, having picked up a left ankle injury, but he had courageously played while not fully fit, his commitment undiminished.

Ever since Alex Ferguson had chosen to make him his captain, Roy Keane had harboured the ambition of stepping up to receive the magnificent Carling Premiership trophy. Now he had achieved it and it was a moment he knew he would remember and treasure all his life. Then, with his two little daughters by his side, Keane joined the rest of the players in a walk around the stadium acknowledging the cheers. Back in Cork there was a feeling of tremendous pride among those watching Keane's great moment on television. He was only the third Irishman ever to captain an English title-winning team.

Next evening there was time for the team to celebrate and it was agreed among the players that they would all meet up at Henry's Cafe Bar in the centre of Manchester. Past experience had taught Keane never to go into Manchester as it tended to invite trouble and in recent years his excursions into the centre of town had been about as rare as a snowflake in June. Against his better judgement, this time he decided that here was one occasion when he couldn't avoid doing so. As captain he could hardly duck out of his team's celebrations and he duly arrived to join his teammates, who were enjoying a few drinks.

But when two girls came into the bar trouble began – a champagne glass was thrown, and Keane received a cut below the eye. Police were called and to his astonishment Keane was arrested in another bar called Quo Vadis. It should have been a night to remember. Instead it turned into a night to forget, with Keane spending a night in a police cell. He had been arrested after a woman complained – falsely as it later turned out – that she had been assaulted. Next morning he was interviewed about the incident and released on bail without charge after Alex Ferguson had arrived at the police station and spoken to him. The incident, of course, made headlines and although the accusation against him proved to be false, the damage had been done. It was an unwelcome distraction for Keane with the FA

Cup final just a few days away and coming within 48 hours of his finest moment at Manchester United.

Keane was not going to let the nonsense spoil his day when on a warm and sunny May afternoon he led his team out at Wembley against Alan Shearer's Newcastle with United chasing a record third Double in the 1990s and the second leg of their Treble.

Sadly for Keane, his participation in the 1999 FA Cup final amounted to just eight minutes. Brought down by a scything foul from Gary Speed in the second minute, Keane knew at once he was struggling and soon realised that he had suffered an injury to an ankle that made it impossible for him to continue. Still suffering from the injury to his right ankle he had picked up against Middlesbrough a fortnight earlier, now it was his left ankle that was damaged and he was forced to hobble off six minutes later and hand over the captain's armband to Peter Schmeichel. Sympathetic applause rang out around Wembley from a crowd totalling just over 79,000 for the player who would miss out on the Champions League final through suspension and was now missing out on all but a few minutes of the Cup final. United fans continued to chant 'Keano' sporadically throughout the game to show their captain that although he may have gone from the field he was certainly not forgotten.

With Nicky Butt held back in Keane's absence for Barcelona, Alex Ferguson opted to send on Teddy Sheringham as Keane's substitute and the stricken skipper had barely had time to take his seat on the United bench at the side of the Wembley pitch before United were ahead thanks to the man who had replaced him. Sheringham made a darting diagonal run spotted by Scholes who rolled a pass invitingly into his path. Without checking his stride Sheringham swept the ball firmly into Newcastle's net.

From that moment onwards United looked the only likely winners and the game was killed off when Sheringham returned the favour to Scholes in the second half by laying on a shooting chance that Scholes converted into a fine goal struck low and firmly into the corner.

At the final whistle Peter Schmeichel was quick to hand back the captain's armband to Keane and the rest of the United team motioned for Keane to lead them up to collect the FA Cup. The skipper had played his last game of the season and the ankle injury hampered him so that he could barely walk but that wasn't going to prevent him from mounting the 39 steps to receive the trophy from Prince Charles. 'I didn't struggle up the Wembley steps,' he pointed out later. 'When you see that trophy, walking suddenly becomes easy.'

All pain was momentarily forgotten as the cup was handed to him by Prince Charles. Keane couldn't help exclaiming, 'You beauty!' as he got his hands on the trophy and lifted it triumphantly in salute towards the United fans. Stepping gingerly back down towards the pitch he turned to drink in the scene of his players receiving their medals one by one. United had done the Double again and Keane was rightly proud of the achievement and of the way the fans had chanted his name during the game, although he had been forced to play so little a part in it. He got a special cheer when he managed to join in United's lap of honour and hobbled round Wembley with one shin pad still in place. For United, it was two down and one to go for what would be an incredible Treble.

> **'I DIDN'T STRUGGLE UP THE WEMBLEY STEPS ... WHEN YOU SEE THAT TROPHY, WALKING SUDDENLY BECOMES EASY.'**
>
> Roy Keane, on picking up the FA Cup after a final in which he hobbled off injured

Although Keane would not be playing against Bayern Munich in Barcelona four days later his presence in the squad that flew out to Spain was much welcomed and appreciated by the others. Keane had played twice against Bayern Munich in the group stages, he had observations to offer and his innate will to win was infectious. His colossal presence would be missed out on the pitch but the FA Cup final had proved to the team that they could win the big game without him.

**KEANE COULDN'T HELP EXCLAIMING, 'YOU BEAUTY!' AS HE GOT HIS HANDS ON THE CUP AND LIFTED IT TRIUMPHANTLY IN SALUTE TOWARDS THE UNITED FANS.**

But it was when the Manchester United and Bayern Munich players trained in the vast Nou Camp stadium the day before the game that it hit home to Keane just what he was missing. He was out on the pitch in his tracksuit but largely set himself apart from the other players. He was there in mind, body and competitive spirit but as a footballer he wouldn't be required. For five and a half weeks he had endured a mental picture of what it would be like to miss out on the biggest occasion and now he was experiencing it for real.

The thousands of travelling United fans who filled Barcelona's main square, the Plaza De Cataluna and the city's main thoroughfare were mostly fearful that Keane's absence would be a telling factor in deciding the outcome of the match. They expected that David Beckham would play central midfield, which meant the team would miss Beckham's telling crosses from the right that had produced so many goals for Yorke and Cole during the season.

Nicky Butt, who would shoulder a greater midfield responsibility with Keane missing, agreed the skipper's absence was a blow, as indeed was that of Paul Scholes, but his rallying cry was that it was now up to the rest of the team to go out and win the trophy for them.

Bayern Munich's midfield star Steffan Effenberg sportingly admitted that it was a great shame Keane would miss the final as he would have relished the challenge of playing against him once more, this time with the cup at stake. 'I'm a big admirer of Keane,' he said. 'He's one of the best midfield players around. He defends well and can also get forward and score, as he showed against us. I enjoyed our battle in the two previous games.' Effenberg's Bayern colleague Sammy Kuffour was more forthright about Keane's enforced absence. 'That is good for us,' he said. 'He is such an important player. He holds the midfield together and helps them use so many attacking forces. He is their driving force.'

> **'HE'S ONE OF THE BEST MIDFIELD PLAYERS AROUND. HE DEFENDS WELL AND CAN ALSO GET FORWARD AND SCORE, AS HE SHOWED AGAINST US. I ENJOYED OUR BATTLE IN THE TWO PREVIOUS GAMES.'**
> **Bayern Munich star Steffan Effenberg on Roy Keane**

Keane was, of course, desperately missed. He could only sit up in a stand with Jim Ryan, manager of United's Reserves, Scholes and Berg and wish he and they were all out on the pitch. The estimated 50,000 United fans in the vast stadium would have dearly loved to have had Keane on the field to get the game by the scruff of the neck after United had gone behind from a Mario Basler free kick bent around a deeply flawed defensive wall of United players. As the game wore on without United carving out the clear-cut chances that might have changed the game, Keane's sheer determination would have been invaluable, despite Beckham's admirable display in central midfield.

In the event it was Beckham's two in-swinging corners that led to what has been described as the most sensational two minutes in sport. At the end of the scheduled 90 minutes the ribbons of Bayern Munich had already been tied to the trophy in preparation for the presentation to the German team when Bayern failed to deal decisively with the first of Beckham's two last-gasp corners. The ball eventually came back out to Giggs, whose half-hit shot was helped on its way into the net by Sheringham, who had come on as a substitute. Moments later Sheringham rose to flick on another Beckham corner and Solskjaer, also on as a substitute, stabbed the ball high into the roof of the net. On the night when Sir Matt Busby would have been 90, Manchester United were once again champions of Europe. They had pulled off the most unlikely of victories, snatched so dramatically from the jaws of defeat, against a team from Munich, a city that since 1958 had held such irrevocable links for United.

Behind the goal where Sheringham and Solskjaer had so memorably scored, there had been euphoric bedlam among the massed ranks of Manchester United supporters as the two late-late goals went in. Utter despondency had been transformed into sheer ecstasy in a flash. Now, long after the final whistle and the cup presentation, the fans stayed behind to salute their heroes. The acclaim was deafening as the team carried the cup towards them, each player cheered long and loud while the cup was paraded and passed among them. But in the extraordinary elation of a victory so totally unexpected and so emotionally destabilising, the fans had not forgotten Roy Keane.

Ground officials were urging the supporters to head for home after a suitable period of celebration nearing one hour had elapsed. But the fans wanted to stage a remarkable tribute

**ON THE NIGHT WHEN SIR MATT BUSBY WOULD HAVE BEEN 90, MANCHESTER UNITED WERE ONCE AGAIN CHAMPIONS OF EUROPE.** to Keane and refused to leave until he had come back out on to the pitch.

Bathed in the glow of red smoke flares, the fans began chanting 'Keano, Keano,' calling for their idol who had modestly left the field as he didn't want to take away the limelight from his colleagues who had performed so creditably. Finally a runner had to be sent to urge Keane to come out on to the field again as the chants of 'Keano' became ever more insistent. The team also refused to leave the stadium until he had reappeared and eventually he came back out, insisting Paul Scholes and Henning Berg also accompany him.

Slowly Keane, dressed in a smart suit, moved somewhat sheepishly forward while repeatedly casting a glance back at the United officials and non-playing players as if seeking for permission to sample some of the ecstatic applause. An equally reluctant Paul Scholes was also waved forward and together they inched forward towards the United end of the stadium. Finally they reached the group of broadly smiling United players, some of whom had by now joined in to add their voices to the chant from the crowd of 'Keano, Keano!' They formed a guard of honour for their captain and, with Scholes by his side, Keane reached the cup he should by rights have lifted. It was a bittersweet moment for him when he did finally raise the trophy aloft to another crescendo of applause from the United team and their appreciative supporters.

Back once more in the dressing rooms, the party was ready to start. Keane grabbed a champagne bottle and showered his colleagues with bubbly. Of course, he shared the excitement and jubilation of his colleagues at such a thrilling victory. After all, it was the squad that had achieved the trophy and he was part of the squad. But to Keane at that moment it didn't feel that way.

Somehow the sharp contrast between his smart-suited appearance and the sweat-soaked kit of the players around him who had earned such a famous victory in the Nou Camp, said it all. Keane had played an indispensable part in the 12 games leading up to the Champions League final, but number 13 had proved cruelly unlucky for him. On the plane bearing the team back to Manchester, Roy Keane sat by himself at the back, alone with his own thoughts.

Right throughout the summer of 1999 Manchester United's players and Alex Ferguson, who had recently been elevated to Sir Alex Ferguson, were right royally feted wherever they went, either individually or collectively. After the astonishing last-gasp heroics of Barcelona, Keane and his team had paraded the three hard-won Treble trophies from the open top of a bus in a triumphal drive through Manchester. The bus, bearing the numbers 2-1 to signify the extraordinary result in Barcelona, was besieged by wildly cheering fans bedecked in United's colours as it inched its way along the streets of Manchester, which had ground to a standstill.

The city had never seen anything like it; nor had Keane and his players. Over the summer months everyone, it seemed, wanted to offer congratulations to the team and the manager on the incredible achievement of winning the Treble. But for Roy Keane in particular, it was a time for looking forward not back. There was much for him to ponder upon during the summer break and uppermost in his mind was whether his footballing future lay with Manchester United.

Keane was at a vitally important crossroads in his career with

In action against Olympique de Marseille midfielder Frederico Brando in October 1999, during a Champions League match.

just one more year of his contract with the club still to run. Under the Bosman ruling, which essentially allows players the freedom to ply their trade at different clubs without restriction once their current contract ends, he would be able to join another club on a free transfer at the end of the 1999–2000 season, if he wished. Given his acknowledged status as probably the best midfield player in his position in Europe, he could expect either a lucrative new contract from Manchester United to keep him at the club or invitations to join Italian, Spanish, German or even French clubs on a huge salary. These monied clubs would be able to pay Keane a huge salary because they would not have to stump up a vast transfer fee as well.

Keane's gut feeling and his respect for Alex Ferguson and the manager's burning ambitions – which were undiminished by the Treble success – were that he should remain a Manchester United player. Tentative talks had begun with Keane in the winter and during the summer the player sat down with his solicitor Michael Kennedy, the club lawyer Maurice Watkins and chairman Martin Edwards to talk about a new contract.

After much discussion the club presented Keane with a new deal that he found had some attractions. Although it was on the table for him to sign, however, he told Alex Ferguson he wasn't sure whether he wanted to do so. The contract fell well short of what Keane believed he was worth. It might have appeared to be

**KEANE WAS ONLY BEING HONEST WHEN HE WENT ON TO TELL HIS BOSS THAT HE WAS THINKING ABOUT A POSSIBLE MOVE TO ITALY OR SPAIN.**

arrogance on his part to want much more but the truth is that Keane and his adviser were determined he should not sell himself short. Keane was only being honest, therefore, when he went on to tell his boss that he was thinking about a possible move to Italy or Spain. Ferguson understood his captain's position and told Keane to think about it although they both agreed that in an ideal world it would be for the best if he could stay at United.

Quite simply, Roy Keane was faced with the biggest decision of his career and he needed to be sure he made the right one. He had to choose where he should spend the best years of his footballing life, to which club he should tie himself for what effectively was the remainder of his top-class career. He had to be mindful in any negotiations that it was probably a final opportunity for one last big pay deal before his powers as a footballer inevitably started to wane when he reached his 30s.

Keane would have preferred his future to have been sorted out sooner rather than later, but at the same time he could afford to be patient. The longer the negotiations dragged on towards the 1 January deadline, the more time any interested clubs would have to put together a package to offer him after that date. Certainly several clubs were casting covetous eyes in his direction – the purchase of Keane was an extremely attractive proposition. At 28 he was nearing his peak, he had shown that he had fully recovered from his cruciate injury, and his reputation as a footballer had never been higher.

Moreover, come 1 January he would be available on a *free* transfer at a time when some very ordinary players were fetching fees of £4 million and £5 million in the transfer market. In Keane's case, a club could soon buy him for nothing but would need to remunerate him extremely handsomely for his footballing services. It was unlikely that Keane would ever again hold such strong powerful bargaining cards when negotiating his future.

Unquestionably Alex Ferguson wanted Keane to remain a

Manchester United player: on more than one occasion he had described Keane as the heartbeat of his team. But both knew full well there were a number of other clubs who would welcome him and that two in particular, Bayern Munich and Barcelona, would take him like a shot once he was available. Bayern, without having to stump up a massive transfer fee, could conceivably offer him a wage of £100,000 a week. Keane was just the sort of midfield player the Bayern coach admired. Juventus were also reportedly casting glances in Keane's direction from Italy as well as Internationale of Milan and Lazio, and Spanish giants Real Madrid. Keane's upcoming availability had not gone unnoticed in France either. No club could officially approach him until January, though.

As the season began, the position for Manchester United was clear-cut. They could pay up to keep Keane, and he most certainly would not come cheap, or if negotiations broke down they could try and cash in on him and sell him for perhaps £10 million or maybe even £14 million. But if they dithered they risked ending up with nothing. There was nothing to stop Keane simply choosing to see out the remainder of his contract and becoming a free agent at the end of the season under the Bosman ruling.

Once Keane had rejected United's first tabled offer, thought to be £28,000 a week, United knew they had to come up with a much more lucrative contract or watch him waving the club a long goodbye through the 1999–2000 season. To do so would be a terrible blow to the team: if Keane were to leave, who could replace him? And at what cost?

Keane certainly wanted to be paid what he believed he was worth. But there was much else besides for him and his family to consider. For five years now the Keane family had been settled in

Manchester, two of his three children, daughters Shannon and Caragh, were now at school, and during the summer the Keane family had moved into a magnificent new £900,000 home in one of the most sought-after locations in Cheshire.

The new six-bedroom, hi-tech home was a veritable mansion, a sprawling, sumptuous, mock-Tudor property built to Keane's own specifications in an area favoured by sports stars and stockbrokers that reputedly has more millionaires per square mile than anywhere in Britain outside London. Keane's pile included three bathrooms, four reception rooms, a conservatory,

**Roy relaxes by taking his dog for a walk near his home at Hale Barnes in Cheshire.**

a triple garage, a state-of-the-art security system and was set in acres of grounds in the leafy suburb of Hale. The garden, set behind a high wooden fence, included beech trees and lawns manicured to the standards expected on putting greens.

The house was little more than a mile away from the Keanes' previous home on the outskirts of the posh Cheshire village of Bowdon, which meant as little re-acclimatisation and disruption to their family life as possible. It also afforded an easy journey to work for the master of the house in his £87,000 Aston Martin.

Moving to another club abroad would be a considerable upheaval for the entire Keane family. Having spent just a year in their new surroundings, they might now be uncomfortable with a move to a strange land and there was the risk that they might find the task of adapting to a new culture intimidating. Any move to Italy, Spain or France would mean language difficulties, particularly for the children and their education, and they would all have to face the problem of trying to make new friends, of finding new schools and a new home. Almost certainly there would be times when one or other or all of the family would be homesick.

Manchester United were able to use the potential difficulties of uprooting as a bargaining tool. Deep down Keane really did not want to move but although his family were firmly settled he indicated he would not be afraid to do so if he had to. And anyway, he could always tell himself, it might just be for only three years.

On a footballing level, a move to a top European club would certainly broaden Keane's horizons, offer him new challenges and the experience would undoubtedly make him an even better player. But initially there would be a tricky transitional period when he would need to be integrated into a new team, get to know his new colleagues and new manager on a professional and personal basis, and learn different methods of playing with different colleagues. There would be moments when he would miss the banter of the dressing room at Manchester United and certainly the close companionship and friendship of his great Cork colleague Denis Irwin.

Another very important consideration for Keane about staying with United was whether the players under him were still ambitious and hungry enough for more European success. On that fabulous night at the Nou Camp they had won the Champions League trophy without him. But would they still have the burning desire to do it again? Since 1968 there had always been an aura of mystique at United about the European Cup and successive United teams had had to live with the burden of being compared with the team who won it then. Now the trophy had been won once more, would the players still be motivated enough to go after it again?

Missing out on that famous occasion and the greatest night in the club's history for 31 years had been a terrible blow for Keane, far worse than everyone realised or the player was prepared to let on. 'I thought it was a tragedy,' he finally admitted one year on. At home he had a medal that told him he had been a

Roy gives his daughters Shannon and Caragh a hug.

member of United's European Champions team. It was a medal he treasured but somehow it didn't feel to him like a European medal, even though he had played in the 12 European games that took United to the final. Keane knew that Henning Berg and Paul Scholes, who had also missed the final, felt exactly the same way.

The opportunity of playing European football had been one of Keane's main motives in joining Manchester United rather than Blackburn Rovers in the first place. When he originally signed for United in 1993, the club were League champions and would be involved in European competition straight away. Judging by the strength of the team, Keane could not merely dream of European glory, he could almost expect it. He could tell from Alex Ferguson's approach that he was determined to make it a reality.

While growing up in Cork, Keane had been brought up on the glory of Manchester United's 1968 European Cup 4-1 success over Benfica. And since he had embarked on a football career, he had played in a lot of very big games for Nottingham Forest, the Republic of Ireland and Manchester United – but it was the European Cup that had brought Keane to United in the first place. He had watched nearly all the European Cup matches down the years, with envy, as far back as he could remember and the game that had always stood out for him was the 1968 final against Benfica. That particular game had taken place many years before he was born, of course, but the great victory had become folklore in the part of Ireland where he was raised and he had subsequently seen that night of triumph for United literally dozens of times, over and over again, on video.

As United went from strength to strength through the 1990s

under Alex Ferguson's stewardship, it became the burning ambition among everyone at the club to emulate, even eclipse, the deeds of 1968. Now United had done it. In years to come the record books would show that Manchester United had become champions of Europe in 1999 – and who would remember that Roy Keane should have been playing but for suspension? Fans of the future would recount the names of the 11 players who triumphed in the Nou Camp. The name of Roy Keane would not be in that famous 11.

Keane still had the loftiest of ambitions and now he was entitled to wonder whether he would ever achieve his dream of captaining Manchester United to European glory. He needed little reminding that Alex Ferguson was not the type of manager to rest on his laurels and that he would be driving the team towards repeating their Champions League success. Ferguson's avowed intention was for Manchester United to be strong enough to dominate Europe. Having found out how to win in Europe, he was anxious to keep on winning, again and again. The really great European sides, Ferguson stressed, were those who won the Cup year after year like Real Madrid, who won five years running, like Ajax and Bayern Munich, who won three, and Liverpool, who won four times in eight years.

But how many teams in the modern era had consistently won the European Cup? Keane could have been forgiven for questioning whether he might have a better chance of ultimate European glory with Barcelona, Bayern Munich or Juventus but Ferguson genuinely felt United stood a good chance of winning the Champions League regularly in what he he felt might possibly turn out to be a golden period for the club.

The notion of a move to Turin, Barcelona, Munich or Rome may have been appealing to Roy Keane since he had made no secret of his admiration for Juventus, AC Milan, Inter Milan, Barcelona and Real Madrid. But whether he chose to go or to stay, he could not lose out financially. Either choice offered riches beyond comprehension for a man who ten years before had been a semi-professional with Cobh Ramblers and seemingly not destined for higher things.

It was therefore from a position of great strength that Keane and his solicitor Michael Kennedy were able to commence negotiations for a new Manchester United contract. Their hand was strengthened still further by the knowledge that United would have serious difficulty in replacing him. Keane knew there were a lot of good midfielders in European football but once wages and a transfer fee were thrown into the equation, the price of getting them to Old Trafford would be prohibitive.

**THE REALLY GREAT EUROPEAN SIDES, FERGUSON STRESSED, WERE THOSE WHO WON THE CUP YEAR AFTER YEAR LIKE REAL MADRID WHO WON FIVE YEARS RUNNING, LIKE AJAX AND BAYERN MUNICH WHO WON THREE, AND LIVERPOOL WHO WON FOUR TIMES IN EIGHT YEARS.**

As the 1999–2000 season opened, stretching ahead of Keane was the most demanding of seasons for himself and his team. Almost immediately after United had won the European Cup against Bayern Munich, it had become apparent that Keane could potentially look forward to leading the team in no less than seven top competitions – World Club Championship, World Club Cup, European Supercup, Champions League, Premiership, FA Cup and League Cup.

The Football Association and the government's sports minister Tony Banks were hopeful that United could challenge for all seven but it soon became apparent that this was an impossible dream. Because of the sheer weight of fixtures something would have to give. United would have to choose between the various competitions.

Amid huge controversy, United sacrificed a domestic trophy in the pursuit of international glory and pulled out of the FA Cup. But it was with the utmost reluctance and under enormous pressure exerted by the government. The politicians saw Manchester United's presence at the World Club Championship in Brazil as vital in gaining votes for England's chances of staging the World Cup in 2006. This competition would, however, clash with the FA Cup dates and with United's season already at fixture saturation point, it was the FA Cup competition that had to go. 'What else could we do?' asked a frustrated Alex Ferguson. 'You cannot go on and on adding fixtures. Something had to give.'

Relinquishing his grip on the FA Cup without his team being able to defend it on the pitch was especially hard for Ferguson. The FA Cup was special to him, since it was the first trophy he had won with United. The only silver lining for Keane and his teammates was that by not competing in the FA Cup, some fixture strain on the second half of the season would be eased. Against that, the fall out from the Rio trip might be fatigue. It might prove to be more draining than expected.

Faced with such a gruelling season, Keane was desperately anxious not to let any contract talks unsettle him on the pitch or affect his form. He had always been a whole-hearted footballer and there was no way he would not give of his best for Manchester United. If this was to be his last season with United he wanted to make it one to remember.

Even when the talks stalled there was no loss of commitment from Keane on the field. His performances on the pitch were nothing less than Ferguson and Keane's colleagues had come to expect from him, even if his pay demands frequently made more headlines.

United's fans had expected an announcement on his future early in August. Ferguson was optimistic after several lengthy discussions with his captain and the indications that Keane was staying were further strengthened by Luciano Moggi, the general manager of Juventus, who commented, 'I got the impression Keane would renew his contract at United and that's the end of the matter as far as I am concerned.' Eventually it became clear that Keane's Old Trafford future would not be decided until the end of the season. In fact the fans would have to wait almost another four months before they would learn of Keane's fate.

**AMID HUGE CONTROVERSY, UNITED SACRIFICED A DOMESTIC TROPHY IN THE PURSUIT OF INTERNATIONAL GLORY AND PULLED OUT OF THE FA CUP. BUT IT WAS WITH THE UTMOST RELUCTANCE AND UNDER ENORMOUS PRESSURE EXERTED BY THE GOVERNMENT.**

If anybody in the Old Trafford boardroom had any doubts as to whether they should be striving so hard to retain Roy Keane as a United player, then the away game to Arsenal on 21 August would have given them an emphatic early season reminder of his worth.

Priceless was the word indelibly attached to Keane by the soccer experts after watching him not only put in a typically ebullient and determined midfield display at Highbury but also dart forward on perfectly timed runs to score the two goals that gave United a remarkable 2-1 win over the Gunners after coming from behind.

Keane's well-taken goals stunned the Highbury crowd into

silence on each occasion and his second, decisive strike broke the stranglehold Arsene Wenger's side had taken on United in recent meetings. The last two visits to Highbury had ended in 3-0 and 3-2 defeats for United and in the previous eight matches between the two sides over the past two seasons, United had emerged victors only once.

This time Keane's two goals gave United a vital win, a psychological advantage over Arsenal and three precious points over the team many felt would be their chief challengers in the Premiership. To cap a memorable afternoon for Keane, he was even the innocent party in a flare-up that could have seen Arsenal's midfielder Patrick Vieira sent off for an attempted butt and slap. Theirs had been a hotly contested confrontation in midfield all afternoon.

Ljungberg, who had developed a habit of scoring against Manchester United, did it again to give Arsenal their 1-0 half-time lead. But Keane cajoled, urged and shouted for greater effort from those around him, and then demonstrated the perfect example of practising what he preached.

A swift exchange of passes from Scholes, to Keane, to Cole and back to Keane, saw the skipper surge past the last defender to side-foot an equaliser firmly past the right hand of Manninger, who was standing in for David Seaman in the Arsenal goal. It was a delightfully conjured move executed with great precision and Keane couldn't help showing just how pleased he was about it. He veered away to stand proudly in front of the United fans to the left of Manninger's goal and smiled broadly as Yorke jumped up on his shoulders and then the rest of his teammates piled in.

Keane's winner did owe something to good fortune but it was only what he deserved for the indomitable spirit he showed all afternoon. Giggs dispossessed Parlour in midfield, turned quickly and drove at the heart of the Arsenal defence and when his shot ricocheted off defender Martin Keown it fell to Keane, surging forward, who neatly chested it down and nudged it past Manninger. It was a sweet moment for Keane and earned him a kiss on his newly shaven head from Beckham. 'I think I've proved the talk of me leaving the club doesn't affect my performances on the pitch,' said Keane. 'It was great to score two goals. I didn't expect to get the chances but when they come to you against a team like Arsenal, you have to take them.'

Over the following three months, barely a day went by without press speculation as to where Roy Keane would be heading at the end of the season with Juventus predicted as the most popular destination. Significantly, almost all the experts who were tracking the protracted negotiations every step of the way agreed on one thing – United would be insane not to keep him. Keane was looking for a deal around £40,000 a week, which would shatter Manchester United's wage structure, but they felt a player of his quality and type was irreplaceable. The fans, too, by and large, were sympathetic to Keane's demands. In fact they made it clear to Martin Edwards how disgusted they would feel if Keane was allowed to leave. It seemed that everyone realised Roy Keane's worth except those who paid his wages at the richest football club in the world.

**'I THINK I'VE PROVED THE TALK OF ME LEAVING THE CLUB DOESN'T AFFECT MY PERFORMANCES ON THE PITCH.'**

Roy Keane, after his two goals against Arsenal

With just eight weeks to go before the 1 January deadline, it was becoming increasingly clear that Manchester United would have to improve their offer to Keane quite significantly if they wanted him to remain at the club.

The sticking point was the wage structure in place at the club. United, of course, could point out that they were a legendary club, they had a magnificent stadium with plans to expand it and that under their wage structure they had produced a team that had just become champions of Europe. They could argue that the wage structure had brought them tremendous success down the years. But now Keane felt there had to be some flexibility if Manchester United were to continue enjoying success, that they had to move with the times if they didn't want to wait another 31 years before they could put the Champions League cup in their trophy room. It was hard for anyone to begrudge him his demands when he was earning £10,000 a week less than Desailly and Leboeuf at Chelsea and £8,000 less than Michael Owen and Robbie Fowler at Liverpool.

Keane was confident that so long as Alex Ferguson remained as Manchester United's manager then the club would try to bring in the best players that they possibly could. But if the club persisted with its rigid wage structure then the very best players wouldn't entertain the idea of coming to Old Trafford when the difference in wages they could expect from other clubs was up to £40,000 a week. 'They could have bought some good players over the years – Ronaldo, Desailly and Batistuta and people like that,' said Keane, 'but they wouldn't come because of the wage structure. And that's fine. I respect the club's position. But they have to respect my position as well.'

Keane, for whom Juventus were reportedly prepared to cough up £70,000 a week, was also able to argue that when he first came to Old Trafford he could have earned more money by signing for another club and financially the situation was no different when three years later he signed to stay with

Manchester United. At that point, again he could have opted to go abroad for higher earnings at a different club. Now, however, his attitude had changed. 'As much as I love the club, I'm not going to sell myself short,' he reasoned. 'OK, it's a team game but it didn't feel that way when I was out with my cruciate. At the end of the day you are on your own.'

On 18 November, just 33 days before Keane would have been entitled to begin negotiations and talk in earnest with

**IT SEEMED THAT EVERYONE REALISED ROY KEANE'S WORTH EXCEPT THOSE WHO PAID HIS WAGES AT THE RICHEST FOOTBALL CLUB IN THE WORLD.**

other interested clubs, United's chief executive Martin Edwards told Manchester United's annual general meeting that the future of the captain was a top priority and that Alex Ferguson would have fresh talks with Keane in the next few weeks. 'Sir Alex is going to have another chat with Roy,' he said. 'We would obviously like to put it to bed but Roy has said that he doesn't want to do it until the end of the season. We would need some feedback from him on that. But if there is any possibility of doing it before the 1 January deadline then obviously we would be delighted to do so.'

Sir Roland Smith, plc chairman, went on to stress that Keane's future was uppermost in the board's mind. 'We are going to do whatever needs to be done to keep him,' he said. 'But until he has made up his mind what he wants, we can't do anything.'

There was a renewed urgency but the issue was still unresolved when Manchester United travelled to Japan at the end of November to contest the unique footballing honour of being able to call themselves champions of the world. It's an unofficial distinction United's fans have long proclaimed for their team at football grounds all over Britain and the rest of Europe, of course, but on 31 November 1999, in Tokyo, at the World Club Championship, of all places, that cheerful declaration finally gained a legitimate ring of truth. By beating Palmeiras 1-0 in Tokyo, Manchester United became king of clubs. They became champions of the world and at last their fans and followers could claim that status quite legitimately.

'THEY COULD HAVE BOUGHT SOME GOOD PLAYERS OVER THE YEARS – RONALDO, DESAILLY AND BATISTUTA AND PEOPLE LIKE THAT ... BUT THEY WOULDN'T COME BECAUSE OF THE WAGE STRUCTURE ... I RESPECT THE CLUB'S POSITION. BUT THEY HAVE TO RESPECT MY POSITION AS WELL.'

Roy Keane

Fittingly it was Roy Keane who wrote a new chapter into Manchester United history by scoring the only goal of the game in the 35th minute. Equally fittingly it was Keane who went up to lift the Toyota Cup in Japan's packed National Stadium to signal that Manchester United had achieved something no other British club had done before. It was a cherished moment for Keane, the rest of the players, and for the club as a whole. Financially Keane's winning goal was worth many millions of pounds to United, a point that would not have escaped the notice of Old Trafford's boardroom, nor Roy Keane, in the continuing negotiations over his new contract.

A fabulous pre-match fireworks and laser display had set the tone for the game at which an astonishing number of Japanese fans of United made their voices heard and their presence felt. If the match could never live up to the dazzling pyrotechnics staged before the kick-off, it was still an often entertaining clash in which Mark Bosnich excelled in goal with two exceptional

saves and Keane exuded control of the midfield in a manner
that the huge crowd could only sit back and admire.

With United playing in a 4-5-1 formation, Keane had the
chance to go forward and when Giggs's pace took him racing
along the left with a chance to put in a long cross, there was
Keane coming in on a timely run to side-foot the ball into the
net. 'I nearly didn't connect,' he said afterwards. 'It would have
been a long old journey back if we hadn't won.' But they had,
it was an historic moment, and Keane's goal had once more
hammered home his importance to the team.

The trip to Tokyo had not been without its critics but, as
Keane pointed out, it was nice to have one trophy in the bag
halfway through the season and the five days away helped build
team spirit that was to show itself in the upcoming Champions
League game against Valencia.

Once back in England there was scarcely time to draw breath
before the crucial Valencia match at Old Trafford and there was
an added buzz about the preparations. In the build-up to the
game, rumours had been sweeping Old Trafford for days that
Keane would, after all, be staying with the club. The fans had
heard such whispers many times before, of course, over the
preceding months but there was a very positive feeling that this
time it really was true. The anticipation was that, if Keane really
was staying with United, an announcement to that effect was
likely to be made just before the Valencia game. The timing of
such a popular declaration would be an important
psychological boost for the team and for the fans for what was
a crucial match. Anything less than a victory would send
United into a two-month Champions League break with very
real worries about their ability to retain the trophy.

Everyone, not least the players, was aware that the 2-0 defeat away to Fiorentina in their opening Group B game had left Manchester United precious little room for manoeuvre. Probably more aware than most was Roy Keane, whose careless back pass had given Fiorentina such a soft goal. He was desperate to make amends for that uncharacteristic aberration. It's not unusual for clubs to progress from the fourteen Champions League groups having suffered two defeats, but failure in the first two games would have left United with the toughest of tasks to catch up.

**KEANE'S WINNING GOAL IN TOYKO WAS WORTH MANY MILLIONS OF POUNDS TO UNITED, A POINT THAT WOULD NOT HAVE ESCAPED THE NOTICE OF OLD TRAFFORD'S BOARDROOM NOR ROY KEANE IN THE CONTINUING NEGOTIATIONS OVER HIS NEW CONTRACT.**

There was also an added edge to the Valencia match in that it would be refereed by Kim Milton Nielsen, the Danish ref who had dismissed Beckham so controversially in France in 1998 during England's World Cup match against Argentina in St Etienne. Now they were to meet again.

When Roy Keane led his players out on to the pitch he was greeted with a deafening, joyful crescendo of 'Keano, Keano', the crowd sensing that the official announcement was imminent and Roy acknowledged the adulation with a familiar clap of the hands above his head.

Many of the fans already knew of his decision. He had told his teammates over dinner that he had spurned offers from foreign clubs to remain a United player. Now, millions of television viewers tuning in to watch the Valencia game on ITV were also being given the news that Keane had signed a new four-year contract and the good tidings had filtered through to the Old Trafford crowd.

The broad smile on Alex Ferguson's face as he emerged from the tunnel for the start of the game told the happy story but it wasn't until the match had kicked off that Keane's new contract with United was officially announced over Old Trafford's public address system to roars of approval and thunderous applause. The relief and excitement among the United fans in the 54,606 crowd was almost tangible. But the renewed chants of 'Keano, Keano' almost died in thousands of throats after just 40 seconds of the match.

Denis Irwin, playing his 53rd game for United in Europe, a new club record, was suddenly dispossessed just inside Valencia's half moments after the kick-off and the visitors' captain, Mendieta, drove purposefully and speedily down the right wing, beat Gary Neville with a deft turn and pulled the ball back from the by-line for Farinos to race on to from the edge of the box. Unchallenged, he was able to shoot powerfully, but fortunately for United, straight at Van der Houw, who beat out his effort. It was Farinos again who was first to the rebound but once again his shot was straight at the goalkeeper, who this time caught the ball comfortably with both hands. United could, and should, have been a goal down in the very first minute in the very midst of the crowd's celebrations over the retention of United's skipper.

After this initial scare United took time to settle and find their rhythm but eventually began to look the more threatening team. Beckham rattled the crossbar with the goalkeeper nowhere but if there was one certainty that night it was that Roy Keane would make his own mark on the game. Before the first half was over he would show in one brief moment why United were so delighted to be hanging on to him and why so many other clubs coveted his services.

In the 38th minute Gary Neville chipped over a cross that a

Training for a clash against Valencia with the Man United team with Jordi Cruff, Andy Cole and Jaap Stam.

Valencia defender, under pressure from Solskjaer, could only nod weakly away. Anticipating the knockdown Keane was on to it in a flash and although the ball was at an awkward height, almost at his hip, he powered a shot from 18 yards low through a melee of players past goalkeeper Palop's despairing right hand and into the corner of the net.

It was a clinical finish, his fifth goal in nine games, and Old Trafford erupted to acclaim the talisman they now knew would be an integral part of Manchester United's foreseeable future. 'Keano!' they bellowed in unison as their hero allowed himself a smile and raised his arms to clap his hands above his head once more. It had taken him six months to put his signature to Manchester United's future but he had needed just 37 minutes to demonstrate why the club spent so long chasing it.

Keane's aptly timed, stunning goal was the difference

between the two sides at half-time and within two minutes of the restart United went 2-0 up. Beckham fooled the Valencia full-back on the right by shaping to meet a pass then allowing the ball to run across his body before turning and whipping in a sharp cross to the near post. Solskjaer, preferred to Dwight Yorke after a four-goal spree against Everton the previous weekend, was quickest to react and adroitly stabbed the ball past Palop from close range.

**HE HAD TOLD HIS TEAMMATES OVER DINNER THAT HE HAD SPURNED OFFERS FROM FOREIGN CLUBS TO REMAIN A UNITED PLAYER. NOW, MILLIONS OF TELEVISION VIEWERS TUNING IN TO WATCH THE VALENCIA GAME ON ITV WERE ALSO BEING GIVEN THE NEWS THAT KEANE HAD SIGNED A NEW FOUR-YEAR CONTRACT.**

Beckham was also the provider for the third goal in the 69th minute, which effectively clinched the tie. Scholes soared to meet a perfectly delivered free kick from the right and directed a powerful glancing header into the top corner. The 3-0 result, which ended with Beckham making a point of shaking the hand of the referee, sent the Old Trafford faithful away in good heart and still further cheered by the knowledge that their inspirational captain was remaining a Manchester United player.

At the end of the match Alex Ferguson led the celebrations with a tribute to his captain. His delight and relief that Keane was staying with United was plain. 'When he delayed his decision I thought it was a good idea,' said the manager. 'To everyone associated with the club it's marvellous news. I always felt he would do that. I get on well with Roy. I have a good relationship with him. Roy Keane epitomises everything I believe in in footballers – his determination, his will to win, his hunger. They are all qualities I can identify with.' Later he added, 'Roy Keane has always proved his value. He didn't have to do anything to convince me of that. The reason we signed him is that we know what he gives us every week. I was always confident he would stay.'

Ferguson said he felt his players had responded to Keane's decision: 'I think it lifted them,' he said. 'They want the best players here and they all respect Roy Keane. They think he is a great player and they are all pleased.' Of Keane's wonderful strike Ferguson said, 'It was a marvellous goal. He did well to keep the ball down. He struck it very well into the corner of the net.'

Valencia boss Hector Cuper, who had witnessed United set the tone for the night by engineering the announcement of Keane's new contract at the first whistle, generously paid his own tribute. 'Roy Keane's goal was excellent,' he said. 'If you let a ball drop for him you know he has such quality in that position.'

For Roy Keane it had been a red-letter day in every sense. 'Everybody must be sick of hearing about it and writing about it,' he said of his new contract. 'It's been a bit of a burden. The last six months I've always been patient. I said I wouldn't sign a contract until I was ready and United, to their credit, have come up with a contract I felt I was deserving. I said from day one my priority was to stay at Manchester United. The fans had a big say and Alex Ferguson who pushed for this contract and hopefully I can repay the manager and the fans with some more silverware over the next few years.'

Keane, it emerged, had agreed a deal that would earn him £45,000 in basic wages a week and with win bonuses that would rise to £52,000 a week, making him easily the highest paid player in the English Premiership. He would be paid considerably more than Newcastle's Alan Shearer, Chelsea's Marcel Desailly and Liverpool's Robbie Fowler. That £52,000-a-week salary was the equivalent of almost every member of the crowd at Old Trafford paying £1 for Keane each week. There was not a Manchester United fan who would begrudge paying it if asked. Significantly, while the negotiations had dragged on Keane had not personally encountered a single United fan who had been critical of the stance he had taken.

Back home in his beloved Cork, his good friend John Delea added his own endorsement. 'And the blessings of God should go with the £52,000 a week,' he declared. 'Roy is a man who deserves it. No one really knows about the good work Roy does because he and his family like to keep it quiet. He's always up at the local kids hospital, visiting the children with leukaemia and spending hours with them, yet he wouldn't want a photographer there and wouldn't even mention it to people. He was over a while back and a women we knew told Roy about a very ill young girl who was mad on Manchester United. The next day Roy went round and spent two hours with that little girl.'

Keane's £52,000 in gross earnings represented an increase of 75 per cent from £30,000 during a period when United's own turnover had climbed from £53.3 million to £88 million which, although not a comparable rate, was still a significant and thoroughly healthy leap.

With sponsorships and his testimonial, Keane could see his earnings over the next four years amount to £17 million. The new deal, brokered by Keane's solicitor Michael Kennedy, had been almost the last throw of the dice by United. In just three weeks' time he would have been entitled to negotiate with any interested club. 'Deep down,' said Keane, 'I always felt that if United came up with the contract I'd sign it. As time went on I thought this might be my last season at United. I knew my position was a very good one. You must remember that I was eligible to move on a free transfer.

Roy meets with disabled children at Carrington Training Ground.

'All I was concerned about was getting the right deal, which I eventually did. As for United, I'm not sure where they would have looked. There are a number of players around but clubs are only prepared to sell at ridiculous prices. Perhaps deep down they knew my contract would be sorted out.'

Even right up to the weekend before the Wednesday on which United secured his signature, Keane had thought he would be leaving the club. 'They seemed rigidly sticking to their wage structure, which had brought them success,' he said. 'The new contract was only put in front of me on Wednesday. I was only too willing to oblige.' It may have been coincidence or merely good timing but on the Saturday Sir Bobby Charlton in a newspaper salute to Keane had described him as the player every Premiership manager would want.

'Ask any manager, if he wants to build a championship team, which one player he would want with money no object. In all honesty, they would all go for Keane,' said Sir Bobby who went on to praise the way Keane dictated the pace of a game, ran non-stop, was one of the few penalty-box players since Bryan Robson and didn't lose a pass. 'It hurts him if he makes the wrong pass or the wrong decision,' said Sir Bobby. 'I saw a survey recently analysing passes and Keane had an amazing completion rate of 97 per cent.' It was a timely eulogy from such a distinguished Manchester United stalwart.

Alex Ferguson had, of course, played a major role in the manoeuvring of the last few days. The delay gave him time to impress upon the board one final time just how much Manchester United needed Roy Keane. He had told Martin Edwards that the club simply could not afford to lose Keane and Edwards knew Ferguson was being totally honest in his assessment. Edwards then acted decisively and got the board to up their 'final' tabled offer. 'I owe him a lot,' Keane later said of Ferguson. 'He really helped me get the deal. He was pushing the board behind the scenes for the last six months to ensure I stayed. I've had a few problems off the field and last year when the League celebrations got a bit out of hand but he has always been very understanding. He's a terrific man-manager, not afraid to put you in your place when you have done something wrong.'

As it turned out, United plc could look upon the retention of Keane as a great triumph. They had been forced to break their rigid wage structure but the club had become the first who had managed to hang on to a star player since the Bosman ruling. They had been cautious, as they needed to be, and they had bargained long and hard to keep Keane. But Keane had held the whiphand all along and Martin Edwards speculated that it would have cost around £50 million in transfer fees and wages to replace him with the Brazilian star Rivaldo.

Replacing Keane could in fact have cost double the amount United were finally prepared to pay to retain him. If Keane's worth on the transfer market was between £15 million and £20 million, that figure would have had to have been written off over the next four years alongside a player demanding an equal if not higher salary. It was no surprise that Keane's record contract was greeted warmly in the City. Manchester United's shares shot up 4.5p to 191.5p, a rise of more than 2 per cent.

In the week before the deal was concluded, Gary Neville described his captain as 'the most influential player in Europe'. If that was the case, then Keane would have felt entitled to demand similar wages to the other great players in Europe such as Del Piero of Juventus, who was on £70,000 a week after tax, or Internazionale striker Vieri on £55,000 a week.

> **'ASK ANY MANAGER, IF HE WANTS TO BUILD A CHAMPIONSHIP TEAM, WHICH ONE PLAYER HE WOULD WANT WITH MONEY NO OBJECT. IN ALL HONESTY, THEY WOULD ALL GO FOR KEANE.'**
> Sir Bobby Charlton

During the drawn-out negotiations, Keane may have been stubborn in his demands and annoyed that the board were taking so long to see sense. But in the end he was a very happy man and so, too, was Alex Ferguson who knew that Keane deserved every penny. Keane had been handed a lucrative contract but Manchester United had done good business too. Richard Baldwin of Deloitte and Touche, the accountancy company that produces the official report on the state of soccer, declared, 'It was actually a very good deal for United. If they had lost him they could have ended up paying about £80,000 a week rather than the £52,000 they are going to pay.'

As Keane and Alex Ferguson faced the television cameras to

talk about his decision to stay, Keane admitted, 'Yes, talks over my new contract were an unwelcome distraction. But I've signed and it's a great relief.'

When the size of his contract was mentioned by sports reporters Keane looked faintly embarrassed but he was forthright when he said, 'Manchester United have been wonderful to me over the last seven years. I wouldn't have got to where I am without them. There was much agonising over the last few months and

**'THE MOST INFLUENTIAL PLAYER IN EUROPE.'**
**Gary Neville on Roy Keane**

I was flattered by the interest of the top clubs in Europe. I had to look at my options. I couldn't imagine coming back to Old Trafford with another English team. There was only one decision once United came up with the right contract. It wasn't about the money, people are getting carried away by that. If it was I would have left this club three years ago. It was about the big picture and that big picture always pointed to Manchester United, no one else. People underestimated just how big United are. My heart is here. The fans have understood my situation very clearly. My signing shows that I'm happy here, at a club with ambitions like my own.'

Waiting patiently nearby for Keane to conclude his talks with the media was Denis Irwin. 'Has he offered to lend you a fiver?' Irwin was asked in jest. Irwin looked thoughtful for a moment then said, 'A bit more than that I hope. A lot more than that, in fact.'

Keane was absolutely correct in saying that the fans had understood his situation and they were delighted with the outcome, not least that it proved that Martin Edwards, the man who had wanted to sell out to Rupert Murdoch, and the institutional investors, could not call all the shots in the dressing room. At no time during the protracted negotiations had the fans accused Keane of greed, treachery or of holding the club to ransom.

Keane's record new contract inevitably caused reverberations within British football. There were those, not just within Manchester United but in British football generally, who had questioned Keane's asking price, considered it extortionate and wondered whether the breaking of Manchester United's carefully nurtured wage structure would open the floodgates. After all, they pointed out, the contracts of Giggs, Scholes and Beckham would all be up in 2002 and they surely would soon be knocking on the manager's door asking for similarly hefty pay rises.

But the bean-counters at United could take some comfort from Gary Neville's assessment of the situation. He felt that Keane's was a one-off case, a contract for a player who was more important than any other at the club. To lose Keane, he stressed, would have been a massive loss and would have sent out a thoroughly negative message to the rest of the team. Neville felt no other player could complain about Keane's fee because of his influence on the team. 'If he's earning more than five times what I am, then he deserves it,' he said.

All the United players to a man were delighted Keane was staying. In a column in the *Daily Telegraph*, Jaap Stam said it was a massive relief for everyone at the club and pointed out that it would have been a sign of weakness if Manchester United had lost one of its best players. 'Some of us were worried that he might leave and that would have seriously harmed the club's progress,' he said. 'You can't go into the transfer market and replace someone like Roy Keane. He is the best in the world at what he does.'

In what was always going to be a long and hectic season for United, Keane's contract was not the only issue which was being hotly debated in soccer circles. Under pressure from the government, United had duly pulled out of the FA Cup with the utmost reluctance in order to enhance England's bid for the 2006 World Cup by taking part in FIFA's inaugural Club World Championship in Brazil.

In Rio de Janeiro the team disappointed in tropical heat and came home with nothing more than a light suntan and no trophy, all of which appeared to vindicate the critics who had argued that United's participation in the competition was not worth the time and the effort and sacrificing the FA Cup. But, as captain, Keane remained positive about the whole experience and declared that the exercise had been great for the club in terms of playing against top players in unfamiliar conditions and on pitches very different from those in England. The time to assess the trip, he said, was at the end of the season.

Fortunately for United, their Premiership rivals Leeds and Arsenal failed to capitalise on United's temporary absence in Brazil but just how much the trip had taken out of United was soon to be put to the test: their first Premiership fixture on their return from Brazil was against Arsenal at Old Trafford on 22 January. Keane recognised that it was a huge game for United and that if the team performed poorly and did not get a result then people would point to them having had a jolly-up in the Rio sun.

United started sluggishly and the game ended in a 1-1 draw with Sheringham scoring a late equaliser. But Sky Sports pundit Andy Gray was just one of the soccer experts who singled out Keane for special praise. 'We were all waiting and watching and wondering to see how Manchester United would perform,' said Gray. 'Arsenal flew out of the traps and it took Manchester United half an hour to get going. But Roy Keane was absolutely sensational.

'Anyone who has a video of that game can look back and see just how Roy Keane got his team going. He went out and started kicking a few, started getting in amongst them. Suddenly his team just rose from there and that typifies why Alex Ferguson has decided to pay such a huge salary to keep him at Old Trafford. It's a team brimming with international quality but Keane's is the first name on the teamsheet. He's the one player Alex Ferguson wouldn't want to do without, particularly in big games. At Forest, Keane was always a goal-scoring midfielder. He hasn't done that at Manchester United. But this season he's gone up a gear, scoring goals, making runs, a real threat. Coupled with his leadership qualities, it's understandable that Manchester United were prepared to break the bank to keep him.'

The fuss had barely subsided when Keane found himself making the back-page headlines again by getting sent off for the sixth time in his United career at Newcastle where United crashed to a 3-0 defeat. He was dismissed for two yellow card offences: showing dissent to a linesman by implying he needed glasses, and for a foul on Robert Lee, although TV cameras later showed it was nothing of the sort. It prompted Ferguson to suggest that the referee had been a little too eager to send Keane off and wondered whether the decision might have been a bit of a hangover from Keane's attitude towards referee D'Urso against Middlesbrough two weeks before.

In the Champions League, United's next opponents in Group B after the winter break were Bordeaux and it proved a difficult tie both at home and in France. In the first leg at Old Trafford United found it hard to enforce their superiority although they might have gone ahead when Beckham hit the bar with a trademark free kick after Irwin had been brought down.

Then, four minutes before the break, Beckham delivered a perfect cross into the six-yard box and Giggs darted in to guide the ball smoothly with his left foot into the bottom corner. It was a good time to score.

In the second half United had a real scare when Bordeaux sprang the offside trap and Laslandes ran free and bore down on United's goal. He could have elected to go for goal himself but instead squared the ball for Wiltord. It should have been a simple tap-in but the Bordeaux striker astonishingly allowed the ball to run further to his left than he needed and he ended up tamely hitting the side-netting. It was a lucky escape for United.

Roy Keane had the chance to make the game safe when a clever late run saw him clean through but the Bordeaux keeper Rame smothered his shot. Later Rame was fortunate to stay on the pitch and to receive only a yellow card when he raced outside his box and sent Keane tumbling. United's decisive second goal finally came when another surging run by Giggs ended with the Welshman supplying a perfect cross for Sheringham to head home from three yards after 84 minutes.

**'IT'S A TEAM BRIMMING WITH INTERNATIONAL QUALITY BUT KEANE'S IS THE FIRST NAME ON THE TEAMSHEET. HE'S THE ONE PLAYER ALEX FERGUSON WOULDN'T WANT TO DO WITHOUT, PARTICULARLY IN BIG GAMES.'**

Sports pundit Andy Gray

The return match at Bordeaux was an ill-tempered affair with Beckham going down from a tackle by Laslandes who was promptly sent off, having minutes earlier been booked for dissent. The crowd felt Beckham had overreacted and jeered him for the rest of the match. But the real flare-up came when Bordeaux's captain Michael Pavon became incensed at something and appeared to spit at Keane. It could have been from sheer frustration because Keane was once again magnificent, setting a battling example to his team, upping the tempo of the game when it needed it and generally controlling the pace of it.

United had got off to an embarrassing start when Van der Houw, normally so reliable, allowed a speculative 30-yard shot to slip through his hands. Despite a desperate backward dive he was unable to grasp it at the second attempt. It was a bad and uncharacteristic blunder and after only nine minutes United were 1-0 down. But Keane scored an excellent equaliser after Beckham, Cole and Sheringham had combined to slip him through the Bordeaux defence. Goalkeeper Ulrich Rame came out to block his shot but Keane was able to prod home the rebound.

United had several scares in the second half, especially when Bordeaux hit the post with Van der Houw well beaten. Then Ole Gunnar Solskjaer scored a wonderful winner just 30 seconds after coming on as a substitute for Irwin after 83 minutes. He produced a superb first touch to control a long clearance from Van der Houw, so good that he didn't have to break stride. Then he jinked one way and went the other to confuse two defenders before slotting his shot home. The game was won.

At the end Pavon insisted on continuing his private contretemps with Keane but the Corkman had had the last laugh. He had paid off yet another slice of his new contract with a brilliant display.

Keane's rich vein of form continued with a phenomenal strike in an impressive 3-1 win at Old Trafford against Fiorentina in the Champions League. From a corner swept over by Beckham, Henning Berg leaped at the far post to head powerfully against the crossbar. Keane was first to the rebound and smashed in an unstoppable volley of stunning velocity and force, which glanced a post as it flew high into the net to put United 2-1 up. It was a magnificent goal, another stand-out moment during a period in which Keane was displaying formidable consistency even by his own high standards.

It was hard not to connect the awesome form Keane was now enjoying with relief he must have felt at no longer having to worry about his future. 'I wasn't playing particularly well before the contract,' Keane did admit. 'I thought I could have done a lot better. I don't care what people say, contract negotiations do affect the player especially with me because it was so high profile, as I was captain and could have gone free. Any mistimed tackle, any ball I might have lost, people were questioning whether I was one hundred per cent focused on my game. It did affect me a bit, the goals probably papered over a few cracks.'

Already there was talk that Keane would be voted Player of the Year by the Professional Footballers Association and he was a good bet to pick up the Football Writers' Player of the Year award as well.

As support swelled for Keane from football pundits and players alike, West Ham's Frank Lampard was just one who publicly nominated Keane for the PFA award. 'For me, Roy Keane has to be top dog,' said Lampard. 'Keane is the complete player and has shown in the Champions League this season that he's the best midfielder in Europe. Harry Redknapp's right in saying Paulo Di Canio's been a genius this season but I think Keane should win the award.'

Keane's reaction to the growing support for his nomination was typical. 'It doesn't bother me and that's not being disrespectful to my fellow members or to the writers but individual awards don't bother me in the least. It's a team game and as long as we win the Championship and the European Cup that's all I'll be worried about.

'The driving force comes from the manager down to everyone at the club. We're hungry for success. People go on about last year but amongst the players that's forgotten about, that's history. You can't live in the past and we want to win the European Cup and League championships every year. Obviously you can't do it every year but we're going to do our best.'

By April the Premiership title was in sight and Keane's contribution had been conspicuous in almost every game, not least when United went 2-0 down at Sunderland and he started the fightback to a 2-2 draw with an excellent goal. But the title was still not assured as Manchester United travelled on 10 April to take on Bryan Robson's Middlesbrough, who had been showing ominously good form in their previous few games. United arrived at the Riverside Stadium having given West Ham a 7-1 thrashing in their previous League outing, the seven-goal deluge coming after Wanchop had given the Hammers a shock early lead. The drubbing dished out to the Hammers on April Fools' Day prompted the West Ham keeper Craig Forrest to declare that United were better than Brazil and it induced Boro's manager Bryan Robson, who had witnessed West Ham's annihilation, to single out Keane as the man who was sustaining United's charge to the title.

Robson unequivocally voted Keane his player of the season. He said, 'There's no better midfielder than him anywhere and they were right to give him the money. Think how much it would have cost to replace him with the fee and wages. He is absolutely top class. He has tremendous stamina, he's quick, he is a great tackler, he never gives the ball away, and he's good in the air. Roy has matured. He has kids now, is settled in his life and has learned to control his temper.'

In the subsequent see-saw 4-3 victory over Boro, Keane did his best to live up to Robson's assessment, not only cajoling his teammates and galvanising them after they went a goal down in the first half – it could so easily have been two – but also managing to keep his temper during two flashpoints involving Summerbell and then Ziege. The latter earned Keane a yellow card but Alex Ferguson quickly defused the situation by taking him off, much to the skipper's obvious disgust. Once again Keane's whole-hearted display earned him admiring plaudits and a TV recommendation from the great ex-Scotland striker Joe Jordan that he should be the PFA's Player of the Year.

**'KEANE IS THE COMPLETE PLAYER AND HAS SHOWN IN THE CHAMPIONS LEAGUE THIS SEASON THAT HE'S THE BEST MIDFIELDER IN EUROPE.'**

Frank Lampard, then a West Ham striker

United followed up the victory over Boro with a 4-0 win against Sunderland that saw Keane showing his great commitment and work ethos even when the match was comfortably won. There was Keane sprinting on to a pass from Quinton Fortune, colliding with goalkeeper Thomas Sorenson and collecting a shin injury in the process that had Ferguson frantically signalling for him to come off. But Keane ignored it and then gave a wave indicating he had no intention of coming off because all three subs had been used. The win took United's League goal tally for the season to 84, a record for the Premiership – and there were still several games to go.

Just as everything appeared to be going so well for Keane, there came an unwelcome distraction for the skipper during the

April charge to the title and before the crucial second leg Champions League tie against Real Madrid at Old Trafford. Having convincingly proved his worth week after week since signing his new contract, it came as a bitter pill for Keane to have to swallow when a letter was sent to all season ticket holders by United secretary Ken Merrett hinting that Keane's £52,000 contract was the major reason behind an upcoming rise in the cost of tickets, an increase in an average season ticket from £380 to £399. The rise was more than twice the rate of inflation. Understandably Keane was livid that Merrett's letter had appeared to use the player's increased salary as an excuse to hike up the prices. Fans were told that they had to renew their season tickets before 15 May. Merrett's notification read: 'There was a huge collective sigh of relief when Roy Keane agreed to a new contract which will ensure he remains a Manchester United player for at least a further three years.

'In making this commitment to Roy, the directors believe they are also making a commitment to supporters.

'Manchester United fans have grown accustomed to the best. It is our duty to ensure that we remain in a position to be able to provide the best.' He went on: 'Price increases are never popular but we are sure that supporters will recognise the importance that we place on staying competitive and being able to compete not only in the transfer market but in our endeavours to retain our existing players.'

Keane maintained a dignified silence on the matter and it was left to his solicitor Michael Kennedy to put the issue in a true perspective. He admitted Keane was livid and pointed out that had the player decided to leave United, then ticket prices really would have to have been jacked up to pay for his successor.

The motive behind the wording of Merrett's letter may have

Holding the PFA Player of the year award 2000.

been wholly innocent but to single out Keane and make him a scapegoat was highly insensitive to the player and a needless, naïve and unfortunate mistake in public relations. Realising their blunder, the board tried to explain that it was just their way of informing the fans that prices were going up because the club wanted to expand and strengthen. But Keane was rightly incensed that the blame for the ticket hike was apparently being laid squarely at his door. It was undoubtedly an embarrassing own goal by the United hierarchy that the club and Keane could have done without, particularly at a time when their biggest game of the season to date loomed large.

Following a disappointing 0-0 performance against Real Madrid in the quarter-finals of the Champions League, United faced a tricky second leg against a very competent Spanish team and Keane was suitably wary. Assessing the task ahead, he stated, 'I'm pretty confident that every game we enter we can win it and generally I think our performances have been quite good. But we need to improve on our performance against Madrid. We were fortunate to come away nil-nil. We went to Madrid and knew that attacking-wise Real are as good as anybody. They came at us from all angles, they really went for it and I think they'll do the same at Old Trafford. Even if they nick a goal, I think we're pretty confident we can score two or three goals against anybody but they are more than capable of beating us, don't worry about that.' They were to be horribly prophetic words.

The game was 20 minutes old when United were exposed down their left flank and it resulted in a cross and an unlucky own goal, scored by Keane of all people. Trying to cut out the low cross with a despairing lunge all he managed to do was divert the ball into his own net past an agonised Van der Houw.

It was a devastating blow, all the more demoralising in that it was a mistake out of the blue and so unexpected from the skipper. Poor Keane could scarcely believe his misfortune. The momentum of his lunge had left him lying prone on his back and there he lay prostrate in disbelief for a couple of seconds, eyes closed, before rising rapidly to his feet with renewed determination written all over his face. Sympathetically the crowd roared out 'Keano, Keano!' and the skipper responded soon afterwards with a powerful run into Real's box and a shot that almost brought an equaliser. Keane fell as he shot but it typified his desperation to redeem himself when even on the floor he managed to half-rise to head for goal again when the ball rebounded off the goalkeeper. Inevitably from ground level his header was too weak to trouble the keeper.

**A LETTER WAS SENT TO ALL SEASON TICKET HOLDERS BY UNITED SECRETARY KEN MERRETT HINTING THAT KEANE'S £52,000 CONTRACT WAS THE MAJOR REASON BEHIND AN UPCOMING RISE IN THE COST OF TICKETS, AN INCREASE IN AN AVERAGE SEASON TICKET FROM £380 TO £399. THE RISE WAS MORE THAN TWICE THE RATE OF INFLATION.**

From Keane's own goal, United were always chasing the game and with Fernando Redondo giving as good as he got in midfield, United's uphill task suddenly looked ominously formidable. It looked bleaker still when they conceded a second goal five minutes after half-time and then a third that effectively killed off the match two minutes later, just after Keane had blazed over a gaping goal from close range. A superb individual goal by Beckham gave United a glimmer of hope and a late penalty by Scholes after Keane, battling his way into the penalty box, had been brought down by McManaman, restored some pride to bring the score on the night to 2-3. But the trophy that Roy Keane and United wanted most of all had been torn from their grasp. 'We keep leaving ourselves mountains to climb, and you just can't do that,' a bitterly disappointed Keane later reflected. 'Yet that is the way we play and right now I can't see it changing. You can't concede three goals against a very good side like Real.'

There was a deep sense of shock around Old Trafford when the result sank in. United and their fans had hoped to go on and win the Champions League again, and go on winning it as Liverpool and Juventus had in the 1980s and 1990s. But the revelation next day that Ruud van Nistelrooy was on his way to United from PSV Eindhoven for £18.5 million signalled Ferguson's intention to keep strengthening the squad with the obvious ambition of winning back the Champions League trophy as quickly as possible.

Then, three days later, United clinched the Premiership title at Southampton with an emphatic 3-1 win in which their inspirational captain showed himself the true professional. The game and the title were comfortably in the bag and yet Keane was still conspicuous for his fiercely competitive display, so much so that he picked up a yellow card. It had been noticeable all season how quick the captain had been to look after, protect and stand up for his young colleagues when there had been any hint of trouble on the field and when Southampton's Chris Marsden had a spat with Beckham after decking him with a robust challenge, Keane moved quickly to stand astride the grounded Marsden and volubly give him a piece of his mind.

Two goals in the first fifteen minutes had virtually ensured United would leave the Dell as champions but only around 1,500 United fans were in the ground to witness it although hundreds more were outside listening to the action on radios after hours of unsuccessfully pleading for tickets. At the final whistle Keane and his team cavorted in the Easter sunshine in front of those fans who had managed to make it inside. Moreover, United's three goals against Saints set a new Premiership record of 87 goals – and there were still 4 matches remaining.

It was a measure of how high the United players set their standards when Keane declared after the game that winning the Premiership was a slight anticlimax compared with the success of the Treble year and coupled with the disappointment of losing to Real Madrid in midweek. But, he stressed, 'We've got to be proud of ourselves.'

Keane also expressed disappointment that United had lost three games during the season. 'It may sound impossible to go through the whole League programme without a defeat but that's what we want to do,' he said.

Asked about Manchester United's continuing desire and hunger for success, Keane traced it back to the first day the players returned for pre-season training. 'The first question the manager asks us every pre-season is, "Do you want to win any trophies?" He says, "I do," and then asks, "Do you share my ambition?" We just go from there. In the first few days of training and in the first few games, if your desire is not there I'm sure you would be shown the door.

'It's a short career and you've got to make the most of it by trying to win every competition you enter. That's my aim. Hopefully that will continue for the next few years because that's where a club like Manchester United belongs, winning championships and European Cups.'

Alex Ferguson had nothing but the most fulsome praise for the players and went so far as to say he felt Keane's team was the best ever in Manchester United's colours. 'I'm delighted that, rather than sitting back on the Treble, the players have gone on to prove themselves all over again,' said Ferguson. 'That's why they are the best, the finest of all the teams there have ever been at Manchester United.'

The Old Trafford faithful had to wait until two days later, Easter Monday, to greet the newly recrowned 1999–2000 Carling Premiership League champions when Chelsea, once thought to be possible title contenders themselves, were the visitors.

The Chelsea players sportingly offered their own salute by lining up to applaud the United team on to the field but

Roy Keane signs autographs for fans during an open Manchester United training session on the second leg of their USA Tour in Los Angeles in July 2003.

inexplicably the Carling Premiership trophy itself was not there to be lifted in front of the crowd of nearly 61,600 who were there to hail their heroes. Premier League chiefs in their wisdom had decided not to let Roy Keane have the pleasure of getting his hands on the silverware until 6 May, when United were to play Spurs in their last home game of the season. Not everyone was convinced. United old boy Mark Hughes spoke for many when he said, 'It was a bit of an anticlimax without the trophy.'

Instead the fans had to make do with the team making a lap of honour after a strangely muted match in which Chelsea, with a place in the Champions League to play for, surprisingly failed to get up any real head of steam and United failed even to get out of first gear. United won 3-2 with Keane substituted with what was later revealed to be a hamstring problem that put him out of action for the remainder of the season.

Off the field, however, Keane continued to capitalise on his fine season, winning two major individual awards and putting his signature to a lucrative new boot deal. Having displayed his loyalty to Manchester United when he could have gone abroad, he displayed a similar kind of loyalty to Diadora by re-signing with the sportswear company in a deal reputedly worth a seven-figure sum. Not long afterwards he was to figure in an amusing new Diadora advertisement that emphasised Keane's power game. The ad featured the back view of a toy model of Roy Keane and littered behind him were the models of two other players – in pieces.

> 'THE FIRST QUESTION THE MANAGER ASKS US EVERY PRE-SEASON IS, "DO YOU WANT TO WIN ANY TROPHIES?" HE SAYS, "I DO," AND THEN ASKS, "DO YOU SHARE MY AMBITION?" WE JUST GO FROM THERE.'
>
> Roy Keane

Andrew Ronnie, Diadora's managing director UK, enthused over the re-signing of Keane to promote his brand. 'Having the captain of Manchester United, the biggest club in the world, as an ambassador for the brand has been fantastic for Diadora,' he said. 'We're delighted to have Roy as a member of the team for the next three years. He's without doubt one of Europe's highest-profile players. He's a great player and a great captain and the spirit he embodies on and off the pitch fits perfectly with the Diadora brand.'

Roy Keane has always regarded football as a team game and, as such, he has never attached much importance to winning individual awards. But he was nonetheless delighted when he capped his season by completing his own personal Double, winning both the Football Writers Association Player of the Year award and the Professional Footballers Association Player of the Year award.

In the FWA's poll, Keane won 53 per cent of the vote, which was the biggest margin in the 52-year history of the award. Chairman of the association, Paul McCarthy said, 'Roy is a worthy winner because he is the heartbeat of a magnificent side and his levels of consistency and excellence are unmatched this season.'

Keane was informed he had won it when he arrived at Vicarage Road for United's League game against Watford and responded, 'This is a fantastic honour. I am very excited personally but it's also a great reflection on the whole Manchester United team.'

The PFA awards were inaugurated in 1974 as a means of giving footballers the opportunity to laud their own fellow professionals. Players from the lower divisions as well as the Premiership are invited to recognise and honour their members and traditionally the PFA Player of the Year has been the individual accolade that the winner treasures above all others since it is an acknowledgment of excellence by his peers. The name of the Player of the Year is arrived at via voting forms distributed to every player in the top flight by each club's PFA representative and each player is allowed one vote. Each is first asked to nominate his Premiership XI, position by position, and then name Player of the Year and Young Player of the Year.

By the time the PFA awards were to be handed out at the end of April there was a general consensus among everyone in the British game that it would be a travesty if Roy Keane did not win Player of the Year. Even England coach Kevin Keegan, who would have dearly loved an England player to have won the accolade, admitted that none had lived up to the standards of Keane. 'It would definitely be Roy Keane,' Keegan enthused. 'You could make a case for a lot of people but for me he has been outstanding. He would get my vote. Even with my England cap on, I think I would say he has been the outstanding player all season. Other players have dipped in and out of form and had great spells. Alan Shearer, Kevin Phillips and Andy Cole have scored lots of goals and David Beckham has been fantastic since Christmas. But over the whole season it has to be Roy Keane.'

On the day before the PFA awards were to be officially announced, the soccer journalists had already voted Keane the Football Writers' Footballer of the Year, an award that gave Keane immense pleasure since he had not always enjoyed a good press. Kevin Phillips, who had produced a prolific season of goal-scoring with Sunderland, came second and Harry Kewell, Leeds United's exciting young Australian import, came third.

As usual, the 27th PFA Awards dinner was a prestigious

occasion, a Black Tie dinner in the chandeliered grandeur of the Grosvenor House Hotel in Park Lane, London. The evening kicked off with a sumptuous four-course meal including cream of broccoli and stilton soup to start and a cream of duck with sherry vinegar main course before the formalities began. Hopes were high for Keane at his Manchester United table, which also included Alex Ferguson, Andy Cole and Mark Bosnich, and as the awards were handed out they were a reflection of Manchester United's superiority all season. The names of the PFA Divisional Award Winners for the Premiership included no less than four United players. The 'perfect' Premiership team, according to those who voted, would have Cole, Stam and Beckham from United as well as Roy Keane in the line-up.

> **'ROY IS A WORTHY WINNER BECAUSE HE IS THE HEARTBEAT OF A MAGNIFICENT SIDE AND HIS LEVELS OF CONSISTENCY AND EXCELLENCE ARE UNMATCHED THIS SEASON.'**
>
> **FWA chairman Paul McCarthy on Keane's winning the FWA award**

Five other players apart from Keane were nominated for the Player of the Year award – Sami Hyypia of Liverpool, Andy Cole, Harry Kewell, Kevin Phillips and Alan Shearer of Newcastle.

Even as Sepp Blatter, the president of FIFA, stepped up to announce the Player of the Year award there were calls of 'Keano' from among the dinner-jacketed audience. Announcing the top three in reverse order, Blatter called out Harry Kewell – who had already picked up the PFA's Young Player of the Year award – in third place, Kevin Phillips in second and, to huge, heartfelt cheers, Roy Keane as Player of the Year. At the announcement it was noticeable that Ferguson, Cole and Bosnich all rose instantly to their feet and applauded Keane, resplendent in a dapper wide-lapel dinner jacket, as he picked his way past the tables of his cheering fellow professional footballers and mounted the four blue-carpeted steps up to the dais to receive the magnificent silver trophy.

Paul Dempsey of Sky Sports, compere for the evening, asked Keane how unsettling he found it to have so many question marks about his future and how he managed to set them aside to do so well on the field of play. 'I've always said that sometimes the easiest place for a player is being out on the pitch,' was his reply. 'I won't lie to you, I think speculation can affect a player but sometimes, as I said, the best place to be is out on the pitch because the media can't get in touch with you. So I tried to put it in the back of my mind and things went fairly well.'

Referring to the cruciate injury that threatened his career, Keane added, 'It did affect me a little bit and a lot of people were glad to see me get an injury like that. But you've got to go on. You get setbacks in your career, players get injured and it's part and parcel of the game and so you react to it and I like to think I've reacted quite well because it was a serious injury.'

Keane also paid tribute to Brian Clough and Alex Ferguson. 'To play under Brian Clough and for him to bring me over from Ireland at such a young age and to put me in the first team after a couple of weeks was fantastic and I owe him a lot. But I suppose Alex Ferguson – Sir Alex Ferguson – would be the main person who has helped me in my career, not just on the pitch but off the pitch as well, which has been a great help.'

He was further asked as a family man and for all the young players looking up to Roy Keane, what would be the best piece of advice he could give them? 'I'd basically say do as hard as you can, not just in games but in training, work as hard as you can, and I think eventually you will get your rewards.'

'You're a fiery lad, and there's nothing wrong with that,' said compere Dempsey. 'I just wondered if you had any thoughts on the new ten-yard rule next season?' This was a reference to the new ruling to be introduced the following year that would allow referees, having awarded a free kick, to have the kick taken a further ten yards towards goal if their decision was contested.

'We'll see, we'll see,' smiled Keane, to much laughter around the room.

Keane said of winning the PFA trophy, 'Of course it's special. I'm very surprised. I got a shock when I won the Writers' one, probably a bigger shock tonight from my fellow professionals, because the players who had all been nominated had a good chance of winning. It was just fortunate that it was me this year and I'd like to thank again all the fellow professionals who voted for me and even the ones who didn't.'

Keane added that he had always dreamed of being a professional with a top club like Manchester United and that there were so many people he would like to thank but admitted that if he did everyone would be there all night. 'People have had enough talking up here,' he said to laughter and another round of amused applause, 'so I'd just like to thank everybody who has helped me in my career. It's been a fantastic ten years I've been in England now, three years at Forest and seven at United and long may it continue.'

For Roy Keane the PFA award as Player of the Year crowned a season of superb achievement. There was the added satisfaction for a Corkman that the award had once again gone to an Irish footballer. Previously, the only Irish winners had been Pat Jennings in 1976, Liam Brady in 1979 and Paul McGrath in 1993.

In the past Keane had regularly made it on to the shortlist of six but United players had often lost out on the award previously because they had to contend with a split vote for more than one candidate. In 2000 both Stam and Beckham were on the shortlist of nominees. This year Andy Cole had also been in contention.

Keane was considered unlucky not to have previously won on more than one occasion, especially in 1999 for his outstanding contribution to the Treble. That year, the award went to the flamboyant David Ginola instead, although many independent observers felt the Spurs winger had won it for a handful of spectacular goals that had caught the eye rather than for consistent performances throughout the season. That year the PFA voters had once again favoured frontmen and goalscorers, as had largely been the custom down the years. Indeed, for the PFA Player of the Year 2000 award, Keane himself had made it known that his vote was going to Sunderland striker Kevin Phillips because of the number of goals he'd scored. 'He's come up from the First Division last year,' Keane explained, 'he scored plenty of goals there and people had their doubts whether he could do it in the Premiership because there really is a big gap. But he's put the ball in the back of the net.'

The PFA vote for Keane in 2000 encompassed his captaincy, which had been exemplary, his 11 goals from midfield which had led the way, and his general all-round play including his passing. An end-of-season statistic showed that in Premiership games Keane had astonishingly made no less that 1,919 passes, more than any other Premiership player. But his chances of winning the award were also boosted by his controversial breaking of Manchester United's wage structure, which had set a new benchmark for the game's top earners. Fears that some players, envious of his salary, and others who had clashed with him on the field, would not vote for him proved unfounded.

On 18 May at another prestigious dinner in London, Keane was officially presented with the Football Writers Association Player of the Year award, the inaugural Sir Stanley Matthews trophy named after the footballing legend who had died just a few months before. For Keane to have his name associated with Matthews was something very special to him. But in some circles there was a rumble of discontent that an award named after one of the great gentlemen of the game should go to a player famed for his combative approach and one who had been sent off once and yellow-carded seven times during the season.

Nevertheless, a season that had started amid so much uncertainty for Keane about his future had ended on an exceptionally high note. Ever since he had been made captain, Keane had vowed to set a standard for himself that both he and the club could consider worthy of following in the footsteps of Bryan Robson, Eric Cantona and Steve Bruce. He had tried hard not to let his commitment overstep the mark and, apart from the hounding of referee Andy D'Urso against Middlesbrough, which he admitted was unacceptable, his double Player of the Season award had further enforced his view that it was an honour indeed to lead out Manchester United.

Back in August 1999, the speculation at the start had been all about which foreign club would land Keane's signature. Now

> **'TO PLAY UNDER BRIAN CLOUGH AND FOR HIM TO BRING ME OVER FROM IRELAND AT SUCH A YOUNG AGE AND TO PUT ME IN THE FIRST TEAM AFTER A COUPLE OF WEEKS WAS FANTASTIC … BUT I SUPPOSE SIR ALEX FERGUSON WOULD BE THE MAIN PERSON WHO HAS HELPED ME IN MY CAREER, NOT JUST ON THE PITCH BUT OFF THE PITCH AS WELL.'**
>
> Roy Keane accepting his PFA Player of the Year award

there was a very different kind of speculation, namely whether Keane could remain with Manchester United after his newly signed contract had expired. Alex Ferguson felt Keane had the capacity to spend a further seven years at least in top-flight football. He would be only 31 when his contract expired and, if he maintained his fitness, he could prolong his career if he was prepared to move to centre-back, a position he had successfully occupied for club and country. Such speculation was noted with interest by Glasgow Celtic for whom Keane in the past had indicated he would like to play towards the end of his career with a possible move to the Scottish club in the summer of 2003.

But that was all far in the future. On 30 April 2000, Roy Keane was the man of the moment and at the Grosvenor House Hotel in London the toast from his fellow footballers was to 'Roy Keane, Footballer of the Year'.

It was party time at Old Trafford on a gloriously sunny Saturday, 6 May, after United beat Spurs 3-1 in their last home game of the season watched by Keane's predecessor Eric Cantona who earned himself two standing ovations – once when he arrived in the Directors' Box and once when he left. The title was already safely won, of course, but United without the injured Keane ended the season in style with a comfortable win. In the dressing room, captain Keane handed out celebratory bottles of champagne to members of his team and, after shaking up his own bottle of bubbly, Keane proceeded to spray a Sky Sports cameraman, who was recording the joyous scene, along with his camera.

The year before, Keane had raced with exuberance out on to the pitch to be given the Premiership trophy, almost leaving his teammates behind. This time he walked out at a more sedate pace as fireworks went off in salute to an explosive team. The kiss Keane planted on the magnificent Carling Premiership trophy was perhaps more heartfelt than the year before. Pushed out of the FA Cup by politics, the Champions League Cup prised from his grasp by Real Madrid, this Premiership trophy – United's sixth in eight seasons – felt so good to Keane in his hands as he raised it above his head.

The formalities over, a broadly smiling Keane stalked around the pitch spraying champagne over teammates and dousing Ferguson and his staff with bubbly as they posed for a photograph. Then, with one arm around the shoulders of Solskjaer and the other around Beckham, Keane joined in a team jig to the sound of 'Glory, Glory Man United' blaring from the tannoy. Thereafter the on-the-pitch celebrations took on an unprecedented family feel with the players parading not just the cup around the ground but their own children. Keane proudly cradled in one arm his little son, Aidan, dressed in jeans and a little Manchester United shirt complete with the number 16 and the name Keane on his back, while his daughters Shannon and Caragh walked alongside him. As he set off on a lap of honour round the field he had dominated all season, the familiar chants of 'Keano!' rang out in greeting. In other circumstances, if Manchester United had not met his pay demands, this would have been Keane's last few moments on the Old Trafford turf. The poignancy of these joyous moments was not lost on Keane or the fans.

Surveying the happy scene bathed in late spring sunshine, former Manchester United star Lou Macari commented, 'The double Footballer of the Year awards and collecting this trophy today will mean a lot more to Roy Keane than the £52,000 a week that constantly gets rammed down his throat.

'It's not his fault that he's such a good player. And it's not his fault Manchester United are willing to pay him the money.'

Two fine goals from Ryan Giggs got the 2003–04 season off to an excellent start as Manchester United collected three points for a comprehensive 4-0 home victory over Bolton in the opening encounter of the new Premiership season. That followed a niggly draw in the FA Community Shield against main rivals Arsenal, but

**'IT'S NOT HIS FAULT THAT HE'S SUCH A GOOD PLAYER. AND IT'S NOT HIS FAULT MANCHESTER UNITED ARE WILLING TO PAY HIM THE MONEY.'**
Former Manchester United star Lou Macari on Roy Keane

even then Roy Keane was delighted to see his side take the trophy on penalties. The Man Utd skipper knows better than most players that winning is a wonderful habit to get into and two more August victories followed, 2-1 away to Newcastle United and 1-0 at home to Wolves.

But then came a hiccup, and perhaps an illustration of frustration to come. United lost 1-0 at Southampton to a late goal from John Beattie. 'It was a game we should have won,' said Roy Keane. But two convincing victories followed. United beat Charlton 2-0 with Ruud Van Nistelrooy scoring twice and then overwhelmed Greek side Panathanaikos 5-0. But then followed the biggest test of the season so far, the mouth-watering clash with Arsenal at old Trafford.

Roy Keane was determined to lead from the front and he was the first player to be booked for his enthusiasm. But other names followed in a bad-tempered game which boiled over in a clash between Van Nistelrooy and Arsenal's Patrick Viera that resulted in a penalty for the visitors. The Arsenal defenders believed the Dutchman had exaggerated the incident and reacted angrily. Van

Celebrating winning the league in 2003 with David Beckham and Ole Gunnar Solskjaer.

Nistelrooy missed the penalty and the game finished goalless and for Manchester United it was definitely two points lost.

As Arsenal ploughed relentlessly on with their unbeaten season, Manchester United continued to under-achieve by their own high standards. They won several games narrowly and then lost 3-1 at home to Fulham in an embarrassing reverse.

In November, Keane's spirits were lifted as form improved. Rangers were emphatically beaten. Man Utd won at Anfield, beat Blackburn narrowly, completed a comfortable double over Panathinaikos, but then met expensively assembled Chelsea. Roy Keane was booked in a tough match won by the London side by a Frank Lampard penalty.

West Brom dumped a weakened Man Utd out of the Carling Cup, but although the football was rarely flowing, Roy Keane was heartened to see his side picking up Premiership points. Aston Villa, Manchester City, Tottenham, Everton and Middlesbrough were all beaten before the end of the year. But a home draw to Newcastle and a shock defeat at Wolves saw more valuable points leak away. More significantly key defender Rio Ferdinand was ruled out of action with his long suspension and the gap between United and Arsenal grew and grew. By the time Middlesbrough won 3-2 at Old Trafford in mid-February it was clear to all but the most faithful fans that the Premiership title had slipped away.

Attention switched to Europe. Roy Keane, perhaps more than any other player, was desperate to win here. But FC Porto had other ideas. Two remarkable goals from Benni McCarthy put the Portuguese side in front and Roy Keane touched the keeper with a trailing leg in a fairly innocuous incident and found himself sent off and out of the crucial second leg. Keane was desperately disappointed, especially when a cruel late goal at Old Trafford put FC Porto through and Man Utd out.

After that disaster there was the little matter of winning the FA Cup to salvage the season. The effort that went into defeating Arsenal in the semi-final was tremendous so defeating Millwall was almost an anticlimax. By most clubs' standards this was a successful season but Roy Keane knew it was a disappointment. As headlines flew he put himself firmly beside manager Sir Alex Ferguson in pledging his future to United.

But perhaps the happiest match of a long season came right at the end, when Roy Keane took a young Manchester United side back to Ireland to play a fundraising friendly against his old club Cobh Ramblers. Roy played for an hour and then spent the rest of the time signing autographs and posing for photographs. 'He has never forgotten his roots,' smiled Cobh's delighted chairman John O'Sullivan.

## CHAPTER 5

# A WHOLE-HEARTED PLAYER

FOR A DECADE Roy Keane has lived up to his reputation as the hardest man in English football. The past seven of those years have been spent as the steel in Manchester United's heart and his indomitable spirit is one very powerful reason why United have been so difficult to beat.

On the field Roy Keane plays on the edge, his determination on occasion boiling over into naked aggression. His is a muscular, intimidating presence on the pitch, full of menacing intent, with his will to win spelled out with every abrasive tackle he makes.

'Awesome' tends to be the word that opposing players use when asked to describe the experience of coming up against Keane at his most fiery and skilful. At grounds up and down the country, football fans have been left in no doubt of Keane's burning desire to come out on top. For millions more watching on television, the first sight of Keane is of the Manchester United captain standing

**IN HIS OWN WAY, ROY KEANE HAS COME TO REPRESENT THE TEMPLATE FOR THE MODERN MIDFIELDER. HE PLAYS IT HARD, KNOWS NO OTHER WAY TO PLAY AND WOULDN'T WANT TO PLAY ANY OTHER WAY. IT'S HIS BELIEF THAT A GOOD CHALLENGE CAN GET HIS TEAM AND THE FANS GOING, THAT GETTING WIRED INTO AN OPPONENT CAN CHANGE THE COURSE OF A GAME.**

at the head of his team in the tunnel. Not for Keane a Gazza-style wink at the camera, a jokey aside to an opponent, or an Ince-style last-minute pulling on of the jersey for good luck. Keane is a shaven-headed warrior with a job to do, eyes fixed firmly to the front, his mind fully focused on the game ahead, his only thought that of winning.

Following his wilder moments on the field earlier in his career, the slogan 'Killer Roy Was Here' was bandied about and Keane the enforcer started to accumulate an on-field disciplinary record that, he himself admitted, he needed to do something about. But in recent seasons, since being made captain of Manchester United and being able to enjoy a stable home and family life, Keane has curbed his temper and has largely steered clear of trouble on the field.

Now, in his own way, he has come to represent the template for the modern midfielder. Roy Keane plays it hard, knows no other way to play and wouldn't want to play any other way. It's his belief that a good challenge can get his team and the fans going, that getting wired into an opponent can change the course of a game. He's right, because he's proved it time and again as opposing players and managers can testify. Out on the pitch Keane, despite having suffered hernia trouble, kicks and bruises and knee injuries that might have finished lesser players, doesn't think about getting injured. He's fearless and, as he explains, it's his living. He realised long ago as a young boy what his strengths were and takes pleasure in the fact that although people right through his career have told him that everyone now knew his game, they still cannot stop him.

Roy Keane is a footballer who knows his role – to win the ball and give it to the attacking players. It's a role to which his game is ideally tailored and once he has won the ball, very rarely does a Roy Keane pass go astray. He has the ability and vision to make the telling, defence-splitting cross as well as the simple pass when needed. He's good at pressing for the ball and gives the team rhythm and pace to their game. To Alex Ferguson, there is a readiness in Keane to withstand pressure, provocation, intimidation and sheer bad luck that is priceless to his team. He's someone who can take a game by the scruff of the neck and change things if they aren't going right.

**'I'M A WHOLE-HEARTED PLAYER AND I CAN'T SIT BACK AND SPRAY PASSES AROUND, TAKE THE OCCASIONAL FREE KICK AND THAT'S MY NIGHT'S WORK. IF I DON'T GET STUCK IN I USUALLY HAVE A BAD GAME.'**

Roy Keane

But it is when his team loses the ball that Roy Keane's attributes are so invaluable. He can spot the danger in a trice and has the boundless energy, even in the 90th minute, to move swiftly to the danger point and snuff it out. Describing his own game Keane once said, 'I'm a whole-hearted player and I can't sit back and spray passes around, take the occasional free kick and that's my night's work. If I don't get stuck in I usually have a bad game. Workrate is a vital part of my game and I can't change.'

The overriding factor in Keane's make-up is that he hates cheats in any walk of life, most of all on the football field. He abhors sneaky foul play and the theatrics that unfairly win free kicks. 'I just hate people niggling at me and pulling at my shirt,' he once explained. 'If it's a crunching fifty-fifty tackle and we both go down, fine. But even in training I lose the head if someone is pulling my jersey. It's niggling, it's cheating and I hate people who cheat, simple as that. In life in general I don't like people who cheat and on the football field I don't like people who cheat.'

It's the same innate sense of justice and fair play that led him to put a stop to the bullying of his boyhood pal Aaron Kenneally which now leads Keane to dispute decisions from officials if he believes they have patently got it wrong. There was a time when he would naïvely harangue referees to the point where he would get himself booked. There were other times when the red mist would descend, the eyes would blink furiously and the challenge would go in recklessly. But in recent seasons the hot-headed moments of yore, the displays of petulance, the eagerness to get involved in flare-ups, the needlessly overvigorous challenges, the silly bookings, have given way to a new maturity in Keane although his drive and resolve remain as strong as ever. Apart from the odd disciplinary blot, his copybook has stayed commendably clean, the days when he was Sporting Enemy Number One after a much-criticised stamp on Gareth Southgate long gone.

> **'IF IT'S A CRUNCHING FIFTY-FIFTY TACKLE AND WE BOTH GO DOWN, FINE. BUT EVEN IN TRAINING I LOSE THE HEAD IF SOMEONE IS PULLING MY JERSEY. IT'S NIGGLING, IT'S CHEATING AND I HATE PEOPLE WHO CHEAT, SIMPLE AS THAT.'**
>
> **Roy Keane**

Keane's reputation as a hard man may have brought him unwanted back-page headlines but it has to be said that there have been occasions when it has worked in his favour. Indeed, he has played upon it to his considerable advantage. Diadora aren't the only company to have utilised Roy Keane's tough public image for the purposes of publicity. In July 1998 Keane starred in an advertisement for the Snickers chocolate bar that made the very most of his uncompromising image on the pitch. In the advertisement, he was pictured confessing to a priest about shoving, punching and kicking opponents. It featured him confessing to a string of ugly incidents on the pitch and when the priest realises Keane's confessions may take some time, the priest starts eating a chocolate bar.

In the confessional, Keane begins, 'Father forgive me. It's two seasons since my last confession. I deliberately pulled a player's shirt in a game last season. In another I shoved a player when the ref wasn't looking. In a big home game I swore at the linesman. Then I swore at the referee – twice. Or was it three times? In another match I threw a punch at this player – but I did get sent off for that one. Another time I kicked a player. I got away with it so I kicked him again.'

Ever since Roy Keane became a top footballer, there has been a fascination – and inevitably some envy – in Cork, Nottingham and Manchester with his rise to wealth and fame. To his credit, Keane has never been one to flaunt his fame and money and he has never forgotten his roots or how fortunate he himself has been. There was a time when, in the heady excitement of acquiring the trappings of celebrity and the pay that went with being a top footballer, he forsook a sponsored car for the thrill of owning a Mercedes with the number plate Roy 1. But it was a look-at-me invitation to envy and trouble and with maturity came wisdom and an anonymous Golf VR6.

At Forest he made mistakes in coping with the success that

came to him at such a young age. Single and restless and living in digs, he was prone to driving around at night and ending up at the homes of other players 'just pestering people, really'. He was also wont to look for excitement in nightclubs and bars, where he was an obvious target for young men envious of the fawning female hangers-on and interested to find out whether the hard man on the pitch was as hard off it. Suddenly Keane was horrified to find himself on the front pages of the newspapers and even in court.

**'LIKE A TRUE CORKMAN, I STOOD UP FOR MYSELF. I WAS VERY NAIVE. I USED TO GO TO NIGHTCLUBS, DRINK, GO TO KENTUCKY FRIED CHICKENS AND UNFORTUNATELY I DIDN'T REALISE PEOPLE WERE GOING TO HAVE A GO AT ME. I THINK IF I WAS A POSTMAN I WOULDN'T HAVE GOT HALF THE TROUBLE.'**

Roy Keane on the aggro he faced when he first became a top-flight footballer

Keane has learned to keep himself to himself but has readily admitted to some of the mistakes of his youth. 'Like a true Corkman, I stood up for myself. I was very naïve. I used to go to nightclubs, drink, go to Kentucky Fried Chickens and unfortunately I didn't realise people were going to have a go at me. I think if I was a postman I wouldn't have got half the trouble.'

For every newspaper allegation about an insulted girl, a barroom fracas, or a nightclub incident, there are many more untold stories about Keane that paint a very different picture of the Corkman. Keane's charity work often goes unnoticed, unreported at his own request. But occasional examples of his generosity, not just with his money but his time, do surface. In 1994, just after signing for United, he visited a young boy in a Cork hospital who was stricken with cancer and had not long to live. Keane brought along one of his football

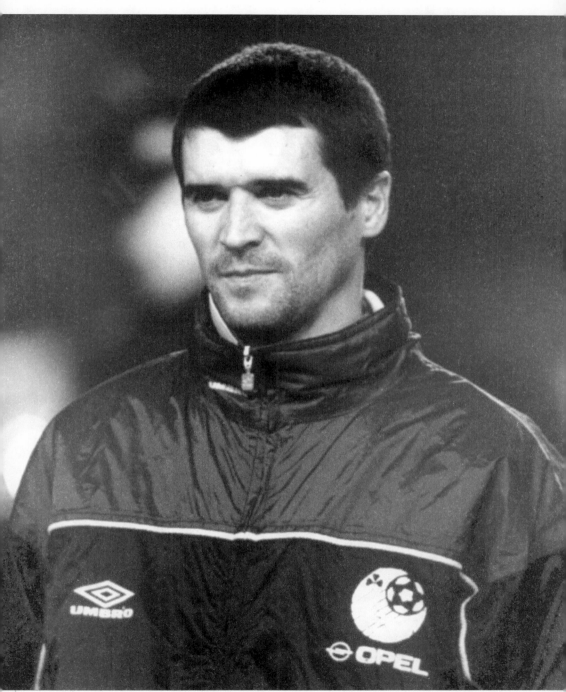

jerseys and a ball autographed by the entire Manchester United team. He spent hours with the lad and made such a favourable impression that when the boy passed away he was buried in Keane's shirt in a coffin that also bore the football. The same year, on his arrival with the Irish team in Dublin after the World Cup, Keane spotted a young fan in a wheelchair who had been brought out to the airport to see his heroes. Keane instinctively took a jersey out of his kit bag and gave it to the boy. And three years ago he was in Cork to promote the Irish Guide Dogs for the Blind Association.

**THE LARGESSE SHOWN TO HIS DAD HAS EARNED KEANE'S FATHER THE NICKNAME IN SOME CORK QUARTERS OF 'STERLING MOSS'.**

In and around Cork there are numerous stories of Keane giving his time and his money to good causes and his generosity to his own family is legendary. Besides buying the beautiful house his parents Moss and Marie now reside in, he regularly sends money home to his father. It is this largesse shown to his dad that has earned his father the nickname in some Cork quarters of 'Sterling Moss'.

Keane realises he relinquished much of his privacy years ago, which is why he relishes the days he can spend back in his beloved Cork with his family. He goes back there whenever he can and intends one day to return to live in the city of his birth. At the Temple Acre Tavern he can still enjoy a drink with his brothers without being pestered. There he is treated as just another customer, the signed shirts in frames on the wall denoting in a low-key manner that this is the Keane family's local rather than bragging that the pub has a soccer superstar among its patrons.

The Temple Acre Tavern is a rare oasis of public calm for

Keane. In public he has had to get used to constant displays of recognition ranging from hysteria and mass adulation, to abuse, to polite requests for an autograph. It's a life in a goldfish bowl that puts a strain on his family when it comes to an outing to a cinema or selecting a holiday where they can enjoy themselves in peace.

Over at O'Flaherty's, another pub in Cork City, there is a different kind of reverence for the most famous footballer the city has produced since Noel Cantwell 30 years ago. On nights when Manchester United are playing European Cup matches, the place is heaving with customers wearing the number 16 Keane Manchester United red shirt, all craning over their pints of Guinness and jostling for a view of the many TV screens showing the match. Denis Irwin's reliability always earns warmly enthusiastic applause from the assembled imbibers for their fellow Corkmen but the roof almost comes off if their favourite son Roy Keane happens to score. Across the city, at White Cross, an African grey parrot that goes by the name of Jake will also react to the goal when asked by his owner Joe Healy, 'Who plays for Manchester United?' The bird's reply, in a distinctive Cork accent, will be, 'Roy Keane – up Cork!'

They say football is a funny game. On the day Kevin Keegan announced his squad for Euro 2000, the England manager met up with former Manchester United and Nottingham Forest manager Ron Atkinson when both were fulfilling ITV promotional duties.

'Why didn't you pick Roy Keane?' Atkinson said impishly and the two men broke into laughter. 'If only,' sighed Keegan.

In September 2001, Roy Keane inspired Ireland to a momentous victory over Holland in the World Cup qualifying tie at Lansdowne Road. Roy was a major influence in a magnificent team performance that snuffed out Holland's hopes of going to the finals. The Dutch, long regarded as one of the major European footballing nations, were eliminated, and it left Ireland poised to join Portugal in the finals if they could win through in a two-leg play-off against Iran.

In the first leg, Roy played through the pain barrier to help Ireland open up a 2-0 lead, which virtually assured them of qualification. He was forced to miss the second leg after aggravating his knee injury. But Ireland came safely through without him, and no one was more delighted than the skipper. Roy could look forward to playing at the very highest level once more. He had waited eight long years since USA 1994 for the chance to demonstrate his class and talents on the world's grandest stage.

Now, when football's greatest players would assemble in June 2002 in Korea and Japan for the finals, Roy Keane knew he would be among them. It was, he conceded, a great feeling and it was clear that his Ireland would give any team a hard game. As one foreign coach admitted, no team would fancy playing Ireland with Roy Keane driving the team forward. He was an opponent who would rightly be feared and respected by the 31 other teams participating.

Roy was an even better player than when he had last pulled on his boots for Ireland at the finals of the World Cup in 1994 in the USA. Everybody in the game acknowledged Keane was truly world class. Now he would have the chance to emphasise it. No one, however, in their wildest imagination, could have foreseen the extraordinary sequence of events that would ultimately find Ireland waging the closing stages of their World Cup campaign without him.

But many months before Roy was destined to become a sensational World Cup figure before the tournament had even kicked off, there were important domestic footballing matters for him to focus upon. As the new 2001–02 Premiership season opened, it soon became clear that his Manchester United team would find it none too easy defending their position as League champions. Arsenal, Liverpool, Chelsea and Newcastle had strengthened their squads and were ready to mount realistic challenges. And, in what was to prove a troubled season for United, controversy and disappointment were never to be far away.

The opening home game of the season saw United concede two goals to newly promoted Fulham's exciting young French striker Louis Saha. Although the match was eventually won, it set an ominous pattern for United's season: opponents were to find flaws in the Reds' defence far too easily, and a series of individual errors also contributed to United woes at the back. That opening Fulham fixture also saw Jaap Stam's last appearance in a United shirt. The sudden transfer to Italy of such a defensive stalwart came as a shock to players and fans alike and sparked a storm of controversy, especially when United went on to leak goals with alarming regularity without him.

Keane, for so long the linchpin of United's midfield, had his own position to worry about too. Alex Ferguson looked to accommodate Veron's undoubted talents into the team and it took time for the Argentinian to bed into United's midfield. Worryingly for the fans, Veron's very presence seemed to leave Paul Scholes out of position and out of sorts. While Keane had to get used to playing with Veron alongside him, his own game wasn't helped by his sending off for the ninth time in his United career after raising his hands at Newcastle's Alan Shearer.

Quite aside from his team's defensive frailties on the pitch, there was something else occupying Roy's mind – a new contract with Manchester United. Looming once again was the question of whether the time was right for a move abroad. As before, such a move naturally held lucrative appeal but would entail a difficult and unsettling uprooting of the Keane family.

Roy's loyalty to his family and to Manchester United was eventually rewarded with a new contract on 2 March 2002, which would see him remain at Old Trafford until June 2006. The four-year deal was reported to be worth around £90,000 a week. Alex Ferguson, who publicly rated Keane as perhaps United's greatest ever player, had by this time unexpectedly gone back on his decision to retire as United's manager and his eagerness to stay on at the helm no doubt helped sway Roy's decision to re-sign.

Despite a remarkably prolific run of goal scoring by new recruit Ruud van Nistelrooy, United's defence of their 2001–02 League championship was brought to a sorry end by Arsenal, who virtually clinched the title by winning what was regarded as a six-point game at Old Trafford. Surrendering the title to arch-rivals Arsenal on home turf was a painful blow for Roy Keane in more ways than one. He also picked up two dead legs in the game.

Having unexpectedly crashed out of the FA Cup to Middlesbrough, the Champions League now offered the only hope of a trophy. Roy's teammates were all too aware how much a winner's medal would mean to him, and several of them came out and stated they considered it their duty to their captain to see that he got it. But their deeds failed to match up to their words.

United's progress through the rounds was both nervous and

erratic, and Roy himself suffered a severe blow when he was carried off with a hamstring injury on 2 April in the game against Deportivo La Coruna. With typical determination, he was back for the crucial semi-final away leg against Bayern Leverkusen and showed tremendous skill, pace and anticipation to put United ahead in the second leg. But United failed to hold on, and that much-coveted medal remained a dream for another year. When the skipper looked back over United's trophy-less season, he was able to say quite truthfully that some players had fallen short of their capabilities.

## CHAPTER 6

# KEANE THE MAN

## KEANE'S CHARACTER

'I always say I'm from Cork first, Ireland second.'

ROY KEANE

'Wherever he ran the ball seemed to be tied to his feet. It was like an extension to his leg. It seemed like part of him he was attached to it so often. He was only a small boy, smaller than the others of his age, yet he had a strength and a presence about him even then, when he was only seven or eight years old.'

CHILDHOOD NEIGHBOUR MARY KENNEALLY

A schoolfriend recalls an incident on the number eight bus into the centre when an older boy pushed Roy roughly off his seat and ordered him to stand. He remembers, 'Roy just refused. He dragged at the lad's jacket and had him almost on the floor before he realised what was going on. We were only ten or eleven and this other lad was fifteen at least. And he was with a gang of his mates. He clouted Roy and sent him half the length of the bus. But still Roy would not let it be. It was his seat and he was not going to give it up. In the end some adults stepped in and told them to pack it in but Roy would still not stop and the big lads were by then threatening to punch us all in. Fortunately we got to the stop by then and the conductor put us all off and it broke up. But Roy was totally fearless. He would never back down an inch over anything. I don't know whether he was brave or barmy but he was different from anyone else I've ever known.'

'He was never very big at school but he was always very hard.'

DENNIS O'CONNELL, CHILDHOOD NEIGHBOUR

'There is no doubt I was a bit of a tearaway when I was younger at home. I always seemed to be getting into trouble. There are five of us kids in our family. In England that is big but for Ireland it is just average really. Undoubtedly I was the black sheep of the family.'

ROY KEANE

'If Forest had not come in for me I would be on the dole now. I was just a YTS lad when they took me on, I'll always be grateful to Mr Clough whatever happens next.'

ROY KEANE IN HIS NOTTINGHAM FOREST DAYS

'The lads had warned me about how much Gazza tries to wind people up with chat. But I still couldn't believe it. He was at it all the game. He never stopped talking for 90 minutes. He was telling me I was rubbish and that was one of the compliments. Some of the things he was saying to me were unbelievable. Most of them were unrepeatable. That is just the way he is.'

ROY KEANE ON HIS FIRST ENCOUNTER WITH PAUL GASCOIGNE

'I was absolutely knocked out when the boss Brian Clough told me I'd be getting a car, a Ford Orion. Back in Ireland I'd never been able to afford a decent car and I'd always been jealous of lads I knew who had one. But more than that it was a concrete symbol that I was a real live professional footballer. I used to wash it on Sundays and drive around all over the place. I've never been as proud of a car since.'

ROY KEANE AS A YOUNG NOTTINGHAM FOREST STAR

'I still have trouble understanding him and I'm sure he has problems understanding me. But we talk the same language when it comes to football.'

BRIAN CLOUGH, KEANE'S MANAGER AT
NOTTINGHAM FOREST

'When I left school at forest I had no qualifications. I went on a couple of courses which paid me a few quid a week. But the outlook in Ireland was pretty gloomy. Tourists might paint a picture of prosperity but it's not quite like that. There was a lot of unemployment in and around Cork. Jobs were scarce. It makes this fairy-tale thing even more complete if you like. Because if I hadn't got a contract with Forest and wasn't playing football for my living now, I know I would be on the dole back in Cork.'

ROY KEANE

'Keane is like a kid who wakes up on Christmas morning and finds an apple, an orange, a box of Smarties and 50 pence in his stocking. He wants more.'

BRIAN CLOUGH

'Maybe if it was any club other than United, I might have thought about it. But what's the point in me leaving United?'

ROY KEANE ON HIS DECISION TO STAY WITH<br>MANCHESTER UNITED

'I haven't forgotten how low I was at times at home. I tried to put on a brave face to the press but there were times when it was so hard. There was no other way than to come back strongly. What was I to do? Sit back and think, "Well, that's the end of it"? I was only 27. I had no choice but to battle back.'

ROY KEANE ON HIS CRUCIATE INJURY

'I actually live quite a boring life.'

ROY KEANE

## KEANE THE INSPIRATION

'Roy Keane's great ambition was always to become a footballer. He spent every spare minute practising his skills. The funny thing is that he was very, very small for his age and although he was very keen on sports, he only made the junior school team once or twice.'

PADDY FLYNN, TEACHER

'I used to call him the Boiler Man. You know, the fellow who mans the furnace, who gets things heated up and keeps them that way. He was the motivator, the leader. When things were going bad for Rockmount, all you had to do was roar at Roy. He would do the rest.'

TIMMY MURPHY, EX-MANAGER ROCKMOUNT BOYS

In his early Rockmount years Keane often played up front but there his size told against him. 'I was kicked about a bit,' he admits. 'While everyone got bigger, I never grew. The centre-halves were just kicking lumps out of me so I had to go back into midfield.' It didn't stop him coming forward, however, and scoring his share of goals. In midfield his natural dynamism helped him to shine and in confrontations with bigger opponents he was constantly reminded of the old adage that the bigger they come, the harder they fall. 'I used to get stuck in,' he says.

'For training Roy would have to get the train from Cork to Cobh but at seven o'clock Roy would always be the first one there at the gates waiting in all weathers, often soaking wet. When training was over, the other players would all go into the dressing room but Roy would stay on and do another ten laps of the field.'

COBH RAMBLERS GROUNDSMAN JOHN O'DRISCOLL

Scout Noel McCabe's carefully compiled detailed notes on the game that changed Roy Keane's life: 'Very Good. Roy is a player who is good at finding players with his passes and aggressive with his tackles, involved in all the activities in the middle of the park.' He praised his broad and strong upper body and his enthusiasm for taking on players. And McCabe firmly concluded, 'A strong looking boy to go on trial to Forest right away.'

Archie Gemmill was deeply impressed in an early Forest

Reserves game by the astonishing effort of the young Irish player. He said, 'I think it was the first time I saw evidence of Roy Keane's amazing will to win. He put in an inspirational performance that night that seemed to transmit enthusiasm throughout the whole team. It is very unusual for one player to be able to make his teammates lift their game but Roy Keane has that ability. It is part of what makes him different. I don't think Arnold Town ever quite knew what had hit them.'

'Enid Blyton could not have written a better script. I am the last one to get carried away about a player who has played in the First Division for just 90 minutes but after that first game I knew Roy Keane had the makings of a great player.'

BRIAN CLOUGH

'Keane sums up United. So competitive and powerful. He doesn't know when he's beaten, he just keeps going.'

ALLY MCCOIST, SPORTS PUNDIT

'Every time I watch him he's outstanding. I haven't even seen him have an average game yet. He's already a United legend and more. He is the captain of the team that won the Treble, and that's an unbelievable achievement. This is the best United team ever, they've won more than anyone else and if I had to pick a world XI, Roy would be in it.'

BRYAN ROBSON, EX-MANCHESTER UNITED STAR, IN 2002

'He's a player's player. He's a fantastic player but he's taken the manager's instructions and desire to win on to the field of play and that's why the Manchester United players round about him, great as they are, look for his inspiration. Against Middlesbrough he was the player who did that when things weren't going too well for Manchester United. In that first 45 minutes when they weren't at their best, he was the one that dragged them through that first 45 minutes until Alex Ferguson sorted it out at half-time and we saw what happened second half, they were tremendous. He is now the best midfielder in Europe.

'He very rarely gives the ball away, he wins his tackles, he gets behind the ball, he organises. The way he differs from other players at Manchester United is that he takes what the manager wants from the dressing room prior to the game and puts the manager's influence, that drive, that determination on the field.'

EX-SCOTLAND AND MANCHESTER UNITED STAR JOE JORDAN

## KEANE AND CONTROVERSY

'Roy Keane is no angel but I'd say he was the one of us least likely to cause any trouble. He was such a quiet lad when he came over from Ireland. Whenever we went out and some lads would be larking about after a drink he would be the one watching mostly. But sometimes when he'd had a drink he could get involved. I never ever saw him start any trouble. But at first he found it hard to back off when we encountered some guys who wanted to make a name for themselves after a few beers. I reckon at least 99 per cent of people are just fine but there is always the lunatic fringe who want to start a fight. Roy is no coward and he found it hard at first to just walk away from insults or abuse.'

A FOREST TEAMMATE

'Brian Clough kissed Roy in public and in front of his mum and dad. Roy was spitting feathers in the dressing room afterwards. The boss was always over the top but that was going too far.'

'I always remember the kick-off. The ball went back to Robson and Roy absolutely cemented him! I said, "Bloody cheek of him! How dare he come to Old Trafford and tackle like that!"'

ALEX FERGUSON ON HIS FIRST SIGHT OF ROY KEANE PLAYING FOR NOTTINGHAM FOREST AGAINST MANCHESTER UNITED AT OLD TRAFFORD

'I cannot and will not tolerate being spoken to with that level of abuse being thrown at me so I sent him home. I've made the right decision, not only for the benefit of me but the squad as well. He is one of the best players in the world, but he is a disruptive influence. Roy Keane will be taking no part in the World Cup – he is going home.'

THEN REPUBLIC OF IRELAND MANAGER MICK MCCARTHY

As United strove to maintain their assault on the Premiership in 1999, Keane was rarely far from the thick of the action – and the headlines. He caused a huge furore when Middlesbrough visited Old Trafford and referee Andy D'Urso awarded a penalty to Boro for a foul by Jaap Stam. Keane led a posse of vehement protests from United players that had the referee physically back-pedalling and the United group of players pursuing him, but to no avail. D'Urso was unmoved. Pictures of the incident showing Keane screaming with vein-bulging ardour at D'Urso caused a tabloid frenzy and much debate about the intimidation of officials. 'I feel the referee made the wrong decision,' was Keane's explanation. 'I've seen it on video a few times. But don't get me wrong, we shouldn't have reacted the way we did. But at the time it was in the heat of the moment, we're going for the championship and we thought we could lose this game one-nil. The ref made the wrong decision on Jaap, I thought he got the ball. It's something you regret, but that's life and you've got to get on with it. Hopefully people won't have to see that again.'

Not long afterwards Keane expanded his views on the incident in Dublin, where he had joined the Republic of Ireland squad for their friendly against the Czech Republic. 'Referees deserve better than the way they have been treated of late,' he said. 'Yes, there are pressures in the the game, pressures to get results. But is is part of the job to handle all that. We went over the top and the manager has had a word with us about it. It won't happen again from us. At the time we did not think what we did was that bad but when we saw the photographs it did look bad and referees deserve better than that because they have a hard enough job as it is.'

Keane, however, did manage to see the funny side of the Middlesbrough incident. 'What happened when the referee gave the penalty was unfortunate,' he said, 'though if he had stood still I don't think we would have been chasing him. But he kept running and we kept chasing!'

## KEANE CURIOSITIES

'My hero was Mike Tyson as a boy. I had four fights as a young boxer and I was seriously thinking about making a career in the ring. But at the time I was also playing soccer and Gaelic football. In the end there wasn't enough time to do all three.'

ROY KEANE

'I'm not a good spectator when it comes to football, and when I'm injured I don't like the idea of going down to the club and hanging around. I feel I'd almost be making a nuisance of myself.'

ROY KEANE

'It's funny, when I first lived in Nottingham, people would ask me if I wanted to go and do a bit of fishing. Or perhaps if I wanted to have a few pints of Guinness. They must think that all Irish people do all day is fish and drink Guinness. As a matter of fact I don't do either!'

ROY KEANE

'I flew to Manchester and met Alex Ferguson but we didn't discuss any contracts, just talked football. That's when I decided, it didn't really matter what contract I was going to get – because obviously I was going to do well anyway – but that I was going to go to Manchester United.'

ROY KEANE

'Roy Keane is soccer's youngest millionaire at the age of 22.'

BUSINESS AGE, MAY 1994

# KEANE'S BEST GAMES

Nottingham Forest fans still argue about which was Roy Keane's best game for the club. But many faithful followers pinpoint a game on 10 December 1991 when Keane scored both goals in an emphatic 2-0 win at Tranmere Rovers in the exotically named Zenith Data Systems Cup northern area semi-final.

Forest were always in control of an entertaining encounter that did much to warm the freezing crowd of just over 8,000 who had to watch the match through drifting fog in spite of the Arctic temperatures. Tranmere started well and pressed for the first 20 minutes with the alert Gary Charles twice robbing John Aldridge just as the always dangerous striker looked on the point of getting the home side in front. But Roy Keane was back to the form that had made him the sensation of the previous season and neatly slotted home the first goal after Eric Nixon could only palm away a shot from Charles after an enterprising interchange with Scott Gemmill. Keane looked on fire that night. He had already narrowly missed with two early chances and was clearly decided he was going to finish on the winning side. Just after half-time Roy made the game safe as he stylishly finished off a sweeping move involving Nigel Clough, Teddy Sheringham, Gemmill and Charles. Leicester in the next round went on to secure another Wembley appearance and won the trophy in a 3-2 thriller against Southampton with Scott Gemmill grabbing the winner in extra time.

There are many fine performances to choose from in Roy Keane's early years in English football. Nottingham sports reporter Ian Edwards favours a famous victory over old rivals Tottenham Hotspur: 'The day that really sticks out for me is when Forest got to the semi-final of what was then the Rumbelows Cup on 1 March 1992. They played Spurs at White Hart Lane and there had been a bomb scare before the match and kick-off had been put back half an hour. It was played in the pouring rain. Forest were winning 1-0 and it went to 1-1 and into extra time. The shirts were so wet they were hanging round people's knees. The pitch was like a mudbath. And there was Roy charging around while everyone else was flagging. He was dominating a game that he had no right to dominate when you looked at his frame and his age. Then he scored the winner from an absolutely incredible header from a Gary Crosby corner. He was above everything, the conditions, the pitch, everything that night.'

'One game stands out in my mind that tells you everything about Keane and his influence on those around him. United were two down early in the game against Juventus and no one thought they could overcome such a big hurdle, especially in Italy. But it seems to me that Keane truly believed that United could still win even though the notion seemed crazy. He scored the goal that gave them hope and, even though he was booked and knew he would miss the final, he drove the team into the final.'

FABRIZIO RAVANELLI

His remarkable display prompted Alex Ferguson to write in his biography *Managing My Life*, 'I didn't think I could have a higher opinion of any footballer than I already had of the Irishman but he rose even further in my estimation in the Stadi Delle Alpi. The minute he was booked and out of the final, he seemed to redouble his efforts to get the team there. It was the most emphatic display of selflessness I have seen on a football field. Pounding over every blade of grass, competing as if he would rather die of exhaustion than lose, he inspired all around him. I felt it was an honour to be associated with such a player.'

# KEANE'S MOST IMPORTANT LESSON

Manchester United were hot favourites for the 1995 FA Cup but in the semi-final replay against Palace, Roy Keane hit the headlines for all the wrong reasons. The match against Palace was always likely to be charged with tension both on the field and on the terraces because it was against Palace at Selhurst Park in January some 11 weeks earlier that Eric Cantona had executed his now infamous kung-fu-style kick at an abusive spectator after being sent off. Now, as the teams were to meet again in a Cup semi-final and because a possibility of crowd trouble was on the cards, both Alex Ferguson and Palace's manager Alan Smith appealed for calm before the kick-off. On the pitch the two teams were still locked at 2-2 after extra time. And there was the prospect of even more trouble when after the game a Palace supporter died following an altercation with United supporters.

In such an emotionally charged atmosphere, the replay at the same Villa Park venue turned out to be a thoroughly stormy affair. The first half ended with Keane having seven stitches inserted in an ankle gash during the interval. But after the break Keane received the first red card of his career for stamping on defender Gareth Southgate following a dangerous and clumsy tackle. Keane may have considered that he had taken enough of a battering that day – and an X-ray later revealed he had sustained ligament damage and a chipped ankle bone – but his reaction was ugly in the extreme and he could have no complaint when the referee banished him from the field.

United won the game 2-0 but Keane's actions inevitably caused a furore in the press, with some observers going so far as to call for him to be barred from playing in the Cup final. The on-field act of violence, coming so soon after the death of the Palace fan and with Eric Cantona's act of madness at Palace still strong in the memory, inevitably had the Football Association bristling and it was no surprise when Keane was subsequently charged with bringing the game into disrepute. He would have to serve an automatic three-match suspension and in the run-up to the disciplinary hearing there was still such a hysterical outcry over the incident that Keane and United had very real fears that he would be given an extended match ban on top.

United's chief executive Martin Edwards was quick to call for calm and reason. 'Everyone has gone completely overboard on this,' he said. 'He should not have retaliated but to talk about punishment beyond the usual three-game ban sounds crazy. He will be fined by the club. What do people want us to do, sentence him to two weeks in jail? I don't see how they can suspend him for more than three games.

'What about all the other players who have been sent off this year for a similar offence? Are they going to have their cases reconsidered? Manchester United have responsibilities to the game. I believe we carry them out. We dealt with Eric Cantona and we have dealt with Roy Keane.'

It was an anxious wait for Keane before he was to know his fate. In the event, the FA three-man disciplinary panel met at the FA's Lancaster Gate headquarters in London to consider what punishment to mete out and decided that Keane should merely be fined. There would be no further match ban beyond the statutory three for the sending-off, which was a huge relief to Keane and to United. The fine of £5,000 was the second biggest handed out by the FA that season and Keane was also fined a week's wages by United.

Keane had made use of his three-match suspension to take the opportunity to have a hernia operation for a long-standing injury and by the time he arrived at the FA hearing he was still feeling the after-effects of the 72-hour operation. With him to add their support were United's assistant manager Brian Kidd and Old Trafford director Maurice Watkins.

Keane made no comment as he limped gingerly to a waiting car after the 90-minute hearing but David Davies, the FA's director of public affairs, was adamant: 'We were always perfectly happy to go ahead with this hearing. We needed to find a balance because the offence was regarded as serious. It was a sensitive issue and it was judged in the circumstances of that game and that night.

'Roy Keane made no attempt to justify the offence but he said he bitterly regrets what happened. We are satisfied that this is the appropriate punishment.'

The appropriate punishment did not warrant Keane missing the FA Cup final against Everton, as some had called for. He was in the line-up for United, whose League form suggested they were hot favourites in Wembley's 50th post-war final on 20 May in front of a crowd of 79,592. But the absence of Cantona – suspended for eight months for his behaviour at Selhurst Park – and the aftermath of the Keane controversy proved critical and United lost 1-0.

## CHAPTER 7

# FACTFILE

| | |
|---|---|
| **BORN:** | Roy Maurice Keane August 10, 1971 |
| **BIRTHPLACE:** | Cork, Ireland |
| **HEIGHT:** | 5ft 11in |
| **WEIGHT:** | 76kg (12st 10lb) |
| **SQUAD NUMBER:** | 16 |
| **POSITION:** | Central midfield |

## 1987

Joins semi-professional League of Ireland club Cobh Ramblers after building reputation with Cork junior club Rockmount.

## 1990

**June:** signed by Brian Clough for Nottingham Forest for £10,000.
**August:** makes debut for Nottingham Forest first team against Liverpool at Anfield.

**8 September:** home debut for Forest v Southampton.

**October:** makes Under-21 Republic of Ireland debut v Turkey.

**December:** wins Barclays Young Eagle of the Month award.

## 1991

**May:** FA Cup runners-up medal as Nottingham Forest lose 2-1 to Tottenham Hotspur.

**May:** makes debut for Republic of Ireland in 1-1 draw with Chile in Dublin.

## 1992

Named Nottingham Forest's Player of the Year.

## 1993

**May:** plays last of 154 games for Nottingham Forest after scoring 33 goals for the club.

**16 July:** turns down offer from Blackburn Rovers to join Manchester United for a then British transfer record of £3.75 million.

**7 August:** makes debut for Manchester United against Arsenal at Wembley in Charity Shield. United win 5-4 on penalties after 1-1 draw.

**14 August:** makes League debut for Manchester United away to Norwich.

**18 August:** scores first two goals for Manchester United against Sheffield United on home debut in front of a crowd of 41,949.

**15 September:** scores twice in his first European Champions Cup match in 3-2 away victory over Honved.

**7 November:** scores late winner in his first local derby game against Manchester City at Maine Road in 3-2 victory.

## 1994

**30 January:** scores his first FA Cup goal for United in 2-0 win v Norwich City.

**May:** helps Manchester United become League champions.

**14 May:** wins FA Cup winner's medal as Manchester United beat Chelsea 4-0 in the final at Wembley to complete the Double.

**June:** helps Republic of Ireland reach second round of the World Cup in the USA figuring in all four matches. Oustanding in successive games against Italy, Mexico, Norway and Holland. Voted team's best player by RTE viewers.

**November:** scores first goal for Republic of Ireland v Northern Ireland.

## 1995

**12 April:** having had seven stitches inserted in an ankle gash at half time, received first red card of his career for stamping on Gareth Southgate during FA Cup semi-final replay which United won 2-0. Later fined £5,000 by the Football Association on disrepute charge.

## 1996

**March:** sent off on his 30th appearance for the Republic of Ireland against Russia in Dublin after taking captain's armband for the first time in Mick McCarthy's first match as manager.

**May:** helps Manchester United to win Premiership title.

**11 May:** helps clinch historic second Double with 1-0 FA Cup win over Liverpool on his 130th appearance for Manchester United.

Named Republic of Ireland captain by McCarthy but fails to report for both Manager's testimonial and Republic training, and is stripped of captaincy and handed six-match ban by his national boss.

## 1997

**May:** helps Manchester United to Carling Premiership title.

**August:** named United's skipper following the departure of Eric Cantona.

**3August:** leads out Manchester United in Charity Shield game against Chelsea at Wembley.

**27 September:** injures himself against Leeds at Elland Road and cruciate ligament tear diagnosed.

**2 October:** Manchester United announce Keane will miss the rest of the season.

## 1998

**July:** despite picking up a yellow card, makes a successful return to football with Manchester United.

**September:** celebrates his election as Republic of Ireland skipper by scoring in the 2-0 victory over World Cup semi-finalists Croatia.

## 1999

**21 April:** scores his side's first goal to inspire United to a 3-2 victory over Juventus in Turin in the Champions League after United went 2-0 down after just 11 minutes. But he receives a yellow card which will rule him out of the final.

**16 May:** helps Manchester United to first part of historic Treble when United beat Tottenham Hotspur 2-1 at Old Trafford to clinch Premiership title. A crowd of 55,000 see Keane lift the trophy.

**22 May:** injured after just six minutes in FA Cup final against

Newcastle United. Substituted but team insist he lifts the FA Cup after 2-0 win completes the Double.

**26 May:** just a spectator at the Nou Camp in Barcelona as suspension rules him out of the Champions League final against Bayern Munich which United win 2-1 in a dramatic finish. But he is given a medal as a member of the squad who played in the tournament.

## 2000

**April:** captains Manchester United to Premiership Title. Voted Player of the Year by the Football Writers Association. Voted Player of the Year by the Professional Footballers Association.

**May:** receives Carling Premiership trophy as Manchester United captain.

## 2002

**June:** Roy Keane makes his controversial exit from Ireland's World Cup squad after a bust-up with manager Mick McCarthy.

**August:** Roy Keane is sent off at Sunderland after a scuffle with fellow Irishman Jason McAteer. Keane was due to serve a three-match ban for his dismissal, but decided to have a hip operation, taking him out of action and the limelight. The hip injury proved more serious than first thought, as Keane spent almost four months on the treatment table.

## 2004

**22 May:** Roy Keane captains Manchester United to FA Cup victory over Millwall by 3-0.

**28 May:** Roy Keane returns to the international fold in Ireland's

1-0 friendly win over Romania. Despite the controversy which heralded his departure, or perhaps because of it, he is cheered to the rooftops of Lansdowne Road.

- Keane is only one of four players to win the League and FA Cup Double on three occasions.

- Keane played in more FA Cup finals than any other player in the 1990s. He played four times for Manchester United and once for Nottingham Forest.

## MAJOR HONOURS

European Cup 1999
Premier League 1994, 1996, 1997, 1999, 2000
Football Association Cup 1994, 1996, 1999, 2004
Champions League 1999
Toyota Cup 2000
Football Writers Association Player of the Year 2000
Professional Footballers Association Player of the Year 2000

Last season: 2003-04

|  | Gls | Apps |
|---|---|---|
| League | 3 | 28 |
| FA Cup | 0 | 5 |
| League Cup | 0 | 0 |
| European/Others | 0 | 5 |